# Maritain and America

PUBLICATIONS OF THE

**AMERICAN MARITAIN ASSOCIATION**

General Editors:
Anthony O. Simon (1990 – 2004)
Michael D. Torre (2009 -)

*Jacques Maritain: The Man and His Metaphysics*
Edited by John F.X. Kansas, 1988
ISBN 0-268-01205-9 (out of print)
Distributed by the University of Notre Dame Press

*Freedom in the Modern World: Jacques Maritain, Yves R. Simon, Mortimer J. Adler*
Edited by Michael D. Torre, 1989, Second Printing, 1990
ISBN 0-268-00978-3
Distributed by the University of Notre Dame Press

*From Twilight to Dawn: The Cultural Vision of Jacques Maritain*
Edited by Peter A. Redpath, 1990
ISBN 0-268-00979-1
Distributed by the University of Notre Dame Press

*The Future of Thomism*
Edited by Deal W. Hudson and Dennis Wm. Moran, 1992
ISBN 0-268-00986-4
Distributed by the University of Notre Dame Press

*Jacques Maritain and the Jews*
Edited by Robert Royal, 1994
ISBN 0-268-01193-1
Distributed by the University of Notre Dame Press

*Freedom, Virtue, and the Common Good*
Edited by Curtis L. Hancock and Anthony O. Simon, 1995
ISBN 0-268-00991-0
Distributed by the University of Notre Dame Press

*Postmodernism and Christian Philosophy*
Edited by Roman T. Ciapolo, 1997
ISBN 0-8132-0881-5
Distributed by The Catholic University of America Press

*The Common Things: Essays on Thomism and Education*
Edited by Daniel McInerny, 1999
ISBN 0-9669226-0-3
Distributed by The Catholic University of America Press

*The Failure of Modernism: The Cartesian Legacy and Contemporary Pluralism*
Edited by Brendan Sweetman, 1999
ISBN 0-9669226-1-1
Distributed by The Catholic University of America Press

*Beauty, Art, and the Polis*
Edited by Alice Ramos, 2000
ISBN 0-9669226-2-X
Distributed by The Catholic University of America Press

*Reassessing the Liberal State: Reading Maritain's Man and State*
Edited by Timothy Fuller and John P. Hittinger, 2001
ISBN 0-9669226-3-8
Distributed by The Catholic University of America Press

*Faith, Scholarship, and Culture in the 21st Century*
Edited by Alice Ramos, and Marie I. George, 2002
ISBN 0-9669226-5-4
Distributed by The Catholic University of America Press

*Jacques Maritain and the Many Ways of Knowing*
Edited by Douglas A. Ollivant, 2002
ISBN 0-9669226-4-6
Distributed by The Catholic University of America Press

*Truth Matters: Essays in Honor of Jacques Maritain*
Edited by John G. Trapani, Jr., 2004
ISBN 0-9669226-6-2
Distributed by The Catholic University of America Press

*The Human Person and a Culture of Freedom*
Edited by Peter A. Pagan Aguiar and Terese Auer, O.P., 2009
ISBN 978-0-9669226-7-7
Distributed by The Catholic University of America Press

*Maritain and America*
Edited by Christopher Cullen, S.J. and John Allan Clair
ISBN 978-0-9669226-8–4
Distributed by The Catholic University of America Press

# Maritain and America

Edited by

Christopher Cullen, S.J.

and

Joseph Allan Clair

AMERICAN MARITAIN ASSOCIATION

Distributed by The Catholic University of America Press

Washington, DC 20064

**Library of Congress Cataloging-in-Publication Data**

Maritain and America / edited by Christopher Cullen and Joseph Allan Clair.

p. cm. -- (American Maritain Association publications)

Includes bibliographical references and index.

Summary: "Jacques Maritain was a leading French philosopher of the twentieth century. He came to know America first hand and taught at four American universities. This book explores his thought in its engagement of the American political system and the American culture of liberal individualism"--Provided by publisher.

ISBN 978-0-9669226-8-4 (alk. paper)

1. Maritain, Jacques, 1882-1973. 2. Political science--United States--Philosophy--History--20th century. 3. United States--Politics and government--20th century. I. Cullen, Christopher M. II. Clair, Joseph Allan, 1980-

B2430.M34M27 2009

194--dc22

2009037217

Manufactured in the United States of America

Distributed by The Catholic University of America Press

620 Michigan Avenue, N.E. /240 Leahy Hall

Washington, DC 20064

# CONTENTS

# INTRODUCTION

## I Prologue

The French philosopher Jacques Maritain (1882-1973) left war-torn Europe for America in 1940 for what was to be a brief visit. As things turned out, he took academic appointments in New York and Princeton and, excluding his three year tenure as French ambassador to the Vatican after the war, ended up living in the United States until 1960. Maritain's work on political philosophy written during this period (*The Rights of Man and Natural Law*, *Christianity and Democracy*, *The Person and the Common Good*, *Man and the State*, and *Reflections on America*) evidence a cheerful enthusiasm for the American political experiment in liberal democracy. But why, one wonders, was Maritain so optimistic about the religious and political potential of America? It has certainly never been in vogue for European intellectuals to fawn over America, particularly not French ones. Maritain did have good luck and found favorable reception among the most elite universities during his exile, but still his critical reflections on American ethical and political life found throughout the writings of his American period are far more than the unthinking applause of a grateful refugee.

The richest and most intellectually elaborate part of Maritain's work on America is found in his presentation of the unique relationship between religion, specifically Christianity, and the political liberalism found in the United States. Maritain proposes that the American political experiment exemplifies a "secular democratic faith" that organizes temporal, political life, yet without abandoning the super-temporal, spiritual dimension of the Christian faith. American democratic society is able to cling to its Christian heritage without excluding other creeds or privileging churches with unwarranted political power, according to Maritain. America is also more strictly secular than many European countries in its original distinction between church and state, yet without drifting toward a wholly non-religious form of cultural secularism. This unique harmony between things human and divine had been struck in the original documents of the country's founding and was still reverberating, Maritain thought, in the religious and political life of the postwar period that he experienced firsthand.

When faced with the liberal "achievements" of modern political life (e.g. representative democracy, human rights, the ideals of equality, liberty, and fraternity), one is forced to ask how this new historical epoch came about. To answer this question requires that one tell some sort of story. Was the Enlightenment's break with the past responsible for this new era in human history? Or are the traditional resources of Greek and Roman philosophy, coupled with the revealed resources of Jewish and Christian traditions, responsible for the relative achievements in human flourishing found in modern democratic society? Is modernity a story about the unfolding development of the self-consciousness of human freedom, as Hegel would have it? Or has the age of modern democratic society only been made possible by the Christian heritage of the West and will it be lost insofar as living Christian faith disappears?

Maritain argued that modern democratic society is a human achievement, yet it is also only made possible by the Christian origins of democratic ideals. He inherited the notion from his teacher, Henri Bergson, that modern democratic society is a temporal, "secular" expression of true Christian spirituality.[1] Thus, there is both an intellectual component–in the sense of historical inheritance–as well as a spiritual component that animates political society through the vitality of faith. That is, democratic society is the secular expression of the deep Christian recognition of universal human dignity and fraternal love summarized in the scriptural exhortation to love one's neighbor as oneself. Maritain calls the Christian roots of modern democratic society (both intellectual and spiritual), the evangelical inspiration of authentic democracy.[2] By "evangelical," Maritain is appealing not to a group of church denominations, but to a universal sense of the Christian Gospel message enshrined in the double commandment of love and the life and work of Christ. Maritain notes that the achievements of modern democratic society–such as the consent of the governed, respect for the rights of people, and proper

---

[1] Jacques Maritain, *Christianity and Democracy & The Rights of Man and Natural Law*, trans. Doris C. Anson (San Francisco: Ignatius, 1986), p. 49.

[2] Ibid., p. 49.

concern for the common good–are all rooted in a certain transcendent conception of the human person that exceeds the Enlightenment rationalism of thinkers like Kant and Rousseau and has its source in the heritage of Christian thought as well as the animating spirit of the Christian concept of universal neighborly love. In his work on political philosophy, *Christianity and Democracy*, written just after World War II, and very early on in his sojourn to North America, Maritain writes:

> Not only does the democratic state of mind stem from the inspiration of the Gospel, but it cannot exist without it. To keep faith in the forward march of humanity despite all temptations to despair of man that are furnished by history, and particularly contemporary history; to have faith in the dignity of the person and of common humanity, in human rights and in justice–that is, in essentially spiritual values; to have, not in formulas but in reality, the sense of and respect for the dignity of the people, which is a spiritual dignity and is revealed to whoever knows how to love it; to sustain and revive the sense of equality without sinking into a leveling equalitarianism; to respect authority, knowing that its wielders are only men, like those they rule, and derive their trust from the consent or the will of the people whose vicars or representatives they are; to believe in the sanctity of law and in the efficacious virtue... of political justice in the face of the scandalous triumphs of falsehood and violence; to have faith in liberty and fraternity, an heroical inspiration and an heroical belief are needed which fortify and vivify reason, and which none other than Jesus of Nazareth brought forth in the world.[3]

This passage illustrates Maritain's thorough going emphasis on the continuity between modern democratic society and its Christian heritage through highlighting the complementary relationship between faith and reason expressed in the interdependence of the temporal and spiritual domains of human life. This emphasis on the complementarity of Christianity and modern democratic society runs throughout Maritain's work during his American period.

---

[3] Ibid., pp. 49-50.

Since the end of Maritain's exile in America (1960), there has been a popular trend in Christian philosophy and theology in this country toward a much less optimistic appraisal of liberal democratic society, recently dubbed the "new traditionalism" by Jeffrey Stout in his book *Democracy and Tradition.* These thinkers complain that modern democratic society is morally and spiritually empty, rooted solely in a self-sufficient humanism and anti-religious form of secularism born from Enlightenment rationalism.[4] The preeminent exponents and most influential authors in this new form of antimodernism, as Stout narrates it, are Alasdair MacIntyre, a Roman Catholic philosopher, Stanley Hauerwas, a Methodist theologian, and John Milbank, an Anglican theologian. Rather than narrate modernity and the relative achievements of liberal democratic society as part of the Judeo-Christian heritage, as Maritain does, the tone of the new traditionalism is much more apologetic and combative. The goal of the new traditionalism is to return to a coherent premodern moral tradition, such as Augustinian Thomism, from the ruin and fragmentation of liberal modernity. These authors hope to rescue modern democratic society from its own dangerous amnesia by emphasizing the dependence of all rationality upon tradition. The method is no longer that of reconciliation and intellectual alliance with secular, liberal modernity, but rather that of "apologetic out-narration," as John Milbank puts it.[5] The goal of apologetic out-narration is to reveal the sandy, even "nihilistic" foundation of liberal modernity, which is simply the social expression of the Enlightenment project's antitraditionalism.[6] The age of secular liberalism is not the social expression of Christian faith, according to these thinkers; it is rather a narcissistic form of anthropocentric humanism that is doomed to individualism and isolation.

One may legitimately wonder whether Maritain's optimism about the complementary relationship between Christianity and modern democratic society is still tenable today, over fifty years later. One

---

[4] Jeffrey Stout, *Democracy and Tradition* (Princeton, New Jersey: Princeton University Press, 2004), pp. 11-12, 118-39.

[5] John Milbank, *Theology and Social Theory: Beyond Secular Reason*, 2nd ed. (Malden, Massachusetts: Wiley-Blackwell, 2006), p. 331.

[6] Ibid.

might ask this question in an historical way and wonder whether or not a modern democratic society like America has drifted away from its Christian roots and therefore lost the intellectual and spiritual resources for an authentic democracy. Or, one might ask whether the theoretical justification Maritain offers for his vision of the complementarity between Christianity and modern democratic society is viable. It is this second question that I shall consider in this essay. Was Maritain's perception of the complementary relationship of Christianity and modern democratic society skewed by a false emphasis on a secularized, political version of Christian faith? Is Maritain's attempt to reconcile Christianity and modern democratic society simply an attempt to reinterpret Christianity in terms of the dominant political discourse of modernity? These questions hinge on how one understands the concept of the secular and whether or not there is a legitimate temporal or secular expression of Christian faith that can be invoked to organize political society.

In the first section of what follows, I shall consider Maritain's conception of secularization and the "democratic secular faith" that he proposes in *Man and the State* as an alternative to the thoroughgoing rejection of the autonomy of the temporal, secular sphere found in the new traditionalism. Maritain sought to provide theoretical legitimacy for the process of secularization through resources that he found in the Christian tradition itself. The new traditionalist, and founder of the Radical Orthodoxy school, John Milbank, on the other hand, offers that the secularization of political society in modernity is a parody of the Christian distinction between the temporal and spiritual domains of life rooted in misinterpretations of Augustine and Aquinas. I suggest that Maritain's version of a "secular faith," which does include both the neo-Augustinian and neo-Thomist elements that Milbank dismisses, is primarily a practical response to the fact of pluralism in modern democratic society and provides a useful model for a religiously renewed democracy that is secular yet open to the practical conclusions drawn out of theological beliefs. Maritain's understanding of the secularization of political life in modern democratic society is more nuanced than is often recognized and provides an important response to antimodern traditionalists like Milbank.

In the second and final section of this introductory essay I shall turn to Maritain's *Reflections on America* and argue that they are a case study of the "democratic secular faith" that Maritain proposes in *Man and the State*. His reflections exemplify how one might interpret modern democratic society, not as a secular parody of true Christian faith, but as one possible version of Christian faith expressed in secular terms in the political sphere–or what Maritain calls a "temporalization" of Christian faith for the sake of political society. I shall also suggest that Maritain's cautious optimism about the modern democratic society he found in America is an example of both translation and Christian discernment that can and should be recovered and employed once again in the present moment.

## II Maritain's conception of secularization

To answer the question of whether or not Maritain presents an overstated pact between Christianity and modern democratic society requires that one understand Maritain's conception of secularization. Maritain argued in numerous places that modernity is the legitimate secular progeny of Christendom, born in the aftermath of the sacral medieval era, which was "a great attempt... to build the life of the earthly community and civilization on the foundation of the unity of theological faith and religious creed."[7] This arrangement succeeded for a period of time but failed after the Renaissance and Reformation, and "a return to the medieval sacral pattern is in no way conceivable."[8] During the medieval epoch, the vitality of the political order was reinforced through the spiritual unity of Christian faith, yet this often required that the spiritual element of Christian faith be enforced through temporal means. This, unfortunately, transgresses the Christian distinction between civil society and the spiritual realm of the church. Regarding the transition from the medieval era to modernity in *Man and the State*, Maritain writes:

> In proportion as the civil society, or the body politic, has become more perfectly distinguished from the spiritual realm of the Church–a process which was in itself but a development of the Gospel distinction between the things that are Caesar's and the things that are God's–the civil society has become grounded

---

[7] Jacques Maritain, *Man and the State* (Washington, D.C.: The Catholic University of America Press, 1998), p. 108.

[8] Ibid.

> on a common good and a common task which are of an earthly, "temporal" or "secular" order, and in which citizens belonging to diverse spiritual groups or lineages share equally. Religious division among men is in itself a misfortune. But it is a fact that we must... recognize.[9]

These comments given by Maritain on the distinction between the secular and spiritual domains of human life represent a broader trend among Christian intellectuals in the middle of the twentieth century to attempt to show that the secularization of political life in modernity is actually a legitimate expression of Christian thought.[10] As Maritain suggests in the quotation above, the distinction between the secular and spiritual realms of human allegiance, and also the autonomy of the temporal sphere, are at the very heart of Christian scripture and theology.[11] Maritain found support for this distinction in Jesus' enigmatic statement to "render unto Caesar the things that are Caesar's," in Augustine's distinction between temporal and eternal goods, and in the neo-Scholastic distinction between the natural and supernatural ends of mankind.

One key feature of the new traditionalism's intellectual project, particularly as represented in the work of John Milbank and Radical Orthodoxy, has been an attempt to upset the security and autonomy of this so-called "secular sphere." The secular sphere, Milbank objects, operates through a supposedly tradition-free and religiously neutral form of "secular reason" that is indebted to Enlightenment rationalism and is rooted in misinterpretations of Augustine and Aquinas. Milbank argues that twentieth century Christian thinkers, like Maritain, offered too much theoretical legitimacy to the autonomy of the temporal

---

[9] Ibid.

[10] The classic neo-Augustinian expression is found in R.A. Markus, *Saeculum: History and Society in the Theology of Saint Augustine* (New York: Cambridge University Press, 1970).

[11] Jacques Maritain, *Integral Humanism: Temporal and Spiritual Problems of a New Christendom*, trans. Joseph W. Evans (Notre Dame, Indiana: University of Notre Dame Press, 1973), p. 6. Cf. James V. Schall, *Jacques Maritain: The Philosopher in Society* (Lanham, Maryland: Rowman and Littlefield, 1998), p. 111.

sphere and thereby unwittingly the formation of a religion-free secularist ideology.

In *Theology and Social Theory: Beyond Secular Reason*, Milbank constructs an alternative narrative regarding the legitimacy of the secular sphere, reminding his readers that in the medieval Christian epoch "secular" primarily refers to a time, not a domain or sphere. Milbank argues that the modern "spatialization" of the secular has reinforced a dogmatic humanism and anti-religious, or beyond-religious, secularist ideology. He begins the first paragraph of the first chapter in his book saying:

> Once, there was no 'secular.' And the secular was not latent, waiting to fill more space with the steam of the 'purely human,' when the pressure of the sacred was relaxed. Instead there was the single community of Christendom, with its dual aspects of sacerdotium and regnum. The saeculum, in the medieval era, was not a space, a domain, but a time.[12]

Throughout *Theology and Social Theory*, Milbank focuses mainly on the Augustinian conception of the secular and its transition from a temporal to a spatial concept–that is, from naming a time to naming a domain. The classic neo-Augustinian expression of the legitimacy of political secularization that Milbank rejects is found in R.A. Markus's *Saeculum: History and Society in the Theology of Saint Augustine.* Markus argues that, for Augustine, the secular names both a time and a domain. Markus argues further that Augustine's spatial and temporal definition of the secular in *The City of God* is the beginning of the Western process of "secularization" and provides the foundation for a secular account of political order.[13] Markus sees Augustine's concept of the secular as "desacralizing" the Roman political sphere and thereby "loosing it from the direct hegemony of the sacred" that dominated it during the classical, pagan era.[14] And, in this way, Augustine's rendering of the secular is effectively proto-modern and liberal in that the "secular" signifies a new phase of neutrality and autonomy for the political sphere to be governed by rational pragmatism, rather than religious

---

[12] John Milbank, *Theology and Social Theory*, p. 9.

[13] R.A. Markus, *Saeculum*, pp. 55-102.

[14] Ibid, p. 173.

discourse.[15] Markus cites Book XIX of *The City of God* as Augustine's definition of a "secular political sphere" wherein the inhabitants of the two cities (earthly and heavenly) are forced to cooperate with one another in specifically non-religious ways for the sake of survival–that is, "for the common goods necessary to this mortal life," as Augustine puts it.[16] This Augustinian insight, Markus argues, was buried during the sacral medieval era and resurfaced in the awakening of the modern epoch.

But does Augustine's use of the Latin words *saeculum* ("age" or "period of time") and *saecularis* ("referring to such a period of time") warrant this rendering of the "secular"? In direct opposition to Markus, Milbank argues in *Theology and Social Theory* that such a neutral rendering of the spatial sense of the secular is not to be found in *The City of God* and furthermore it is not intelligible apart from Augustine's distinctly theological narrative of history. There is therefore nothing transferable about Augustine's concept of the secular for any modern universalized discourse of "secular reason" or "secular order."[17] As Milbank says, "Once, there was no 'secular'" and secularism must remember its own Augustinian story and see itself once again as a distinctly Christian innovation.[18] By highlighting the church as the only truly "political" community, where the virtue of charity is able to unite individuals with deep differences into a community of forgiveness without coercion, Milbank scorns the pretences of liberal toleration and religious diversity in modern democratic society, arguing that this type of toleration is rooted in a smug and soulless form of Enlightenment rationalism. Milbank's presentation of the church as the only truly political community on earth, in time, is rooted in his own

---

15 R.A. Markus, *Christianity and the Secular* (Notre Dame, Indiana: University of Notre Dame Press, 2006), pp. 63-64.

16 R.A. Markus, *Saeculum*, p.102. This quotation from Augustine is found at *De civitate Dei*, XIX, 17.

17 In addition to his *Theology and Social Theory*, see also John Milbank, "An Essay Against Secular Order," *Journal of Religious Ethics* 15 (1987): 199-224.

18 John Milbank, *Theology and Social Theory*, p. 9.

disputed reading of Augustine's ecclesiology in Book XIX of *The City of God* against Markus's interpretation.[19]

Although Maritain does not address the concept of the secular in Book XIX of Augustine's *City of God* directly, he is clearly influenced by Augustine's political thought, particularly Augustine's distinction between the eternal, heavenly city and the earthly, temporal city. Maritain takes this Augustinian distinction to be foundational for the Christian distinction between the spiritual and temporal spheres of human society represented by the church and civil society. He says:

> A genuine temporal community of mankind is not the perfect *civitas* in the Aristotelian sense, but that kind of *civitas* in the Augustinian sense, which is imperfect and incomplete, made up of a fluid network of human communications, and more existential than formally organized, but all the more real and living and basically important.[20]

Throughout his writings, Maritain's favor for Augustine's political realism over Aristotle's idealism aligns Maritain much closer with the secular realism of Markus's reading of *The City of God,* rather than Milbank's idealistic presentation of the church as the only truly political community.

The other distorted theoretical affirmation of the autonomy of the "secular" sphere, according to Milbank, is found in certain neo-Thomist distinctions between nature and grace and the cor-responding notion

---

[19] Milbank argues his case against Markus in *Theology and Social Theory*, chap. 12. For excellent critical discussions, see Michael J. Hollerich, "John Milbank, Augustine, and the 'Secular'" in *History, Apocalypse, and the Secular Imagination: New Essays on Augustine's* City of God, eds. Mark Vessey, Karla Pollman and Allan D. Fitzgerald, O.S.A. (Bowling Green, Ohio: Philosophy Documentation Center, 1999), pp. 311-26; John R. Bowlin, "Augustine on Justifying Coercion," *The Annual of the Society of Christian Ethics* 17 (1997): 49-70; Robert Dodaro, "Ecclesia and res publica: How Augustinian are Neo-Augustinian Politics?" in *Augustine and Postmodern Thought. A New Alliance Against Modernity*, eds. L. Boeve, M. Lamberigts, M. Wisse (Leuven: Peeters, 2008), pp. 237-72.

[20] Jacques Maritain, *The Social and Political Philosophy of Jacques Maritain*, eds. Joseph W. Evans and Leo R. Ward (Notre Dame, Indiana: University of Notre Dame Press, 1976), p. 319.

of a purely natural end for mankind. In modernity, Milbank argues, this neo-Thomist picture of a natural end for mankind has hardened into a fictitious conception of secular, political society that is too distinct from religious institutions and insulated from the intrusion of religious reasoning. Milbank's most thorough treatment of this neo-Thomist distinction is found in his book on Henri de Lubac called *The Suspended Middle*, where he praises de Lubac's understanding of the relationship between the natural and the supernatural. Milbank highlights de Lubac's essay "Nature and Grace," where de Lubac offers a critical assessment of American social and political life, arguing that its errors are ultimately rooted in a misguided neo-Thomist duality of nature and grace.[21] Milbank notes that de Lubac's position on the United States seems accurate and differs intensely from Maritain's "uncritical enthusiasm" for the modern democratic society he found in America. Although Milbank has not developed his own critique of Maritain's neo-Thomist appraisal of secular modernity, Tracey Rowland invokes Milbank's "postmodern Augustinian Thomism" as a critical alternative to Maritain's pro-secular, neo-Thomist description of political society and broader reconciliation of Thomism and Liberalism in her book, *Culture and the Thomist Tradition.*[22]

One should note that the story Milbank tells about the birth of the secularist ideology in modernity is fundamentally an intellectual one. It is a story about the power of ideas in forming culture. Certainly, the inter-traditional arguments among Thomists and Augustinians about the legitimacy of secularization are important, yet it strikes the reader as strange that Milbank thinks the rise of secularization is exclusively

---

[21] John Milbank, *The Suspended Middle: Henri de Lubac and the Debate Concerning the Supernatural* (Grand Rapids, Michigan: Eerdmans, 2005), pp. 22-23 n. 6. Milbank cites a speech that Henri de Lubac delivered in the United States in 1968 that was later published as, "Nature and Grace" in *The Word in History: The St. Xavier Symposium*, ed. T. Patrick Burke (London: Collins, 1968).

[22] Tracey Rowland, *Culture and the Thomist Tradition. After Vatican II* (New York: Routledge, 2003), pp. 22, 50. Rowland's book is published in Routledge's *Radical Orthodoxy Series*, which is edited by John Milbank, Catherine Pickstock, and Graham Ward. Rowland's critique of the reconciliation of Thomism and Liberalism, which includes her reading of Maritain, represents an interesting confluence of *Ressourcement* theology and Radical Orthodoxy.

an intellectual issue. There also seem to be practical and historical reasons for the rise of secularized political society in modernity.

Although Maritain's narrative of the rise and legitimacy of the autonomy of the temporal, political sphere relies on both the Augustinian temporal-spatial sense of the secular, as well as the Thomistic distinction between nature and grace, ultimately Maritain's affirmation of political society as properly "secular" is rooted in a response to the plural and diverse religious and metaphysical outlooks represented by citizens in liberal democratic societies and the need to recognize the differences of religious conscience. The process of the secularization of political society in modernity is a practical consequence of theological plurality. Although religious pluralism is not a good that needs to be celebrated, for Maritain, it is a fact that must be recognized.[23]

### III Maritain's "Democratic Secular Faith"

Maritain's account of the legitimacy of the secularization of political discourse and the autonomy of the temporal sphere in modernity contrasts sharply with Milbank's anti-secular narrative in that Maritain proposes a "secular faith," rather than promoting a form of "secular reason" associated with a version of political liberalism. Maritain also proposes a practical model for democratic society to remain religious, or regain its religiousness, by distinguishing between the second order "practical conclusions" that issue forth from the deeper "theoretical justifications" that are rooted in disputed philosophical systems and religious creeds represented by the diverse members of the body politic.

In *Man and the State*, Maritain rejects the tendency in eighteenth and nineteenth century European political philosophy to ground political society in "mere reason," that is, "reason separated from religion."[24] He argues that the tragic events of the first half of the twentieth century have refuted this type of bourgeois rationalism. He says that "we have been confronted with the fact that religion and metaphysics are an essential part of human culture, primary and indispensable incentives

---

[23] Jacques Maritain, *Man and the State*, p. 108.

[24] Ibid.

in the very life of society."[25] Thus, if modern democratic society is to enter its next historical stage with sufficient intelligence and vitality, "a renewed democracy will not ignore religion, as the bourgeois nineteenth century, both individualist and "neutral," did; and this renewed, "personalist" democracy will be of a *pluralistic* type."[26] This "renewed democracy" that Maritain proposes must either embrace, or at least acknowledge, the Christian intellectual heritage reflected in its own ideal of freedom united for the common good, while still also recognizing that "men belonging to... different philosophical or religious creeds and lineages could and should cooperate in the common task and for the common welfare, provided they similarly assent to the basic tenets of a society of free men."[27]

The democratic "secular faith" that Maritain outlines is practical in nature and not primarily dogmatic or theoretical; that is, secular faith is a practical, political expression of dogmatic or theoretical beliefs. Maritain makes an extremely intricate case for these "practical tenets" of the temporal creed that combines a three-fold appeal to natural law, revealed law, and the historical shape of human reason as it has developed in Western civilization. He proposes that "many can share the same practical secular faith provided they similarly revere, perhaps for quite diverse reasons, truth and intelligence, human dignity, freedom, brotherly love, and the absolute value of moral good."[28]

Maritain argues that one must maintain a sharp distinction between "the human and temporal creed which lies at the root of common life" and is but a set of "*practical conclusions*" or "*practical points of convergence*" on the one hand, and on the other, the "*theoretical justifications*, the conceptions of the world and of life, the philosophical or religious creeds which found, or claim to found, these practical conclusions in reason."[29] Maritain also expects there to be a fluid and deep relationship between these theoretical justifications and practical points of convergence. It is the task of the political society's citizens to

---

[25] Ibid, p. 109.

[26] Ibid; italics in original.

[27] Ibid.

[28] Ibid., p. 111.

[29] Ibid.; italics in original.

translate the relevance of their religious or metaphysical outlooks into the general, practical language of the political society's "secular faith." What, one wonders, is the content of these practical conclusions drawn up in the democratic secular faith that Maritain envisions? In *Man and the State*, Maritain offers a moral charter that outlines the points that the practical tenets of the democratic secular faith must deal with:

> Rights and liberties of the human person, political rights and liberties, social rights and social liberties, corresponding responsibilities; rights and duties of persons who are part of a family society, and liberties and obligations of the latter toward the body politic; mutual rights and duties of groups and the State; government of the people, by the people, and for the people; functions of authority in a political and social democracy, moral obligation, binding in conscience, regarding just laws as well as the Constitution which guarantees the people's liberties; exclusion of the resort to political coups in a society that is truly free and ruled by laws whose change and evolution depend on the popular majority; human equality, justice between persons and the body politic, justice between the body politic and persons, civil friendship and an ideal of fraternity, religious freedom, mutual tolerance and mutual respect between various spiritual communities and schools of thought, civic self-devotion and love of the motherland, reverence for its history and heritage, and understandings of the various traditions that combine to create its unity; obligations of each person toward the common good of the body politic and obligations of each nation toward the common good of civilized society, and the necessity of becoming aware of the unity of the world and of the existence of a community of peoples.[30]

Maritain argues that the cherished practical tenets involved in such a moral charter are not sustained by reason alone, but through a fluid and complex process of practical agreements rooted in theologically diverse theoretical justifications that are welcomed, yet never fully expressed, in the public sphere.

---

[30] Ibid., pp. 112-13.

One may legitimately wonder whether Maritain was too optimistic about the authority and longevity of the "Christian inspiration" that undergirds his "democratic secular faith." One may also wonder if Maritain is subtly relying on an Enlightenment style concept of universal rationality in his appeals to "truth" and the "absolute moral good" that sounds quite similar to the eighteenth and nineteenth century rationalism that he is denouncing–a case of cutting off the branch that he is standing on. I suggest that this is not the case because Maritain is not proposing a variety of "secular reason," but rather a conception of "secular faith" wherein religious believers learn to project their faith into the political sphere through a process of "temporalization," in order to reach practical agreements with other citizens. Maritain's picture of a personalist democracy rooted in a "secular faith" presents a model of dialogue for democratic society that both respects the depth of theological diversity among its citizens, without abandoning the pursuit of universal truth, and also promotes a common morality that might transcend these differences and legitimate the practical conclusions drawn out by the citizens. Ultimately, this dialogue must be done by the citizens and not arbitrated by the administration of the political society itself, according to Maritain, which in itself remains secular.[31]

Maritain's response to the secularization of political discourse and his model of practical agreement is still a compelling and useful model for incorporating religion in democratic society. Rather than hunting the intellectual ghosts responsible for the false ideology of secularism, as Milbank's narrative does, Maritain approaches the secularization of political discourse in modernity as a necessary historical stage after the medieval epoch and as an appropriate response to the fact of religious and metaphysical pluralism. Maritain offers a practical model for retaining religion in modern democratic discourse while not neglecting, nor praising, deep metaphysical differences. Ultimately, Maritain remains hopeful that secular democratic society will give way to a new Christian civilization. This civilization will necessarily look different than it did in the past, although it will not be unrecognizable to those within the tradition.

[31] Ibid., p. 114.

## IV Maritain's Reflections on America

Maritain delivered the Walgreen Lectures at the University of Chicago in 1949 (these lectures became *Man and the State*, published in 1951) and was invited back in 1956 to give a three-day seminar on the topic of America, under the auspices of the Committee on Social Thought. The talks Maritain delivered grew into his *Reflections on America* (published in 1958), which retain the informal character of Maritain's considerations of America offered in the three seminars.

In his reflections, Maritain provocatively says that if a "new Christian civilization is ever to emerge in human history, it is on American soil that it will find its starting point."[32] One way to understand this optimism about the reconciliation of Christianity and modern democratic society in this country is to read his *Reflections on America* as a case study of the "democratic secular faith" that he proposes in *Man and the State*. In this way, one can identify the features of modern democratic society that Maritain praises in American life as secularized fragments of Christian belief. Rather than speak of a "secular faith" in his *Reflections*, Maritain invokes the language of a "temporalization" of Christian belief. In the fourth and final section of this essay, I shall consider what features of American political life Maritain sees as "temporalized" Christian beliefs and conclude by highlighting Maritain's own warnings about the delicate nature of a society formed by a temporalized, that is, a secularized, version of Christian thought and practice.

In any attempt to narrate the "evangelical inspiration" that intellectually grounds and spiritually animates a modern democratic society, like America's, one runs the risk of making a triumphalist appeal to Christian supremacy in a culture of waning political influence on one hand, and on the other, of reinterpreting Christianity in the dominant political discourse of the day in such a way that it corrupts the truly revolutionary character of the Christian gospel, which is both spiritual and political in content. The "new traditionalists" are concerned that the political philosophy of thinkers like Maritain represents both triumphalism and also a modern corruption. Yet, if one

---

[32] Jacques Maritain, *Reflections on America* (New York: Charles Scribner's Sons, 1958), chapter 19; this is hereafter cited in the text as "*RA*," with the chapter number following in Roman numerals.

considers Maritain's *Reflections*, one finds that Maritain himself is keenly aware of both these dangers.

In his *Reflections*, Maritain has high praise for traditional American figures like Abraham Lincoln and the Founding Fathers, traditional documents like the Constitution, traditional institutions like the Supreme Court, and traditional American ideals like natural rights, seeking to narrate how these modern figures, ideals, and institutions were made possible by the inherited Christian notion of the human person. Maritain also highlights and praises what he sees as the contemporary sparks of "evangelical inspiration" flickering in the democratic and spiritual movements of the postwar period. He praises Dorothy Day and the Catholic Worker Movement, Saul Alinsky and the Industrial Areas Foundation, as well as the Reverend Martin Luther King, Jr. and the black people of Montgomery, Alabama. Maritain sees them all as people who embody the Christian ideal of human dignity expressed in the Gospel and in America's Constitution (*RA* VI).

Maritain also suggests that American political life is sustained as much by the founding documents and ideals as it is by the constant stream of immigrants who continue to travel to America from every corner of the world (*RA* IX). He speaks of Americans as "bruised souls," alluding to the wounds and sorrows of American ancestors, who either migrated here or were brought here forcefully (*RA* IX). The "bruised soul," Maritain says:

> bears witness to a kind of bruise or wound which is, I would say, of an evangelical nature: because wounds which cause a human soul to be compassionate are evangelical wounds; and such a sentence offers us, I think, the deepest reason for the sense of mercy and pity, and the sense of responsibility toward all those in distress, which are rooted in the collective American psyche, deep beneath the hardness and harshness of the hunt for material interests and advantages which is the object of ordinary activity and ordinary conversation. This spark of the Gospel lying deep in people who more often than not do not think at all of the Gospel, is not a thing that one speaks of. It is hidden in the secret life of souls, and covered by all the ordinary selfish desires and concerns of human nature. It exists, however, and is active in the great mass of the nation. And what is more valuable in this poor world than to find a trace of Gospel fraternal love active among

men? There is, in the most existential sense, a strain of Gospel fraternal love deep in the American blood (*RA* IX).

Maritain highlights the spiritual importance of immigration for the life of this country–admitting the complexity that immigration will involve as the country's population rises–and suggests that the constant influx of poor, humiliated, and marginalized people is a secret source of strength and energy for the spiritual and democratic life of this country. Maritain also warns the members of the "commercial republic" about the distractions involved in consumerism and the dangers of unrestrained corporate power, encouraging Americans to move into a new phase of capitalism.

In America, Maritain thought he found evidence for his conviction that a thorough account of the separation between the secular, political sphere and the spiritual domain of the church would lead not to isolation, but to cooperation and mutual benefit. This idea runs from Maritain's early work, *Integral Humanism* (1936) through *Man and the State* and on to his *Reflections on America*. Maritain also emphasized how fragile this relationship of institutional separation and spiritual cooperation actually is, warning that any "temporalized religious inspiration runs the risk of terminating in a failure if religion in its own order does not victoriously resist any trend toward becoming itself temporalized" (*RA* XIX). Maritain goes on:

> The risk is that *religion itself* might become temporalized, in other words, so institutionalized in the temporal structures themselves and the temporal growth itself of a given civilization, that it would practically lose its essential supernatural, supra-temporal, and supra-national trans-cendence, and become subservient to particular national or temporal interests (*RA* XIX); [italics in original].

The religious inspiration that is at work in the "temporal consciousness" of this country, Maritain proposes, is not an abstract spiritual force, but "is rooted, of course, in the particular religious creeds to which such or such individuals or families subscribe" (*RA* XIX). The projection of religious belief into the temporal order can "survive for a time even if some have slipped away from religious faith," but it can only preserve its vitality "if in many others it is not cut off from living religious faith" (*RA* XIX).

Given that the temporal projection of religious belief in this country has not resulted in an undeniable "new Christian civilization," one may legitimately wonder whether Maritain's proposal for a democratic secular faith and a religiously renewed personalist democracy has not, on the contrary, simply reinforced an antitraditional secularist ideology that is immune to religious dialogue in public debate, as the new traditionalists fear. In response, I suggest that Maritain's language about the temporalization of Christian faith does not reinforce a secularist ideology, but rather is a useful way of thinking through the role of religion in secular democratic society.[33] Rather than providing an intellectual assault on the validity of the autonomy of the secular sphere and polarizing the debate between adherents of the Christian tradition and liberal secularists, Maritain's approach offers a middle way between antimodern traditionalism and liberal secularism. Maritain's approach also provides a modest attempt to remind modern democratic societies, like America's, that their precious ideals about human dignity, liberty, and fraternity lose their intelligibility when excised from the philosophical and theological conversations in which they have been fashioned. Even more importantly, these ideals lose their vitality when divorced from living faith in the transcendent source to which all temporal human life must ultimately be ordered. The spiritual traditions, namely Christianity, for Maritain, must be remembered intellectually, and more importantly they must be practiced faithfully.

One can now see that Maritain's postwar enthusiasm for American democratic society may have been too optimistic about the ongoing reconciliation between individual rights and the common good, the alliance of religious faith and secular political institutions, and the possibility of a humanism which remains theocentric rather than turning anthropocentric. The new traditionalists' appraisal of modernity has helped many regain the confidence and critical capacity necessary to discern the vast difference between the anthropocentric humanism of secular liberalism and the Christian humanism found in

[33] James V. Schall makes the important point that reading Maritain on democracy and human rights in the contemporary moment requires "constant internal correction to recognize that what he means by these terms is something very different from what is generally meant by them in the culture": James V. Schall, *Jacques Maritain*, p. 95.

the Augustinian and Thomist traditions. The new traditionalists have provided some thinkers, like myself, with the courage to think and live out of the resources of a particular premodern tradition again, something that Maritain himself exemplified. Yet the danger in the new traditionalists' strategy is that it can cause one to forget how to narrate the indebtedness of the achievements of liberal democratic society to the heritage of Christian thought and practice. This ongoing "positive" work that Maritain embodied must be done, not as an act of cultural triumphalism, but as an act of spiritual and intellectual discernment.

Maritain's conception of a "secular faith" in *Man and the State*, which affirms an ongoing fragile process of projecting religious belief into the temporal order, is simultaneously an act of translation and interpretation, as well as an act of critical, spiritual discernment. Each new age and political epoch presents unique dangers and possibilities of misinterpretation. The process of working out the temporal, political expression of Christian faith in an age of unprecedented pluralism, information exchange, and communication is an evolving task. For Maritain, modern democratic society is *a*, not *the*, temporal, "secular" expression of Christian faith. It is an expression particularly focused on the dignity of the human person that is embodied in the revolutionary Enlightenment ideals of liberty, equality and fraternity. A temporal expression of religious belief is necessarily inclusive and pluralistic, which means, for Maritain, that it seeks a "practical," rather than a full-blooded theoretical, agreement among those of diverse philosophies and religious creeds in the body politic. It is this practical response to pluralism that distinguishes Maritain's theory of secularization from that found in the new traditionalism, as I mentioned above, and gives Maritain's theory ongoing significance today.[34] For Maritain, the task is to continue discerning whether or not the culture of any modern democratic society is an accurate temporal expression of the Gospel.

---

[34] In many ways, this brings Maritain's approach to the secularization of political life and the role of religion in modern democratic society much closer to the pragmatic expressivism of Jeffrey Stout, rather than the new traditionalism's absolute refusal of the secular sphere. See Jeffrey Stout, *Democracy and Tradition*, pp. 98-100.

Maritain provides an example of the ongoing task of translation and discernment. Modern democratic society, for Maritain, is a contingent, imperfect version of political society, yet a version that uniquely expresses certain elements of Christian truth about the human person. Although the version of modern democratic society found in America is flawed, there may still be strains of "evangelical inspiration" in the American blood that thinkers like Maritain can help one detect. In this way, Maritain is an example of what it might mean to be both modern and traditional. In the spirit of Maritain, and in the country that Maritain was so critically hopeful and cautiously optimistic about, the essays in this volume contribute to the ongoing process of "temporalization" that Maritain proposes.

## Conclusion

In this essay, I have suggested that Maritain's conception of a "democratic secular faith," that he proposes in *Man and the State* and sees expressed in his *Reflections on America*, is an alternative to the new traditionalism's thoroughgoing rejection of the autonomy of the temporal, secular sphere. Maritain sought to provide theoretical legitimacy for the process of secularization through resources he found in the Christian tradition in order to form a practical response to pluralism. I suggest that Maritain's understanding of the secularization of political life in modern democratic society is more nuanced than is often recognized and that his narrative of secularization provides an important response to antimodern traditionalists like John Milbank. Maritain's *Reflections on America* exemplify how one might interpret modern democratic society, not as a secular parody of true Christian faith, but as one version of Christian faith expressed in secular terms in the political sphere–or what Maritain calls a "temporalization" of Christian faith for the sake of political society. I suggest that Maritain's methodology for interpretation and discernment can and should be recovered and employed in the present moment, as the essays in this volume reflect.

Upon his arrival in New York City from France, Maritain's first impression of America was that it was a hopeful country, freed from the memories and burdens of historical necessity that plague the Old World of Europe (*RA* III). Maritain admits in his *Reflections* that this sentiment of freedom from history is a great illusion, yet it can also be a liberating thought that helps a nation turn forward in openness to the future. And, in this sense, America is "young" and full of hope (*RA* III). When considering the contemporary moment, one may worry that this openness to the future and freedom from the past has simply created a cultural wasteland of tradition-starved consumers marching forward under the banner of progress in America. If America's hopefulness is to become anything more than a cynical joke, it is imperative that the citizens of this "young" country consider the sources–both intellectual and spiritual–that lay underneath its cherished democratic ideals. For these ideals are often the precious and fragile projections of religious belief into the temporal order of a pluralistic society that is trying to find the common good.

In his reflections, Maritain cautions Americans about the dangers of submerging themselves in a frantic cycle of work and consumption without making space for leisure and quiet (*RA* XVIII). He worries that the American attitude toward time may be antithetical to the contemplative activity required for a whole civilization to be formed in the United States. "What the world expects from America," Maritain concludes in his *Reflections*, "is that it keep alive, in human history, a fraternal recognition of the dignity of man–in other words, the terrestrial hope of men in the Gospel" (*RA* XX). Yet this fraternal recognition of the dignity of man, which is the terrestrial, secular hope offered in the Gospel, can only be sustained, according to Maritain, by a living awareness of the eternal source of human dignity. The true end of civilization building, indeed of all human activity, is summarized, for Maritain, in the scriptural invitation to "Be still, and know that I am God" (Psalm 45:11; *RA* XVIII).

Joseph Allan Clair

Princeton University

# Catholicism and the Declaration of Independence: An American Dilemma about Natural Rights

Robert P. Kraynak

Roman Catholics have never been entirely "at home" in America. As we know from history, the first settlers were mainly Protestant Reformers and restless adventurers, along with a few Jesuit missionaries from neighboring colonies. The American Founding Fathers were mostly Protestant by background and often Deists or Masons by conviction; and the only truly American religion is probably Mormonism. The Catholic immigrants who arrived in the nineteenth century from Ireland, Germany, and Italy often faced intense anti-Catholicism and took several generations to become mainstream Americans; and they frequently paid the price of admission by diluting their faith and practice. Pope Leo XIII even referred to "Americanism" in a public letter of 1899 (*Testem Benevolentiae*) as the heretical tendency to trim the faith to fit modern culture—creating suspicions among Church officials about an Americanist heresy that was akin to suspicions about the modernist heresy in the early twentieth century.

Despite these tensions and suspicions, Roman Catholics in America have always had a genuine sense of gratitude for the religious liberty and economic opportunity of America and have been deeply patriotic. Very few returned to the "old country" in disillusionment. Yet, the positive experience of living and prospering in America leaves open the question of whether Catholics have accepted or can accept fully the principles of the American regime. Some think it is impossible, implying that the relation of Catholicism and Americanism is essentially a marriage of convenience or at best a prudent alliance between a medieval, hierarchical church and a modern, democratic, capitalistic society. Others argue that an inner affinity or principled harmony can be found, even if it was not always recognized by past generations. The case for finding a principled harmony between Catholicism and Americanism has been strengthened by the Second Vatican Council (1962-65), which specifically endorsed religious liberty, constitutional democracy, and a qualified version of human rights for the first time in the history of the Catholic Church. These developments have created a complex relation between Catholicism and Americanism that is difficult to untangle.

In this paper, I will try to untangle the relation by sorting out areas of agreement and disagreement. I will begin by describing six sources from which the American political tradition is derived—namely, Protestant Christianity, English common law, classical republicanism, the natural rights theory of the Declaration of Independence (drawn mostly from John Locke), the ideal of gentleman statesmanship, and James Madison's modern republicanism. I will then argue that, of the six sources, the natural rights theory of the Declaration has become the predominant one, transforming and incorporating the others so that we now measure political legitimacy by the protection and expansion of natural rights.

After discussing the sources of the American political tradition, I will turn to the Catholic "connection" and suggest that the contribution of Catholicism to any of the sources has been minimal, and the Declaration of Independence in particular betrays no direct Catholic influence. Yet, Catholicism shares the Declaration's affirmation of natural law, which means, ironically, that Catholicism is closer to the Declaration than Protestantism (which has generally rejected natural law theory). Thus, Catholicism and Americanism have natural law in common, as John Courtney Murray pointed out. But Catholic natural law is traditionally derived from St. Thomas Aquinas who has a different version of natural law than the Declaration of Independence and John Locke. The Thomistic-Catholic version of natural law emphasizes the perfection of the rational creature through virtue and favors constitutional monarchy, while the Lockean-American version emphasizes inalienable natural rights and favors constitutional democracy or republicanism.

The new twist in the relation is the incorporation of natural rights into the Catholic natural law teaching over the last century. This development has been accompanied by the scholarly claim that natural rights actually began in the Middle Ages and were a discovery of Catholicism rather than of the Enlightenment. If this is so, then Catholicism anticipated natural rights and may now be seen as compatible with the Declaration, even though it did not contribute historically to the Declaration and was often hostile to the rights of man in the eighteenth century. According to this revisionist view, Catholicism provides the authentic grounding of the natural rights principles proclaimed in the Declaration of Independence and may further imply, as John Courtney Murray was wont to argue, that only Catholic natural law could save America.[1]

In judging these various claims, I will argue that the Catholic revisionists of the twentieth century have exaggerated the similarities between Catholicism and the Anglo-American natural rights tradition: Catholic natural law is not primarily about natural rights and government by consent of the people, but about the natural ends of man as a rational creature and the use of prudence to apply these ends to politics. The prudent application of natural law, however, does not automatically point to democracy and natural rights as the best regime, because the natural ends of man are often best realized in a mixed regime that includes hierarchical or undemocratic elements. From this perspective, constitutional monarchy is the first choice and constitutional democracy a second choice.

The conclusion I shall draw is that Catholics can endorse the American version of natural law expressed in the Declaration of Independence as a partial version of Thomistic natural law. They can also embrace the American constitutional order as a decent second choice compared to more hierarchical regimes and support it with a high degree of loyalty and patriotism. But prudence also counsels Catholics to be wary of the abstract rights flowing from the Declaration of Independence (especially the sweeping right to pursue happiness as one sees fit) and to nurture instead those strands of the American political tradition outside of natural rights principles which direct

---

[1] See the conclusion of John Courtney Murray's *We Hold These Truths: Catholic Reflections on the American Proposition* (New York: Sheed and Ward, 1960), pp. 334-36. A similar claim is now heard in France, where Jean-Marie Cardinal Lustiger recently argued that the principles of the French Revolution–the rights of man or liberty, equality, and fraternity–should now be seen as Christian in inspiration, even though they were used against the Church at the time of the Revolution. See Jean-Marie Cardinal Lustiger, "Liberty, Equality, and Fraternity," *First Things*, No. 76 (October 1997): 38-45.

citizens to a notion of "ordered liberty" that contains the whole truth about God and man.

## I Six Sources of the American Political Tradition

The American political tradition is a complex and somewhat disparate order that has evolved gradually over four centuries from a variety of sources. To understand the complex relation of Catholicism to the Declaration of Independence, it is necessary to begin with an enumeration of all the sources of the American political tradition with brief descriptions of their contribution to the American way of life.

One important source is Protestant Christianity, especially the radical brands of Puritanism and "free church" congregationalism inspired by John Calvin and Ulrich Zwingli that influenced many early American settlers. The political creed of the American Puritans (as Perry Miller has shown) was "covenantal theology"–a sort of Old Testament Christianity that saw the American Puritans as New Israelites whom God had chosen to build a godly nation in this new land that would be "a city upon a hill" or a New Jerusalem. Their polity was a theocracy governed by a spiritual elite of "visible Saints" who were bound by a covenant with God to implement His divine law and by a covenant with the people to respect their consent.[2] Other dissenting Protestants, such as Baptists, Quakers, and Mennonites, were not tolerated by the Puritans, but the dissenting sects have outlived the Puritans in later centuries because they have been less theocratic than the Puritans and more willing to accept religious liberty. Though the old Puritans are gone, a pale reflection of their original covenantal theology remains today in the vision of a divinely chosen Christian America among certain Protestants of the Christian Coalition (but rarely among Catholics, for whom America has never been a chosen land or New Jerusalem in the Biblical sense). Protestant Christianity has profoundly shaped American political culture, providing the inspiration for many social movements (including intense anti-Catholicism at times), and continues today in various diluted and embattled forms.

---

[2] Perry Miller, ed., *The American Puritans: Their Prose and Poetry* (New York: Columbia University Press, 1956), pp. 1-108.

A second source of the American political tradition is English common law. Unlike natural law or constitutional law, common law is loosely codified customary law—a compendium of practices, statutes, and judicial decisions that together make up the historic rights and privileges of Englishmen. Evolving over many centuries, it has produced protections for liberty against arbitrary power, as well as legal and customary constraints that helped to distinguish "ordered liberty" from license.

Americans inherited the common law from their English forebears, giving them a vivid sense of the rights of Englishmen going back to the Magna Carta. In a recent book, *The Theme is Freedom: Religion, Politics, and the American Tradition*, M. Stanton Evans argues that notions of freedom and consent in America owe more to common law and feudal contracts than to Enlightenment theories of individual rights. James R. Stoner also notes the influence of common law on America's "unwritten constitutionalism." Stoner argues that the long list of grievances in the central part of the Declaration of Independence (largely unread today) were taken from traditional English common law principles, such as trial by jury, opposition to the quartering of troops without consent, and opposition to taxation without consent. Robert L. Clinton also argues in *God and Man in the Law* that many provisions of the U. S. Constitution were specifically taken from English common law (such as, *habeas corpus*, due process, impeachment, bicameralism, the origination of revenue bills from the lower house, executive pardon, prosecuting treason, trial by jury, as well as prohibitions on bills of attainder, on *ex post facto* laws, on double jeopardy, and on cruel and unusual punishment).[3] Broadly speaking, the American founders appealed both to the historic rights of Englishmen embodied in common law (a

---

[3] M. Stanton Evans, *The Theme is Freedom: Religion, Politics, and the American Tradition* (Washington, D.C.: Regnery, 1994), pp. 149-247. See, also, James R. Stoner, "The Common Law Spirit of the American Revolution," in *Educating the Prince: Essays in Honor of Harvey Mansfield*, eds. Mark Blitz and William Kristol (Lanham, Maryland: Rowman and Littlefield, 2000), pp. 192- 204, and Robert L. Clinton, *God and Man in the Law: The Foundations of Anglo-American Constitutionalism* (Lawrence, Kansas: University Press of Kansas, 1997), pp. 96-97.

traditional, particularistic claim) and to the natural rights of all mankind (a rational, universalistic claim) in justifying their actions.

A third element of the American political tradition is also part of the English heritage, namely, an aristocratic notion of gentleman statesmanship. Some of the great Puritan leaders, such as John Winthrop, were gentleman rulers who appealed to social hierarchy as well as to covenant theology for their authority. Many leaders of the American Revolution, as well as many framers of the U. S. Constitution, were members of Virginia and Massachusetts dynasties of political families and social elites. Though not possessing hereditary titles or noble birth in the feudal sense, Washington, Adams, Jefferson, Madison, Monroe and others were not simply men of the people, either. They were gentlemen politicians–members of the social aristocracy (some possessing landed estates) who constituted an educated and cultivated elite enjoying the leisure to devote their lives to politics, manners, war, and scholarship.

The reference to "sacred honor" at the end of the Declaration of Independence is undoubtedly a reflection of the gentlemen's code of honor—a pledge to dedicate their lives, fortunes, and honor to the cause of the Revolution. As Tocqueville noted, "When the American Revolution broke out... the famous men of that time... had a greatness all their own; [whose] renown brought honor to the nation, not vice versa."[4] For the first generation of the American republic, they stood as a quasi-aristocratic counterweight to the democratic revolution that they fostered; and even those among them who were completely self-made men, such as Benjamin Franklin, were molded by the manners of courts and aspired to some of the social distinctions of gentlemen. They were (somewhat inconsistently) gentlemen politicians dedicated to republican government.

A fourth source of the American political tradition is the classical republican tradition—the inheritance of Greece and Rome. The actual influence of this tradition in America is difficult to gauge and is hotly contested by historians. Certainly, there were considerable rhetorical

---

[4] Alexis de Tocqueville, *Democracy in America*, ed. J. P. Mayer (New York: Harper, 1969), I, 2.7, p. 257.

appeals to classical themes, especially to comparisons between the ancient Roman republic and the modern American republic. For example, the founders spoke repeatedly of republican virtue and classical moral virtues; George Washington was depicted in the image of Cinncinatus (the Roman farmer-general who served his country in war and returned to his farm); the anti-Federalists appealed to the small republic model for their idea of liberty and referred to themselves as Brutus and Cato; the authors of *The Federalist* called themselves Publius (after Publius Publicola, a Roman freedom fighter who helped to overthrow kingship and establish the Roman republic); and the architectural style of Washington, D.C. was modeled on classical Rome, with Capitol Hill named after Capitoline Hill and the Supreme Court building modeled on a pagan temple.

Having acknowledged these points, however, one must also recognize the fundamental difference between ancient and modern republicanism—the Roman republic was governed by a Senate made up of a hereditary aristocracy of patricians or "enrolled fathers" whose primary occupations were politics, war, and imperial conquest. The American republic drew its authority from the sovereign people and was intended to be a commercial republic rather than a military republic. The contrast with ancient Rome becomes even clearer when the fifth and sixth elements of the American tradition are described.

The fifth element is the natural rights-social contract theory, proclaimed in the Declaration of Independence as well as in other writings before and after the American Revolution. The basic idea of natural rights is that all men are created equal in the sense of being endowed by the Creator with equal rights to life, liberty, and the pursuit of happiness. These rights are natural and inalienable because they were put into human nature by God ("Nature's God") and cannot be taken away by other men or by states. Governments exist to secure those rights, and they do this best when they are based on the consent of the people. Revolution is justified when natural rights are violated by a series of abuses or when the consent of the governed is thwarted by serious usurpations of power. This is essentially Lockean social contract theory, and some of the language in the second paragraph of the Declaration referring to "a long train of abuses" is directly copied from chapter nineteen of John Locke's *Second Treatise of Government*, "Of the Dissolution of Government."[5]

The reliance on Locke, of course, does not mean that the Declaration is exclusively Lockean. As Walter Nicgorski points out, there are non-Lockean features in the Declaration drawn from the classical and Christian traditions.[6] Jefferson himself referred to a mixture of elements when he described the document as "an expression of the American mind" drawn from common ideas of the time as well as from "the elementary books of public right [by] Aristotle, Cicero, Locke, Sidney, etc." (Letter of Jefferson to Henry Lee, May 8, 1825). This mixture can be seen in the three main sections of the Declaration: I, The statement of general principles, based on the law of nature and nature's God; II, The statement of 27 grievances against the King and British Parliament; and III, The proclamation of freedom and independence from Great Britain.

In the famous first section, Locke's influence predominates in the general principles of God-given natural rights, government by consent, and the right to revolution that I summarized above. Some scholars have also detected the influence of Emer de Vattel's *The Law of Nations* in the opening lines, where the principles are applied to relations among nations ("when in the course of human events, it becomes necessary for one people to dissolve the political bands which have connected them with another..."). The suggestion is that the Declaration is primarily a document of international law, asserting the corporate right of one people or nation to self-determination like the other peoples and nations of the world. This insight, of course, does not

---

[5] Compare Locke's *Second Treatise*, par. 225, "But if a long train of abuses, prevarications, and artifices, all tending the same way, make the design visible to the people ..." with the Declaration of Independence, par. 2, "But when a long train of abuses and usurpations, pursuing invariably the same object evinces a design to reduce them under absolute despotism...". As one can see, the two sentences are virtually identical in phrasing and meaning, which means Jefferson was copying Locke on this point.

[6] Walter Nicgorski, "The Significance of the Non-Lockean Heritage of the Declaration of Independence," *American Journal of Jurisprudence*, 21 (1976): 156-77.

negate the Lockean features of the document; it merely qualifies them by bringing out the concern for national self-determination or corporate self-government in addition to individual rights.

Locke's influence is also qualified in the central section of the Declaration where the grievances against the King and British Parliament are listed to justify the Revolution. As I count them, there are 27 grievances consisting of 16 violations of consent (a collective right of self-government) and 11 violations of property and personal rights (individual rights). Many of these grievances (as noted above) were based on the traditional rights and privileges of Englishmen derived from English common law, although many also overlap with Locke's list of legitimate grievances against tyrannical government found in chapter nineteen of *The Second Treatise of Government* (especially pars. 212-220, describing violations of consent by executives altering the legislature; and pars. 221-222, describing violations of property rights by oppressive legislatures). The list of grievances in the Declaration thus appears to be a blend of Lockean and English common law principles.

The third and last section of the Declaration insists on the necessity of the colonies to become free and independent states—to be self-governing peoples who legislate for themselves—despite the ties of kinship and blood ("consanguinity") between American colonists and Englishmen. This section of the Declaration ends with appeals to divine Providence and with pledges of honor to aid in the success of their revolutionary cause. Like other parts of the document, these sentiments also seem to be a blend of the English heritage, the Christian notion of a providential God, the gentlemen's code of honor, and classical republican ideas of patriotic duty to participate in politics and even to sacrifice one's life for one's country. The Declaration is thus a subtle and complex weaving of the Lockean and non-Lockean elements in the American political tradition.

The main omission in the Declaration of Independence is any reference to the new form of government that the Americans should adopt—the assumption being that it is a matter left open for deliberation and trial and error after the Revolution. As we know, this decision was settled a decade later when Americans adopted the U.S.

Constitution and became a Federal Republic or a "natural rights republic" (to use Michael Zuckert's apt phrase). As James Madison argued, the social basis of the American republic would be a multiplicity of interest groups arising in a large or extensive commercial society in which property rights would be protected from an overbearing majority. Madison also argued that the protections for liberty and the common good could not be based on the assumption that “enlightened statesmen will always be at the helm.” While recognizing the need for virtue and patriotism, he specifically said that the surest protection for liberty would be a set of checks and balances that divided the powers of government into many competing centers. The separation of powers and a multiplicity of economic interest groups would thus be the main features of Madisonian constitutionalism, rather than reliance on the wisdom and patriotism of leaders and citizens.

In summary, the American political tradition arose from several elements mixed together over three or four centuries–Puritanism, English common law, classical republicanism, gentleman statesmanship, God-given natural rights, and the Madisonian constitutional republic. In large measure, the history of the American way of life consists in the playing out of these various traditions, with one or another predominating at different periods.

Over the long term, however, the natural rights principles of the Declaration of Independence have become the dominant tradition. Whether that predominance is for good or for ill is a matter of heated debate. While some scholars like Michael Zuckert and Thomas West think that it is a moral triumph, and others think it creates moral problems (I include myself in this latter group), one cannot deny the correctness of Zuckert’s historical analysis demonstrating the dominance of natural rights over the other traditions, creating a hegemonic Natural Rights Republic. Zuckert's proof is simple, but powerful: All of the other traditions have absorbed natural rights principles (often unaware) and have been transformed and overpowered by them.[7]

For example, the Puritans of colonial America, who began as staunch theocrats led by "visible Saints," gradually incorporated natural rights-social contract language and principles into their political theology. By 1744, a minister such as Elisha Williams could write a lengthy pamphlet on “The Essential Rights and Liberties of Protestants” in which he simply equates the Protestant idea of *sola scriptura* with Locke’s right of conscience, affirming “a Christian’s natural and unalienable right of private judgment in matters of religion.”[8] In similar fashion, William Blackstone’s new codification of the English common law in his *Commentaries on the Laws of England*, which appeared in four volumes from 1765 and 1769, incorporated Lockean ideas into a common law framework. Blackstone defended traditional powers of king-in-parliament (the sovereign legislative power) and the protection of the “absolute rights” of individuals. Following along the same lines, the American founding fathers, who were quasi-aristocratic gentlemen politicians in their personal lives, dedicated themselves to regime principles based on natural rights and republicanism, rather than on aristocratic exclusivity ("the aristocrat as democrat" is how the American historian Richard Hofstadter describes Thomas Jefferson, with both accuracy and irony).[9] Similarly, the opponents of the U.S. Constitution, the anti-Federalists, used the rhetoric of classical republicanism to state their case, appealing to the small, virtuous, participatory republics of the ancient world against the idea of the large, more centralized republic of the Federalists. Yet, the anti-Federalists finally settled on the promise of a Bill of Rights attached to the Constitution as the price of their support, indicating that their highest priority was the protection of rights.

---

[7] For the following discussion, see chapters 4-7 of Michael Zuckert, *The Natural Rights Republic: Studies in the Foundation of the American Political Tradition* (Notre Dame, Indiana: University of Notre Dame Press, 1996).

[8] See Ellis Sandoz, ed., *Political Sermons of the* American *Founding Era, 1730-1805* (Indianapolis, Indiana: Liberty Press, 1991), pp. 85, 97-98.

[9] Richard Hofstadter, *The American Political Tradition and the Men Who Made It* (New York: Vintage, 1973), pp. 23-56.

One may therefore conclude that the Declaration of Independence and the U.S. Constitution together produced the natural rights republic; and this combination of ideas has predominated over the other strands of the American political tradition (although the Lockean conception of natural rights was transformed in the nineteenth and twentieth centuries by statesmen such as Abraham Lincoln and by modern, mainly German, philosophy into the neo-Kantian human rights of present-day America).

## II Catholicism and Natural Rights

What has Catholicism to do with these six sources of the American political tradition and with developments in that tradition since the colonial and founding periods? Not a great deal, as far as I can tell. Of the six elements mentioned above, only English common law could be said to have a direct Catholic connection. In its origins, common law is part of the Christian "higher law" tradition; it arose sometime during the feudal period of Catholic England, as Stanton Evans shows in his book, *The Theme is Freedom*. But I doubt if one could say that English common law is Catholic *per se*, since it did not arise in other Catholic nations (although some scholars such as Kenneth Parrington argue that a *jus commune* or common law tradition, including certain protections for liberty, emerged in the late middle ages on the European continent as well).[10] As for the other strands of the American tradition, one would be hard-pressed to find a direct Catholic connection to Puritanism, classical republicanism, Lockean natural rights, gentleman statesmanship, or Madisonian constitutionalism.

In other areas of America, one can find historical Catholic influences–for example, in colonial Maryland (under Lord Baltimore's Catholic proprietorship, until the end of the seventeenth century, with its brief experiment with religious liberty), in education (in the many distinguished Jesuit universities and parochial schools), in trade unionism and social work (endorsed by Pope Leo XIII and promoted by Dorothy Day's Catholic Workers Movement), in the ethnic-Catholic

---

[10] See Kenneth Parrington, "Sovereignty and Rights in Medieval and Early Modern Jurisprudence: Law and Norms without a State," unpublished paper from the Catholic University of America Law School, Washington, D. C.

neighborhoods of urban America, in New Orleans' Mardi Gras, and in today's pro-life movement. One can also point out, as Michael Novak does in his book on religion at the American founding, *On Two Wings*, that some prominent American Catholic families such as the Carroll family of Maryland had members who were personal friends of George Washington, as well as signers of the Declaration of Independence and the Constitution.[11] And, of course, the remarkable Orestes Brownson converted to Catholicism in the nineteenth century and wrote *The American Republic*. But this is not the same thing as claiming that their Catholic thought directly influenced the colonial or founding periods, or the civil war period, or the great periods of Progressive reform in America.

The crucial questions, then, pertain to *indirect* connections between Catholicism and American principles. One question is whether Catholicism has its own natural rights tradition beginning in the Middle Ages and flowing from its canon law or natural law traditions. This is the claim of Brian Tierney, who maintains that natural rights emerged from the notion of "subjective right" in medieval canon law. A similar claim is made by John Finnis, who argues in his new book on Aquinas that human rights are implicit in Thomistic natural law and its conception of the dignity of the person.[12] A second and more general question is whether natural rights are implicit in the Christian idea of human dignity arising from the Biblical teaching that all human beings are made in the image and likeness of God and redeemed by Christ. Assuming the answers are "yes" to these questions, the third and final question is whether the Catholic conception of the rights and dignity of the person is the same as the God-given natural rights proclaimed in the Declaration of Independence. Let me approach these questions slowly by looking first at scholarly claims about a longstanding Catholic natural or human rights tradition.

---

[11] Michael Novak, *On Two Wings: Humble Faith and Common Sense at the American Founding* (San Francisco: Encounter Books, 2002), pp. 140-43.

[12] See Brian Tierney, *The Idea of Natural Rights: Studies on Natural Rights, Natural Law, and Church Law 1150-1625* (Atlanta: Scholars Press, 1997), and John Finnis, *Aquinas: Moral, Political, and Legal Theory* (Oxford: Oxford University Press, 1998), ch. 5: "Towards Human Rights."

At first glance, it would seem that Christianity in general and Catholicism in particular could not easily develop a conception of natural or human rights. There are several weighty reasons why it could not do so easily. In the first place, Christianity places duties to God and to neighbor before claims of rights and cannot accept the proposition that a right to pursue happiness as one sees fit takes precedence over duties to God and man. After all, the Bible uses the language of divine law rather than the language of rights to express morality and justice: It gives us the Ten Commandments rather than the Ten Bill of Rights, and the commands not to kill and not to steal do not necessarily mean that others have a right to life or to own property.[13] Even the command to love one's neighbor as one's self is not necessarily the same as respecting the rights of others—if, for example, loving others means imposing on them for their own good (to save their souls or to steer them away from sin).

In the second place, Christianity's foundation on divine revelation implies a duty to accept transcendent truth; and Catholicism requires acceptance of authoritative pronouncements about truth by the hierarchical Church. This is crucial for Catholics, but even Protestants who allow individuals to interpret Scripture for themselves have developed means for promoting orthodoxy and suppressing heresy. It is not easy for any devout Christian to accept a blanket right of individual conscience, especially if it leads to a society indifferent to God or to a society in which bizarre New Age cults proliferate and the true faith is marginalized. While orthodoxy does not automatically imply theocracy or a confessional state, it is not easy to square with religious liberty, either.

Third, the Christian notion of original sin implies distrust of weak and fallible human beings to use their rights properly. Belief in original

---

[13] For this reason, Germain Grisez says that "rights" do not even qualify as moral principles in the strict sense and must be derived from duties and human goods. He warns that Catholics should be "cautious in using the language of rights" and observes that "In reading the New Testament, one finds a great deal about the responsibilities of Christians, very little about rights," *The Way of The Lord Jesus* (Chicago: Franciscan Herald Press, 1983), Vol. 1, "Christian Moral Principles," ch. 9, p. 270.

sin instills in Christians a keen sense of how freedom can go awry and seems to imply that any notion of political freedom must be a conditional good, rather than an absolute good and could not be an abstract principle of political legitimacy. Original sin means weak and corruptible human beings need curbs on freedom by social and political institutions, including the legislation of morality by the state. Of course, Catholics have always maintained that the corruption of man by original sin does not obliterate his rational nature; but this implies even greater responsibilities for the state—not only suppressing vice and sin, but also perfecting the rational souls of citizens by inculcating moral and intellectual virtues. Such political responsibilities are hard to reconcile with protections for rights. And they indicate why Christians and Catholics have put more emphasis on "inner freedom"—the freedom of the soul from sinful desires or self-mastery—rather than "external freedom"—the freedom from external political controls, including the controls of a repressive state or the institution of slavery. When St. Paul spoke of Christian freedom, he meant inner freedom, not the external freedom proclaimed by natural rights. Thus, Paul could say without contradicting himself, "For freedom Christ has set us free... do not submit to the yoke of slavery" (*Gal.* 5:1) and "slaves, obey... your earthly masters" (*Col.* 3:22).

Fourth, Christianity, and especially the Catholic tradition, elevates the common good above the rights of individuals and even above the rights of separate groups. Catholic teaching about the family and man's social nature also conflict with the individualism and privacy of rights. Traditionally, Catholicism did not define the common good as simply the condition for individual development (as it does today somewhat naively in *The Catechism of the Catholic Church*, see par. 1906-09). Rather, it viewed the common good in corporate fashion, embodied in corporate groups and upholding "unity in peace" that promotes the harmony of social classes and inculcates moral virtues that perfect the rational soul and promote civic friendship ("solidarity," in today's terms), as well as civic piety. The Catholic conception of the common good is best captured by the concept of corporate hierarchy, rather than by conditions for the exercise of individual or group rights.

Fifth, the Christian teaching about charity—whose essence is sacrificial love—makes the whole notion of rights seem selfish. The culture of rights, when deeply entrenched, seems to create a society in which people feel the world owes them something when they declare, "I have my rights!" As Alexander Solzhenitsyn has said critically of Western rights: "'Human rights' are a fine thing, but how can we be sure that our rights do not expand at the expense of others?"[14] More precisely, rights are a two-edged sword: They are noble and glorious when used against real tyranny and real oppression, but they are base, selfish, and destructive when used against legitimate authority and traditional morality, as they often are in modern society. Although rights have practical or horizontal limits ("my rights end, where your rights begin"), there is no clear guideline within rights themselves to distinguish between the legitimate and illegitimate use of rights—for example, between the rights of Christian marriage vs. the rights of gay marriage, between the right to choose abortion vs. the right to life, between true vs. false rights. This distinction cannot be found in rights themselves, but in an objective hierarchy of goods that explains how rights must be properly used in order to be legitimate. Hence, from a Catholic perspective, it seems that rights are conditional goods—their value depends on the ends for which they are used, which means that rights are not properly speaking rights, but conditional goods subservient to higher goods.

Finally, Christians and especially Catholics cannot accept the premise of the natural freedom of the autonomous self that underlies most doctrines of rights. The most influential doctrines of rights emerged from the philosophers of Enlightenment Liberalism (Hobbes, Locke, Rousseau, Kant, Mill, Dewey, and Rawls). They argue that human beings are "born free," and they posit the existence of a state of nature or an "original position" which proclaims personal autonomy at the expense of human dependence on God or on fellow human beings and which denies natural sociality, as well as naturally given or divinely ordained hierarchies. Natural freedom and equality are antithetical to the notion of divinely ordained religious hierarchy in the church or a natural hierarchy in the family or claims that those who are more wise and virtuous have some legitimate title to rule over those who are less

---

[14] Alexander Solzhenitsyn, *Rebuilding Russia: Reflections and Tentative Proposals* (New York: Farrar, Straus, and Giroux, 1991), pp. 54-55.

wise and virtuous. Since these notions are inherent in Catholic teachings, a Catholic doctrine of human rights cannot begin from the assumption of an autonomous self in a state of nature or an original position. The rights must be derivative from duties, hierarchies, and prior human goods, which raises the question if they are still rights at all, rather than conditional grants from a higher authority to use one's freedom for specified ends and goods.

These objections to Christian theories of human rights are weighty objections. They make one wonder how Catholics today can embrace human rights so readily and incorporate them into Catholic social teaching; they also make one doubt if Catholic natural law has had, all along, an implicit or embryonic idea of natural rights that gradually came to be recognized in the modern age. What is the basis of these claims?

The answer, I think, is the development within Catholicism of a new anthropological doctrine–"the dignity of the human person"–that has enabled Catholics to claim that it has a conception of the person that includes the possession of human rights. The philosophical and theological label for this doctrine is "personalism," the most influential movement in Catholic thought over the last century and the main reason why human rights are now a central feature of Catholic social teaching.

### III The Dignity of the Human Person and Human Rights

Catholic personalism does not have a clear beginning point. Its first stirring seems to be the Thomistic-natural law revival of Pope Leo XIII at the end of the nineteenth century. In *Rerum Novarum*, Leo develops an eclectic notion of higher law from Aristotle, Thomas, Lockean property rights, and some references to "the dignity of the person" as a creature worthy of respect who should not be treated as a mere instrument of production or exploited as a means to others' ends. Leo tells business employers "to respect in every man his dignity as a person ennobled by Christian character.... [and not] to misuse men as though they were things in the pursuit of gain, or to value them solely for their physical powers—that is truly shameful and inhuman"; these moral imperatives are requirements of "natural reason and Christian philosophy" (par. 20).

Pope Leo's embryonic formulations of the dignity of the person were then developed in the twentieth century by many great theologians and church leaders—above all by Jacques Maritain, but also by Emmanuel Mounier, Gabriel Marcel, Heinrich Rommen, John Courtney Murray, Pius XII, John XXIII (especially, *Pacem in Terris*), John Paul II, and by the new natural law theorist, John Finnis. As one might suspect from this list, Catholic personalism comes in several varieties, with important and subtle differences. But all grow out of the same general project of building on Thomistic natural law, by adding features of modern philosophy derived from Kantianism, phenomenology (especially Scheler), and existentialism, in order to offer an enhanced notion of the person as an active, willing subject, as well as to provide a richer consciousness than original Thomism of the interior spiritual life and uniqueness of every human being.

The key point, as Maritain said, is that every human being is not merely an individual, differentiated from others by a material-bodily existence, but a "person"—a rational substance with a supernatural destiny, possessing intrinsic worth or dignity (often characterized as infinite, absolute, sacred, or inviolable) because each one is made in the image of God and (as later personalists add) because everyone is an absolutely unique and unrepeatable creation of God from the moment of conception. In a further refinement of personalism, Catholic theologians have argued that a "person" is not merely a "substance," but a "relation"—a creature possessing reason and free-will with a capacity for relating to others, especially in a dynamic relation of self-giving love (a new formulation for Christian charity).

The crucial political question is whether the human person as such is a possessor of rights that must be recognized by the state and fellow citizens. This was one of reasons for developing the concept of the person, although not necessarily the primary one. In Joseph Cardinal Ratzinger's important article, "Concerning The Notion of Person in Theology," the political implications of personhood are not even mentioned. Ratzinger's focus is on theology and ethics—showing that the Christian development of the term "person" from Greek philosophy is an evolution from the word for mask or dramatic role to a metaphysical substance to an external relation. For Ratzinger, personhood is relatedness to others in self-giving love, modeled on the inner relations of God in the Trinity and, by analogy, existing in man as a social being who relates to others in self-giving love while preserving his own identity. A human person is thus not a substance but a relation—a dynamic, existential reality of relation, rather than a static or closed substance. For Ratzinger, personalism is a new way of fully understanding man as an image of the divine Trinity and of appreciating the interiority of man's spiritual nature.[15]

For Maritain and others, however, personalism is primarily *political*: it is a way of reconciling traditional natural law with the rights of man. Maritain sees human rights as an inference from the Gospels' notion of the intrinsic dignity of the person implied in God's love for every human being and flowing from the Christian duty to love everyone as a child of God. Maritain also believes that the Thomistic notion of natural law, which views man as a rational substance with free-will, can be developed into the modern concept of the person as a rights-bearing agent. But Maritain is aware that Christianity (and Catholicism in particular) has not always recognized the potential of the Gospel for inspiring the rights and dignity of the human person, nor has it found the correct balance of rights and duties. In fact, he admits, the path to these insights has been a rocky road:

> In ancient and medieval times [more] attention was paid... to the obligations of man than to his rights. The great achievement of the 18th century was to bring out... the rights of man also required by natural law. That discovery was due to a progress in moral and social experience, through which the root inclinations of the human person were set free... But that great achievement was paid for by errors in the theoretical field... Attention even shifted from the obligations of man to his rights only. A genuine view would pay attention to both the obligations and the rights in natural law.[16]

With these historic shifts in mind, Maritain sees himself as developing for

---

[15] Joseph Cardinal Ratzinger, "Concerning the Notion of Person in Theology," *Communio* 17 (Fall 1990): 439-54.

[16] Jacques Maritain, *Man and the State* (Chicago: University of Chicago Press, 1951), p. 94.

the first time the proper mix of rights and duties in natural law—synthesizing the traditional natural law duties to perfect the rational soul through virtue with the modern natural rights of the person to be protected from the arbitrary power of the state or the repression of society. The result is a political theology that provides a Christian basis for a "democracy of the person" or "personalist democracy" that would avoid the errors of totalitarianism and liberal individualism.

In assessing the achievement of Maritain and others, I would like to draw attention to the paradox that they themselves recognized and understood as a serious problem. The problem is that the Gospels and Epistles speak about love and respect for all mankind, especially for the poor and powerless, in a way that sounds like respecting their rights as persons and empowering the disadvantaged groups of society. Moreover, Christianity emphasizes the infinite worth of every human being as a creature with an immortal soul, capable of either eternal life or eternal death. But the language of dignity, rights, and personhood and the momentous political implications of these concepts for democracy were not developed in the New Testament nor recognized for a long time in Western or world history. In fact, it took at least twelve centuries of canon law (according to Brian Tierney) or even eighteen centuries of natural law (according to Maritain) to see the Gospel inspiration for human rights and democracy. Until those times, no one really thought that the moral commands of the Gospel and the duties of natural law implied natural rights or human rights–in the precise sense of rights as immunities and protections of the individual from the arbitrary power of the state, or as a neutral zone of personal and private freedom from moral imposition, or as entitlements from the state for a certain level of material welfare and respect. Even when rights were recognized as such by Christians, the proponents of rights still had to make a sharp distinction between true and false rights and to specify precisely the ends for which rights must be used in order to be morally justified.

Brian Tierney, in particular, notes this stubborn fact in his book, *The Idea of Natural Rights,* where he argues against a Thomistic scholar of the old school, Michael Villey. According to Villey, Catholic natural law supports "objective right," but not "subjective rights"–the former being a standard of natural justice that inheres in the moral order of the universe (such as, the justice of the wise ruling over the unwise) and the latter being a power in the soul to choose freely or to claim dominion over property and immunity from the state. Tierney disputes Villey by arguing that "subjective right" or "rights" (*jus* or *jura*) began to emerge in twelfth century canon law before Aquinas and Ockham, eventually leading to the natural rights of modern liberalism. But Tierney honestly admits that no one in the tradition quite saw his point. In an extraordinarily candid admission he says:

> Michael Villey sees rights theories ... as an aberration, [as] a deformed variety of Christian thought. Another whole school of thinkers, represented most eloquently perhaps by Jacques Maritain, sees a doctrine of individual rights as always implicit in the Christian emphasis on the dignity of human personality. If this last point of view is to be defended, the key word must surely be 'implicit.' Perhaps there was always a possibility that Christian teaching on the inherent value of each individual person could be reformulated as a doctrine of subjective natural rights. *But, certainly, through most of Christian history, the possibility was not realized.*[17]

The difficulty that Tierney acknowledges is the stubborn resistance of Christian ethical concepts (such as charity, universal love, the inherent dignity of the individual in the eyes of God, or the Christian preference for the poor) to being reformulated as natural or human rights. It requires Tierney to "smoke it out," as it were, but his scholarly writings leave many readers (including me) with the impression of finding all smoke and no fire in the Catholic canon law and natural law traditions. Many of Tierney's citations from medieval canon law refer to powers in the human soul to do what is right according to natural law, which is more like a virtuous power than a natural right–a power to act properly rather than a subjective right to act freely. Other citations by Tierney refer to *jus* or *jura* as grants from higher authorities to act in accordance with divine law.[18]

---

[17] Brien Tierney, op. cit., p. 215; emphasis added.

[18] Ibid., p. 41: "jus was not a violent power but a 'virtuous power'... a 'licit power'.... a 'rightful power'"; and p. 63: Rufinus says, "natural jus is a certain

Apparently, the Christian idea that everyone is worthy of love is not the same as the claim that everyone is worthy of rights.

But where precisely is the sticking point that prevents Christian charity from leading to natural rights without the creative effort of scholars like Tierney to discover them in hindsight? In my judgment, the problem lies in the six weighty objections discussed above that indicate why the underlying beliefs of Christianity and Catholicism prevent one from arguing from charity to human dignity to human rights. Those six objections were: the priority of duties to God and neighbor over individual rights; the doctrine of original sin; the priority of the common good and man's social nature over the individual; the priority of perfecting the rational soul over letting people be free to express themselves; the selfishness implied in many rights claims; and the rejection of personal autonomy or natural freedom implicit in most notions of rights. To this list, I would add the observation that the Christian concept of human dignity applies primarily to man's relation to God—to the capacity for responding to God's law and God's love that animals and other creatures are not able to do and to the ability to become holy like the Holy God of the Bible. These attributes of human dignity are spiritual rather than political and do not automatically imply the freedom from external control, as well as the protections and entitlements, that we today call human rights.

Thus, it seems that the effort of Catholic personalists to discover in hindsight a doctrine of rights in the Christian tradition and to ground a doctrine of rights in the Christian idea of the dignity of the person is problematic. It does not stand up to careful scrutiny and must be re-thought.

## IV Troubling Conclusions

One of the great attractions of Catholic personalism is that it holds out the tantalizing prospect of a harmonious convergence between Catholicism and modern democracy based on natural or human rights.

---

force divinely inspired in man by which he is led to what is right and equitable."

If a connection between the Gospel, Catholic natural law, and the dignity and rights of the human person does exist—as Tierney, Maritain, Murray, and others suggest—then Catholicism and the Declaration of Independence would share considerable common ground. The documents of the Second Vatican Council of the Catholic Church and statements of Pope John Paul II, a great Catholic defender of human rights, have encouraged us to think this way. As the Pope recently said on the occasion of receiving the new U. S. ambassador to the Vatican:

> The Founding Fathers of the United States asserted their claim to freedom and independence on the basis of certain 'self-evident' truths about the human person: truths which could be discerned in human nature, built into it by 'nature's God.' Thus they meant to bring into being... a great experiment in what George Washington called 'ordered liberty': an experiment in which men and women would enjoy equality of rights and opportunities in the pursuit of happiness and in service to the common good. Reading the founding documents of the US, one has to be impressed with the concept of freedom they enshrine: a freedom designed to enable people to fulfill their duties and responsibilities toward the family and the common good of the community. Their authors clearly understood that there could be no true freedom without moral responsibility... no happiness without respect and support for the natural units or groupings through which people exist, develop, and seek the higher purpose of life in concert with others... [Hence] it would truly be a sad thing if the religious and moral convictions upon which the American experiment was founded could now somehow be considered a danger to free society... [And] the credibility of the United States will depend more and more on its promotion of a genuine culture of life, and on a renewed commitment to building a world in which the weakest and most vulnerable are welcomed and protected.[19]

---

[19] John Paul II, "John Paul II on the American Experiment," *First Things* (April 1998), pp. 36-37.

The striking feature of the Pope's statement is the summary of the founding principles of the United States, including the Declaration and the intentions of the American founders, in such a way that it coincides with Catholic teaching on the human person and the right uses of freedom. He says true freedom is directed toward the true hierarchy of ends; it is responsible freedom under God that is dedicated to the family, to the common good, to the "higher purposes of life in concert with others" (meaning religious and moral ends in natural and spiritual associations), and to the protection of the weak and unborn in "a genuine culture of life." Yet, the proper name for such freedom is not natural rights but "ordered liberty."

The crucial point is that none of the higher purposes of ordered liberty that the Pope mentions in his eloquent statement are actually mentioned in the Declaration itself, which leaves open the question of the proper use of natural rights. While some might suspect the Pope of giving the Declaration a Catholic "spin," there is reason to believe that the American founders themselves, living in a more conservative era than our own, when natural rights did not imply the radical autonomy of today, understood freedom in similar ways. As the intellectual historian, Knud Haakonssen has argued: "In the eighteenth century, natural rights derived from natural law and natural duty. Natural rights were understood as part of a morally well-ordered universe [that is] structured and lent certainty by the law of nature. Natural rights theory was much less individualistic and [less] anti-authoritarian than it was later taken to be."[20] And Thomas West has recently given us a re-interpretation of Locke that brings out the traditional restraints on natural rights that Locke apparently intended—including the promotion of family values, a rationalized version of Christianity, a scheme of moral education in bourgeois virtues, and the moral

[20] Knud Haakonssen, "From Natural Law to the Rights of Man: A European Perspective on American Debates," in *A Culture of Rights: The Bill of Rights in Philosophy, Politics, and L aw, 1791-1991*, eds. Michael J. Lacey and Knud Haakonssen (Washington, D.C.: Woodrow Wilson International Center for Scholars, 1991), pp. 19-61.

preconditions of citizenship in a free society.[21] If these scholars are right, both Catholicism and Lockean-Americanism are converging toward a kind of "conservative liberalism" that includes a system of natural rights limited by traditional moral and religious constraints and directed to higher goods than materialism and individualism. Perhaps all are converging toward ordered liberty.

Yet, much of this strikes me as wishful thinking about the harmony of natural rights and Catholic principles. Not only is Tierney's scholarly claim of an independent Catholic human rights tradition dubious on historical grounds (the subjective rights that he uncovers are not forerunners of modern natural rights but virtuous powers or internal supports for traditional moral virtues). One may also question the consistency of the Catholic teaching that claims that rights are inherent in the dignity of the person made in God's image and in the possession of a rational nature and then adds the qualification that rights are legitimate only when used to serve higher purposes than personal happiness. This means that rights are both absolute and conditional. They are absolute in the sense of being inherent in the dignity of man and therefore inviolable. But they are, in fact, subject to conditions, qualifications, and even repression if they subvert the true hierarchy of ends that Catholics see as the real purpose of life–namely, the moral, intellectual, and theological virtues that direct the soul upward to its rational and spiritual perfection and to its last end, eternal life.

Thus, in the last analysis, Catholics cannot view rights as rights. Their belief in higher ends means that they must see human rights as conditional goods subservient to higher goods that reflect the whole truth about God and man. This view of rights carries the corollary that if voluntary preaching to use rights properly are repeatedly ignored–producing a debased mass culture in a secular democratic society, wholly indifferent to the truth about God and man–then legislating

---

[21] Thomas G. West, "Vindicating John Locke: How a Seventeenth-Century 'Liberal' Was Really a 'Social Conservative,'" *The Witherspoon Fellowship Lectures*, Feb. 23, 2001 (copyright by The Family Research Council and available at www.frc.org/pap...spoon/index.cfm).

morality or otherwise imposing on people to seek higher goods would be justified. The standard of legitimacy for Catholics, in other words, is not merely respect for human rights and the consent of the people, but the realization or the attempt to realize the virtues and perfections specified by natural moral law and the eternal law of God.

Thus, it seems to me that the correct procedure for Catholics in reasoning about natural or human rights ought to be the reverse of what is normally done today. Instead of arguing that natural or human rights are intrinsic to Catholic morality as a development of natural law and then trying to control those rights with moral restraints and appeals to higher ends, one should defend the true hierarchy of ends and then argue that rights are conditional goods whose value depends on their ability to produce the true order of higher goods. As soon as one reverses the procedure, however, one is back to traditional Thomism, which means one is forced to deny the convergence of Catholicism and the modern natural rights found in the Declaration of Independence and to accept instead a prudent alliance between the two sets of principles.

Starting from traditional Thomism, one would have to reason about modern politics and the American regime in the following way. Thomism begins by recognizing that God has ordained four types of law for the governance of the created world—eternal law, divine law, natural law, and human law. Eternal law is God's plan for the entire natural universe. Divine law is the revealed law of Scripture that guides man to his supernatural end, eternal happiness, and governs the spiritual realm of human affairs (the structure and sacraments of the Church, the order of charity and grace). By contrast, natural law directs man to earthly happiness and guides the temporal realm of politics. Natural law does this by articulating the natural inclinations and ends that God has imprinted on human beings as rational creatures made in His image and likeness. Natural law as such is not a theory of freedom or human rights; it is a theory of the hierarchy of being in which man participates as certain type of privileged creature in the universe (although not the highest creature, since angels are higher than men). Hence, natural law is the participation of the rational creature in eternal law, as Thomas says.

The first practical principle of natural law is "good is to be done, evil to be avoided." Thomas identifies three basic goods as those to which rational creatures are inclined by their God-given nature—the good of self-preservation, the good of procreation in the family, the good of rational perfection through living in political society and through knowledge of the truth about God. As Thomas clearly indicates, these goods are grounded in the hierarchy of created being (ascending from inanimate to animate to specifically human goods). These goods are also reflected in the hierarchy of the human soul, whose parts ascend from the appetitive part to the irascible part to the rational part. Natural law is essentially a theory of natural inclinations to the proper ends of man, understood as an objective hierarchy of goods that points to virtue as the perfection of the soul of the rational creature.

As a theory of natural inclinations to the proper acts and ends of man—from preservation to procreation to virtue— natural law does not directly specify which political regime is best. Prudence is needed to make judgments about how to apply the hierarchy of natural ends to politics. Those judgments are made by statesmen or legislators who apply natural law to the concrete circumstances of time and place, producing human law, such as the U.S. Constitution or the unwritten English Constitution. Following Aristotle, Thomas allows a variety of legitimate regimes in the temporal sphere of politics. The best choice in most cases is a constitutional monarchy—a mixture of kingship, aristocracy, and democracy balanced together in a stable order combining virtue and wisdom in the king and his council mixed with an aristocratic senate and the participation of the people in certain spheres of civic life. Other constitutional regimes—such as a polity—are second and third choices. In contemporary terms, this would imply that constitutional monarchy is better than constitutional democracy, because the former makes greater provision for the higher and nobler demands of virtue than the latter In other words, a regime in which monarchical and aristocratic elements are mixed with popular elements is more conducive to the hierarchical ordering of the souls of its citizens—directing them to rational perfection, rather than to comfortable self-preservation or to the freedom to do as one pleases.

Applied to the American situation, Thomistic natural law requires one to judge the work of the American founding fathers by the objective hierarchy of ends which God has ordained for man. Here, the decisive question would seem to be whether the natural law doctrine of the Declaration of Independence which guided the Americans contains some of the elements of a true natural law found in original Thomism. The answer, we now must admit, is that the Declaration contains only a partial or incomplete version of true natural law, because it does not provide sufficiently for the perfection of the rational soul. The Declaration of Independence asserts a right to pursue happiness, but does not provide sufficiently for the higher goods of temporal and eternal happiness, leaving them more to personal choice than to corporate responsibility or leaving them to the larger culture which surrounded the Declaration and the Constitution that still contained vital remnants of classical and Christian culture and of the English common law tradition. Yet, if the American founders had been more attentive to preserving these traditional elements, they might have been Tories rather than revolutionaries. Or, since they themselves were gentlemen politicians of quasi-aristocratic character, they might have waged a war of independence on less sweeping principles than natural rights and established a more hierarchical regime than a constitutional republic.

However, a Thomistic approach to politics requires prudence, which counsels statesmen to seek the best approximation of the true hierarchy of goods in the given circumstances. After the American Revolution occurred and the regime was settled in favor of republicanism, Catholic Thomists could be American republicans—they could have acted like Alexander Hamilton, who favored constitutional monarchy while accepting constitutional democracy or republicanism as the only practical option in the circumstances. Within that basic acceptance and loyalty to of the American natural rights republic, Catholic Thomists could hold reservations about the natural rights basis of the regime and hope to move it in a more hierarchically ordered and less individualistic and less materialistic direction. For, as Robert Bork has argued in the spirit of Thomas Aquinas (and of Edmund Burke and Russell Kirk), the natural rights principles of the Declaration of Independence have the seeds of moral decay within them, because they gave a "blank check" to future generations in the abstract principles of liberty and equality. The Declaration cannot really prevent its sweeping grants of self-evident, inalienable natural rights from evolving over several generations from the ordered liberty of the American founders into the permissive freedom and radical egalitarianism of today, because such rights subvert the traditional moral constraints that held them in check for a hundred and eighty years (until the cultural collapse of the 1960s).[22]

With this prudential judgment in mind, Catholic natural law thinkers and Catholic citizens of America can be patriots who love their country by loving the more conservative elements in the American political tradition rather than the natural rights principles, with their revolutionary and (long-term) subversive tendencies. They can find the greatness of America in all of its cultural and political traditions—including Protestant or evangelical Christianity, classical republicanism, English common law, quasi-aristocratic gentleman statesmanship, and Madisonian constitutionalism—without reducing America to its natural rights principles. And they can heed the critics of Catholic personalism, such as Simone Weil, who remind us that the human person is most dignified or elevated when it subordinates the self to the highest good—which it embraces as a gift, an inspiration, and an obligation—rather than expressing itself freely or pursuing a personal vision of happiness as an inalienable natural right.

At its best, then, the Declaration of Independence is a partial or incomplete version of Catholic natural law based on Thomistic principles. At its worst, the Declaration of Independence is opposed to Catholic natural law when "the pursuit of happiness" as a fundamental right loses all connection with rational or spiritual perfection and promotes a radical egalitarianism and expressive individualism that denies the legitimate hierarchies of church, family, and society. The relation between Catholicism and the Declaration of Independence should be seen therefore as more of a prudent alliance than a principled harmony. Such a relation can be the basis of a deep and enduring but conditional American patriotism that enables Catholics to

---

[22] Robert H. Bork, *Slouching Towards Gomorrah: Modern Liberalism and American Decline* (New York: Harper Collins, 1996), chs. 1-4.

be "at home" here and now, but never entirely "at home" in the American political tradition.

# SOCIAL COHESION OF A PLURALIST CIVIL SOCIETY: A CHALLENGE TO MARITAIN'S POLITICAL PHILOSOPHY

Henk E.S. Woldring

## I Introduction

The central question of this paper reads as follows: under what conditions can the spirit of the American people change socio-economic structures, generate a new phase in its civilization and, consequently, promote the social cohesion of society? The hidden conflict between the spirit of the people on the one hand, and the structure of industrial civilization on the other was a key element in Maritain's first impression of the United States.[1] He characterizes the spirit of the people as souls and vital energy that have the potency to change socio-economic structures. He considers the inner logic of the structure of the industrial civilization as inhuman and materialistic, and acknowledges that this economic structure generates certain patterns of thought, behavior, and moral values. However, Maritain argues that the result of the hidden conflict is that the spirit of the people has vanquished and transformed from within the logic of the structure of industrialized civilization. This transformation inaugurated a new phase in modern civilization that is characterized by a new morality, which includes the idea of social cohesion. However, Maritain does not analyze the precise inter-relationships between socio-economic structures and the spirit of the people, nor how this new morality arises. To clarify Maritain's position on these interrelationships I shall analyze his ideas more extensively with the help of Alexis de Tocqueville, Max Weber, and Max Scheler.

## II Spirit of the People and Socio-economic Structures

Maritain characterizes the essence of the spirit of the American people as "their souls and vital energy, their dreams, their everyday effort, their idealism and generosity." He adds: "freedom-loving and mankind-loving people, people clinging to the importance of ethical

---

[1] Jacques Maritain, *Reflections on America* (New York: Charles Scribner's Sons, 1958), p. 22.

standards."[2] Elsewhere, he adds the good will, the sense of human fellowship, human reliability, helpfulness, and the extraordinary resilience that is "a sign of a perpetual alertness of the spirit."[3] Next, Maritain argues that the spirit of the American people is directed "toward the good of man, the humble dignity of man."[4] Moreover, moral values of the Gospel, like mercy, pity and the responsibility toward all those in distress, are "hidden in the secret life of souls."[5] Maritain believes that these spiritual ideas are decisive for the development of the American society of the future.

However, material factors, such as the structure of industrial civilization, also play a role in the development of society. The inner logic of the structure of industrial civilization, which is originally grounded in the fecundity of money and the primacy of individual profit, is characterized by inhumanity and materialism.[6] Another material factor that Maritain discusses is the social structure of the segregation of black and white population groups. In the southern United States and in the highly industrialized areas of the North, many African Americans and whites live in separate neighbourhoods.[7] At the same time, American society is characterized as a classless society. Maritain argues that the genuine concept of class implies a certain element of fate and inevitability; it refers to both a social condition, which, as a rule, is hereditary, and to a relatively immobile social structure. However, in American society there is no hereditary stability in social conditions. American society is characterized by dynamic material conditions that make everyone liable to shifts in one's social position; this perpetual change is normal. Although Maritain holds that his statement about America as a classless society is basically true, he acknowledges that it will become more true in proportion to the

---

[2] Ibid., p. 22.

[3] Ibid., pp. 33, 36-37, 67.

[4] Ibid., pp. 89-90.

[5] Ibid., pp. 85-86.

[6] Ibid., p. 21.

[7] Ibid., pp. 50, 52

growth of equality of opportunity for everyone and decrease in economic differences between population groups.[8]

Maritain holds that socio-economic structures generate certain patterns of thought, behavior and moral values. The American classless society, for example, generates a climate of freedom of action, competition and career.[9] Moreover, Maritain acknowledges that in industrialized nations "large areas in the common consciousness... have been infected by the miasmata that emanate from the structures... of our modern [industrial] civilization."[10] He acknowledges that there are people who measure everything in terms of success, practical power and personal aims. However, he does not want to pay too much attention to these people because, according to him, they do not represent true American mentality and life style.[11] Maritain also acknowledges that the structural segregation of African Americans and whites pervaded all aspects of social life. Although federal law stood for the complete equality of all citizens, the social structure of segregation generated feelings and behavior of large parts of the white population opposed to the federal law. This social structure of segregation "corresponds not only to ingrained prejudices, but also to ingrained customs and traditions to which the daily activities... have been adjusted."[12] However, Maritain argues that those customs and prejudices are incompatible with the spirit of the American people. He is convinced that spiritual energies will, ultimately, conquer those customs and prejudices.[13]

Maritain holds that patterns of thought, behavior and moral values which are generated from socio-economic structures of society are not strong enough to resist the power of spirit. He argues: "[T]he people... were keeping their own souls apart from it." Next, he concludes that

---

[8] Ibid., pp. 175-78.

[9] Ibid., pp. 155, 160, 178.

[10] Ibid., p. 31.

[11] Ibid., pp. 31-32.

[12] Ibid., p. 50.

[13] Ibid., pp. 53-57.

"the spirit of the people is gradually overcoming and breaking" the logic of the socio-economic structures. Moreover, this spirit has transformed from within the inner dynamic and historical trend of the structures, and inaugurated a "really new phase in modern civilization."[14] However, Maritain does not explain what 'from within' means. What is the precise link between the spirit of the people on the one hand, and the socio-economic structures that generate patterns of thought, behavior, and moral values on the other, that makes this process of transformation possible? Before answering these questions, I will describe Maritain's view of the new phase of civilization.

### III A New Phase of Civilization

Maritain argues that the new phase in modern civilization gave American society a material and moral outlook fit to free human beings and fit to build a civilization genuinely original in character, capable of captivating the "hearts of men."[15] This new phase of civilization is characterized by a general state of mind, a common consciousness, and a coherent social life that is dominated by the original characteristics of the spirit of the American people: generosity, good will, general kindness, a sense of human fellowship, moral conscience, the gradual realization of the American ideal of equal opportunity for all, and progress in social justice.[16] Of course, there are egoistic and greedy individuals, but, according to Maritain, America is neither egoist nor avaricious. On the contrary, American people know the importance of money not only for improving their own lives, but also for improving the lives of others and for the service of the common good.[17]

Maritain does not say that the new phase of American civilization is a new Christendom. He argues that this civilization may become a fertile ground for the development of a new Christendom if the spiritual renewal takes place in souls that will make Christian faith and morality actually prevail in common consciousness and behavior. Next,

---

[14] Ibid., pp. 23, 111, 197.

[15] Ibid., pp. 23, 29.

[16] Ibid., pp. 33-38, 70, 112.

[17] Ibid., pp. 33-35.

he asks the important question: "[H]ow can you have the face to speak of a new Christendom to come, when you see the state of our present world, with all the threats of degradation and even destruction to which mankind is being subjected, and had you not better speak of new barbarism already come?"[18] Although he answers that the ferment of justice is more or less secretly making headway, and that Christian faith is still alive, he does not really answer the question: how can the spirit of the people transform socio-economic structures, and its patterns of thought, behavior, and moral values into a new phase of civilization that might be a fertile ground for a new Christendom, and not for some kind of barbarism?

Regarding this question, Maritain connects the new phase of civilization to democracy. He argues that the inner transformation of socio-economic structures should be aimed at the primacy of *human welfare* and the political *common good.* "These phenomena taken together," he continues, "are great signs foreshadowing a new age in the development of democratic societies."[19] He means an "existential democracy: not as a set of abstract slogans, or as a lofty ideal, but... democracy as a living reality."[20] He argues that a favourable condition for the sound development of democracy is a pluralist civil society: in this type of society, participating citizens belong to a variety of autonomous social communities that are in possession of authority commensurate with their function, and have their proper rights, freedoms and responsibilities (social plurality or differentiation). Moreover, in a pluralist civil society, participating citizens belong to very different philosophical and religious creeds (worldview plurality), and they should cooperate for the ultimate goal of the common good.[21]

---

[18] Ibid., p. 190.

[19] Ibid., p. 197.

[20] Ibid., pp. 161-62.

[21] Ibid., p. 179. See Maritain, *Integral Humanism: Temporal and Spiritual Problems of a New Christendom* (Notre Dame: University of Notre Dame Press, 1973), pp. 162-76.

## IV Pluralist Democracy

To clarify the relationship between the new phase of civilization and pluralist democracy, I will now discuss some theoretical distinctions in Maritain's philosophy on democracy which, although unique with respect to their mutual connection in politico-philosophical literature, are extremely useful. First, he argues that a genuine democracy implies a fundamental agreement with respect to communal life, i.e., it must "*bear within itself a common human creed, the creed of freedom*."[22] This faith is not a religious faith, but a *secular* or *civic* one. He criticizes libertarian theories, which see democratic society as an arena in which all private conceptions of communal life are met without any common thought for the well-being of society. Second, this secular faith is implemented by practical tenets or a *practical charter* that contains a legal structure, articles, formal rules, and procedures that together lead citizens toward the political organization of a democratic state. Third, citizens can try to justify this *practical charter* from very different philosophical or religious outlooks. Fourth, Maritain argues that, notwithstanding the diversity of worldviews, the democratic élan should be kept alive by the adherence to a *moral charter* or the code of public morality that underlies the practical charter and makes its workings possible. The moral charter deals with, for instance, public moral values such as: rights, liberties and responsibilities of persons who are members of associations; human equality; fraternity; mutual tolerance and respect; and the obligations of each person and the state toward the common good. Fifth, Maritain also identifies a *common ethos*: the inner energy of both the secular democratic faith and the public morality that underlies the active participation of citizens in political life.[23]

Maritain wishes to strengthen the practical charter through comprehensive philosophical and religious outlooks in order to revitalize democracy, and, consequently, to promote the new phase of civilization. However, what is the precise link between theoretical justifications of the practical charter on the one hand, and public

---

[22] Jacques Maritain, *Man and the State* (Chicago: University of Chicago Press, 1951), p. 109.

[23] Ibid., pp. 111-13, 145.

morality that characterizes the new phase of civilization on the other? Maritain introduces the idea of a common ethos that includes the idea of social cohesion. However, he does not analyse how a common ethos and, consequently, social cohesion arises.Social cohesion is an inclusive concept that needs to be clarified more specifically. Robert Bellah *et al.* formulate social cohesion as a central problem. They formulate the question as follows:

> The fundamental question we posed, and that was repeatedly posed to us, was how to preserve or create a morally coherent life. But the kind of life we want depends on the kind of people we are–on our character. Our inquiry can thus be located in a longstanding discussion of the relationship between character and society.[24]

Regarding the relationship between character and society, these authors refer to Alexis de Tocqueville's *Democracy in America.* Tocqueville did not use the term *social cohesion*, but he had this idea in mind and related it to a common ethos. In the following sections, I shall discuss the arguments of Tocqueville, Weber and Scheler to gain more insight into the relationship between a common ethos and social cohesion.

## V Alexis de Tocqueville on Mores

According to Tocqueville (1805-1859), the existence and survival of any society depends on an integrated alliance between people's participation in social institutions (material life conditions) and their commitment to certain ideas, behavior and moral values (non-material factors). Material life conditions can be determined by a hierarchical social structure (e.g. feudal structure), relationships of social equality, or other social and political institutions. Material life conditions inevitably generate certain patterns of thought, behavior, and moral values which, at the same time, also maintain and legitimize these conditions. In the introduction of *Democracy in America*, Tocqueville writes:

---

[24] Robert N. Bellah *et al.*, *Habits of the Heart: Individualism and Commitment in American Life* (New York: Harper and Row, 1986), p. vi.

> No novelty in the United States struck me more vividly during my stay there than the equality of conditions. It was easy to see the immense influence of this basic fact on the whole course of society. It gives a particular turn to public opinion and a particular twist to the laws, new maxims to those who govern and particular habits to the governed. I soon realized that the influence of this fact extends far beyond political norms and laws, exercising dominion over civil society as much as over the government; it creates opinions, gives birth to feelings, suggests customs, and modifies whatever it does not create.[25]

Before the Revolution of 1789, the material life conditions of the French people in the feudal era were determined by a hierarchical structure. This social structure seemed to be unchangeable because it produced patterns of thought, behavior, and moral values that legitimized the material life conditions. The revolutionary ideas of freedom and equality of the Enlightenment philosophers could not be realized because of those dominant patterns of thought, behavior, and moral values. However, before the French Revolution, the feudal structure was in a process of disintegration. Many citizens who were striving for more social freedom and equality were encouraged by some revolts that had already occurred. As a consequence, traditional patterns of thought, behavior, and moral values disintegrated more and more, and this process of disintegration created space for achieving ideas of freedom and equality. Tocqueville shows how these ideas supported a process of growing social and political freedom and the equality of citizens to participate in free social and political associations and the state government.[26]

Tocqueville argues that the French Revolution was possible because of the lack of universally shared social consciousness, opinions, and moral values.[27] There was an ideological vacuum that could be filled by the ideas of the Enlightenment philosophy. But this could not happen

---

[25] Alexis de Tocqueville, *Democracy in America* (New York: Harper and Row, 1988), p. 9.

[26] Alexis de Tocqueville, *The Ancient Regime* (London: Dent and Sons, 1988), pp. 140-41.

[27] Ibid., p. 113.

overnight. To achieve this, Enlightenment ideas first had to be rooted in material life conditions and its pattern of thought, behavior and moral values. In French society, in the second part of the eighteenth century, material life conditions and its patterns of thought, behavior, and moral values were changing, which made the people susceptible to new ideas of freedom and equality. Albert Salomon argues correctly that Tocqueville does not defend a one-sided materialistic interpretation of society, because that would diminish the significance of non-material factors.[28] I hold similarly that Tocqueville does not have an idealistic approach, starting with philosophical and moral ideas, because that would diminish the significance of material factors. This position is in contrast with the ideas of Richard Herr.[29]

Many critics of Tocqueville argue, and rightly so, that he uses an integrated alliance of material life conditions on the one hand, and non-material conditions, on the other hand, as a method of social research. However, in discussing his method of research, these critics do not clarify what the precise relationship is between these material and non-material factors. My thesis is that the interaction between material life conditions and non-material factors (patterns of thought, behavior and moral values) generates *mores*: various notions, opinions, and ideas that shape mental habits. I characterize these *mores* as basic elements of a common or *social ethos*. These *mores* make people susceptible to new ideas. In an historical context, these mores linked up with the ideas of the Enlightenment philosophers and were then pursued in a revolutionary direction. These mores or basic elements of a social ethos that shape mental habits show precisely the link of that integrated alliance in Tocqueville's method of research. Discussing the ideas and arguments of the Enlightenment philosophers, Tocqueville writes: "Arguments of this kind can not succeed till certain changes in the conditions, customs, and minds [*moeurs*] of men have prepared a way for their reception."[30] This means that interaction between

---

[28] Albert Salomon, "Tocqueville, Moralist and Sociologist," in *Social Research*, vol. 2 (1935): 417.

[29] Richard Herr, *Tocqueville and the Old Regime* (Princeton, New Jersey: Princeton University Press, 1962), p. 36.

[30] Alexis de Tocqueville, *Ancient Regime*, p. 11.

changing material life conditions and changing patterns of thought, customs and moral values generates new *mores* that shape mental habits.

Tocqueville considers mores "to be one of the great general causes responsible for the maintenance of a democratic republic in the United States."[31] He continues:

> I here mean the term "mores" (*moeurs*) to have its original Latin meaning; I mean it to apply not only to "*moeurs*" in the strict sense, which might be called the habits of the heart, but also to the different notions possessed by men, the various opinions current among them, and the sum of ideas that shape mental habits. So I use the word to cover the whole moral and intellectual state of a people.... I am only looking for the elements in them which help to support political institutions.

Thus, Tocqueville discusses *mores* as the "great general causes" for maintaining the democratic republic. His precise thinking was that these *mores*, or basic elements of a social ethos, which are the result of the interaction between material and non-material life conditions, underlie the idea of social cohesion. Moreover, changes in material life conditions (by a combination of whatever political, social and ideological causes) create space for new ideas and make people susceptible to these ideas. These new ideas may strengthen or weaken the *mores*. He was investigating, in particular, those *mores* that could be strengthened to promote social cohesion.

### VI Max Weber and Max Scheler on Ethos

Max Weber (1864-1919) and Max Scheler (1874-1928) discuss the problem of *mores* in a way that is comparable to Tocqueville. According to Weber, in any given era, socio-economic relationships may produce certain moral values, social norms and other ideas. At the same time, those relationships often are the result of a worldview and life style that transform socio-economic conditions into a particular economic system. Weber argues that one should investigate the processes of socio-cultural development in two ways: in terms of ideas and in terms

---

[31] Alexis de Tocqueville, *Democracy in America*, p. 287.

of socio-economic structures. In his essay *The Protestant Ethic and the Spirit of Capitalism*, he investigates mainly the working of ideas. His study on *The Religion of China* begins with an analysis of the sociological foundations of the development of monetary policy in medieval China, and of the development of the Chinese political structure.[32] His *Economy and Society* begins with an analysis of economic relationships, and continues with analyses of philosophical ideas and religious systems.[33] Weber therefore says:

> [I]t is, of course, not my aim to substitute for a one-sided materialistic an equally one-sided spiritualistic causal interpretation of culture and of history. Each is equally possible, but each, if it does not serve as the preparation, but as the conclusion of an investigation, accomplishes equally little in the interest of historical truth.[34]

Like Weber, Scheler distinguishes "ideal factors," such as philosophical thoughts, moral values, and religious ideas and expectations that people have, and which they intend to realize in society. On the other hand, he also discusses "real factors," such as economic relationships of production, political relationships of power, and family relationships, which are based on human passions. Scheler tries to show that societies develop through an interaction between the ideal and real factors. He presents an insight into the mutual influence of ideas and thoughts on the one hand, and the socio-cultural circumstances in which these ideas and thoughts are active, on the other. In developing these two complementary perspectives, he intends to avoid both an idealistic and a materialistic view of society:

> [S]ociology's ultimate and proper task consists in examining the kinds and the orderly sequence of the *reciprocal effects* of ideal

---

[32] Max Weber, *The Religion of China: Confucianism and Taoism*, ed. by H.H. Gerth (Glencoe, Illinois: The Free Press, 1951), pp. 3-104.

[33] Weber, *Economy and Society: An Outline of Interpretive Sociology* (Berkeley, California: University of California Press, 1978), in particular Part II, Chapter VI.

[34] Weber, *The Protestant Ethic and the Spirit of Capitalism* (New York: Charles Scribner's Sons, 1958), p. 183.

*and* real factors, as well as of the spiritual and drive factors that determine the contents of human life.[35]

Scheler argues that ideal factors manifest themselves in society according to their own "logical meaning" ("*Sinnlogik*"), or their own cognitive and moral steering principles that regulate the origin and decay of ideas. This "logical meaning" determines what possibilities on the idealistic level are present in society. He argues that the development of real factors occurs in quite another manner, that is, according to an "effective primacy" ("*Wirkprimat*"). He rejects the "vulgar Marxian" idea of economic determination. He acknowledges that economic factors have an important significance for constituting society, but he argues that other factors are also active, such as political, religious and moral ideas.[36] The core of his theory is that the real factors determine the conditions and limits of what can be realized from the ideal factors.

However, in what manner does the interaction process between real and ideal factors take place? In other words, how can we conceptualize the interaction between these factors? Scheler answers this question by using the concept "*ethos*": elementary notions of moral values and norms that give direction to people's thoughts and actions.[37] This ethos may be called a social ethos: it not only regulates morality, it is also the link between ideas of a just social order and the factual order.[38] Scheler argues that real factors contain an elementary notion of moral values and, as such, the stirrings of a social ethos. Next, the ideal factors purify the information presented by real factors and they transform that information into a more distinct social ethos. Depending on the normative context in which it operates, the social ethos can be transformed, weakened or reinforced. By changing the social ethos, the development of political and economic power structures can be altered. The social ethos is generated by real factors and shaped by ideal

---

[35] Max Scheler, *Problems of a Sociology of Knowledge* (London: Routledge and Kegan Paul, 1980), p. 36.

[36] Ibid., pp. 44, 50.

[37] Ibid., p. 93.

[38] Ibid., pp. 63-64, 93, 101.

factors. As such, the social ethos serves as a matrix for the development of moral, economic and political knowledge, and actions to change real factors, i.e., socio-economic structures.[39]

To clarify the mutual relationships between material and ideal factors, Weber uses the concept "elective affinity" ("*Wahlverwandtschaft*" or an inner connection). In his essay on the Protestant ethic, he does not describe the entire history of capitalism in the West. He argues that its economic, legal and political institutions produce a certain spirit or what he calls an "*ethos*" that is characterized "ideal typically" by a rational and systematic organization of labour and life style.[40] He does not present a theological examination of the Calvinist ethic, either. He merely describes its "ideal typical" characteristics: asceticism, sobriety, perseverance, avoidance of luxury and frivolous pleasure. Finally, he argues that Protestant asceticism corresponds to the spirit of capitalism and, moreover, that there is an "elective affinity" between the religious ethic of Protestantism and the spirit of early capitalism that came to expression in a mutually reinforcing ethos.

I conclude that Weber and Scheler, like Tocqueville, present a non-deterministic interpretation of the relationship between social structures on the one hand, and thought, moral values and other ideas on the other. They argue that society is constituted by an interaction between material and non-material factors. Tocqueville argues that this interaction is mediated by stirrings of a *social ethos:* notions, opinions, ideas and moral values. Weber and Scheler hold that real factors (institutions) already contain these stirrings, which will be strengthened by ideal factors. All three argue that the social ethos shapes mental habits that make people susceptible to new ideas, which in turn shape the social ethos. They consider this social ethos essential to the social cohesion of society.

---

[39] Ibid., pp. 47-52.

[40] Weber, *The Protestant Ethic*, p. 51.

## VII Common and Differentiated Ethos

Tocqueville, Weber and Scheler not only discuss the common ethos of society at large, they also give an account of a socially differentiated ethos, depending on the social group in question. What is the nature of the relationship between a differentiated ethos and the ethos of society at large? I have already discussed Maritain's idea of a democratic and pluralist civil society in which citizens participate in a variety of autonomous communities. The core of the idea of civil society is not only that society is socially differentiated in order to distribute power, it also refers to the nature and purpose of this differentiation: to promote an effective autonomy of communities according to their characteristics and the freedoms and responsibilities of the group members in accordance with human dignity. Next, we can argue that every community is characterized by an internal social integration and a social cohesion that are related to both material and non-material factors. Although the concept of *social cohesion* is rarely discussed in sociological literature or is used interchangeably with *social integration*, I shall distinguish between these two terms.

Material factors are 1) organizational rules and institutionalized patterns of participation to realize personal and group goals through interdependent activities in the group, and 2) the structural context of relationships with other communities. These material factors of a community generate certain patterns of thought, behavior and moral values, and stirrings of a social ethos, as well. The degree of integration of a community is determined by these material factors and its patterns of thought, behavior, and moral values. It is an empirical variable changing between communities and changing over time within the same community. Not all communities have a high degree of integration, in which every standardized activity or moral value is functional for this community as a unity.[41]

Non-material factors are 1) common ideas about the nature and characteristics of the specific community (school, family, industry, sportsclub, church, etc.), 2) commitment of the group members to

---

[41] See Robert K. Merton, *Social Theory and Social Structure* (New York: The Free Press, 1968), p. 81.

concrete group goals, 3) group-identification, and 4) moral values of personal freedom, dignity and responsibility. The more these non-material factors tend to strengthen or to adjust the social ethos, the more these factors contribute to the social cohesion of a community. Unlike Merton, I hold that social cohesion is not generated solely from common moral values and norms that are internalized by members of a community.[42] Social cohesion is related to a social ethos that arises from the interaction between material and non-material factors. This does not mean that social cohesion refers to a homogenous community in all respects, because every community consists of a heterogeneity of persons, social positions and responsibilities. However, social cohesion implies homogeneity as far as the non-material factors strengthen the social ethos. Ultimately, this is what makes a community a social unit.

Differentiated communities are often characterized as "mediating structures": communities that are located between the government and citizens. With a reference to Tocqueville, Philip Selznick judges them as being extremely important both for the social identity of the participants and the vitality of society. On the one hand, moral values and social virtues are transmitted within these communities to their participants. On the other hand, these communities promote the commitment of participants to the society as a whole; they inform and mobilize their participants to function in society at large.[43]

The material factors of civil society consist of a variety of differentiated communities that act as mediating structures in generating stirrings of the social ethos of society at large. Like Maritain, Selznick considers this differentiated society the "infrastructure" of a pluralist democracy. Amitai Etzioni's idea that society contains a "moral infrastructure" consisting of families, schools, and other communities is compatible in this respect with Selznick's theory of mediating structures. Etzioni considers these communities essential for the cultivation and transmission of moral values and virtues. It is

---

[42] Ibid., pp. 369-70.

[43] Philip Selznick, *The Moral Commonwealth: Social Theory and the Promise of Community* (Berkeley, California: University of California Press, 1992), pp. 517-18. Alexis de Tocqueville, *Democracy in America*, pp. 515-17.

within the family that children learn specific moral values. School education builds further on the moral development of students' personalities–and may even correct it. Other communites also contribute to the student's moral development. In society as a whole, this process of the internalization of moral values and virtues is further broadened. The ultimate goal of Etzioni's theory is to contribute to a morally strong and coherent society.[44] To the extent that these material factors of civil society constitute a moral infrastructure they promote a greater degree of social integration of society. And to the extent this infrastructure contributes to a morally strong society, it promotes social cohesion. The nature of the relationship between a differentiated ethos and the ethos of society at large is precisely this process of learning and the internalization of moral values and virtues that begins in differentiated communities and is broadened in society at large.

## VIII Conclusions

In my discussion of Maritain's thesis that the spirit of the American people has transformed socio-economic structures *from within*, I asked the question: what is the precise link between the spirit of the people on the one hand, and the socio-economic structures and its patterns of thought, behavior, and moral values, on the other, that makes this process of transformation possible? The theories of Tocqueville, Weber and Scheler are very helpful in answering this question. The process of interaction between socio-economic structures and its patterns of thought, behavior and moral values produces certain *mores* or stirrings of a social ethos. In a dynamic society, socio-economic structures and these patterns of thought change continuously, and, consequently, the social ethos will change as well. If, and only if, the stirrings of a social ethos make people susceptible to ideas of the spirit of the American people, can these ideas then, in turn, shape the social ethos. These ideas may enforce the social ethos that gives direction to people's thought and action to transform socio-economic structures and to inaugurate a new phase of civilization. The idea of a social ethos clarifies why Maritian argues that socio-economic structures have been transformed

---

[44] Amitai Etzioni, *The New Golden Rule: Community and Morality in a Democratic Society* (New York: Basic Books, 1996), pp. 175-79.

*from within*. However, since Maritain does not discuss the origin of a common ethos, his theory of the spirit of the people capable of transforming socio-economic structures remains too idealistic.

Moreover, I think that Maritain underestimates the resistance that socio-economic structures and their patterns of thought, behavior and moral values will offer to that transformation. Since neo-liberal capitalism is characteristic of American and other Western societies, economic interests and commercial forms of social organization are dominant in these societies. The material life conditions in such societies produce consumer-oriented, individualistic and competitive thought—behavior and ideas that generate a social ethos that maintains and legitimizes these liberal-capitalist material factors. Since this social ethos is dominant in Western societies, they influence not only the economic sectors of society, but also other sectors (school education, health care, social welfare, etc.). These dominant non-material factors endanger the nature of society as a pluralist civil society.

Maritain is certainly right that spiritual forces can cause changes in those structures and patterns of thought. But not straightaway! We should be aware that the social ethos is a mediating factor. If this common ethos contains advantageous elements for the spirit of the American people, a new phase of civilization can be achieved by virtue of this renewed social ethos. However, if this social ethos does not contain those elements, and offers an enduring resistance to the spirit of the people, the possibility of some kind of barbarism cannot be excluded.

In an analogous way, I can answer the other question posed before: what is the precise link between theoretical justifications of the practical charter, on the one hand, and the public morality that characterizes the new phase of civilization, on the other? This link is what Maritain calls a common ethos: the inner energy of both secular democratic faith and the public morality that underlies the active participation of citizens in political life. However, he introduces this common ethos as an idealist object, because he does not explain how this ethos arises. It may be clarified by the process of interaction between the differentiated civil society and its patterns of thought, behavior, and moral values. This interaction produces the stirrings of a social ethos, which in turn may be enforced by the spirit of the people. This common ethos contains the inner energy of the morality that characterizes the new phase of civilization. This morality includes the idea of social cohesion. Maritain argues, almost romanticizes, the new phase of the American society characterized by material and moral equipment fit to free human beings and capable of captivating the "hearts of men." He seems to refer to Tocqueville's idea of "habits of the hear,t" but, like Tocqueville, he means more than this: captivating the hearts of human beings brings about various opinions and ideas that shape mental habits that are susceptible to a new phase of civilization.

In a democratic and dynamic society, both socio-economic structures and social ethos tend to change continuously, and religious and philosophical worldviews contribute to this process. The crucial and challenging question is what direction this change will take. I argued already that some kind of barbarism cannot be excluded. In this connection, I acknowledge the relevance of Maritain's attempt to promote a new Christendom. However, Christian moral values can only influence actions to change socio-economic structures if a changing social ethos makes people susceptible to them. Christian moral values have the potential to strengthen the social ethos, which in turn will strengthen public morality and social cohesion.

Maritain acknowledges that the common ethos is not the same as social cohesion, but social ethos is essential to social cohesion and contributes to it. Social ethos does not and cannot determine the social cohesion of a democratic civil society in the sense of a homogeneous society. A democratic civil society is characterized by a social and worldview pluralism, but its ultimate goal is the common good. The common ethos is directed precisely at promoting this goal and in this sense it tends to promote social cohesion.

# Resolving the Tension between Tolerance and Truth: Jacques Maritain on the Moral Extremes of Relativism and Fanaticism

John G. Trapani, Jr.

There is an apocryphal Abraham Lincoln story that is as insightful as it is humorous. It tells of a Mississippi River barge that rammed into an abutment of a railroad bridge spanning the river. The railroad wanted to hold the barge company liable, and hired a high-powered law firm from the East. The barge owner questioned the right of the railroad to interfere with navigation, and hired Abraham Lincoln as its sole counsel. After a long, detailed, and complex trial, it was finally time for closing arguments.

> Those for the railroad spoke eloquently, summarizing the evidence, advancing watertight arguments, and clearly impressing the jurors. Then came Lincoln's turn. He rose, strode to the jury box, smiled, and made a single statement: "My learned opponents," he said, "have presented an impressive case. There is no question that they have their facts absolutely right. But they have drawn completely wrong conclusions." The jurors laughed uproariously, adjourned to their deliberations, and after only a few moments returned with a verdict favoring Lincoln's client.
>
> As soon as court adjourned, the railroad attorneys besieged Lincoln with questions. "We had that case won," they told him. "Then you simply tell the jurors that our facts are right and our conclusions wrong, and they decide in your favor. Why? What did you do to them?"
>
> "Well, boys," Lincoln replied, "it just happened that when the court had adjourned for lunch today, I happened into a saloon where the jurors were eating, and I told them a little story. A story about a farmer who was working in his barnyard one day when his ten-year-old boy came rushing up to him, all excited. "Paw," said the boy. "Come quick. The hired man and Sis are up in the haymow, and he's a-pullin' down his pants and she's a-liftin' up her skirts. Paw, they're gettin' ready to pee all over our

hay." "Son," said the farmer, "you've got your facts absolutely right, but you've drawn a completely wrong conclusion."[1]

For however charming and amusing this Lincoln anecdote may be, its simple wisdom also provides us with a useful framework for critiquing the prevailing, popular, and politically-correct understanding of tolerance in a democratic society such as ours: specifically, the theory that, in a pluralist society, where cultural and political differences abound, citizens are truly tolerant only when they suspend any claims to truth and, when making decisions, they let the majority decide.

Living in America in the 1940s and 50s, Jacques Maritain had a first-hand opportunity to reflect on the problems of democracy in general, and on the problem of the tension between tolerance and truth in particular. Some of these ideas are found in his book, *Reflections on America.*[2] In an earlier essay, "Truth and Human Fellowship," however, Maritain addresses Hans Kelson's theory of "relativist democracy," a theory that holds Pontius Pilate, in Maritain's words, as the "lofty precursor of relativist democracy." Maritain's critique summarizes Kelson's position in this way: "Because Pilate did not know what truth is, Kelson concludes, he therefore called upon the people, and asked them to decide; and thus in a democratic society, it is up to the people to decide, and mutual tolerance reigns, because no one knows what truth is."[3] Those who concur with this conclusion might argue that, since American democracy is indeed characterized by great racial, ethnic, political, and religious diversity, how else might we hope to resolve this pervasive pluralism? Isn't the suspension of truth-claims, by leaving the resolution of issues to the majority, at the very foundation of any true democracy? In reply, others may wonder, either

---

[1] P.M. Zall, ed., *Abe Lincoln Laughing* (Knoxville, Tennessee: University of Tennessee Press, 1995), pp. ix-x.

[2] Jacques Maritain, *Reflections on America* (Garden City, New York: Image Books [Doubleday], 1964).

[3] Jacques Maritain, "Truth and Human Fellowship," *On The Use of Philosophy* (Princeton, New Jersey: Princeton University Press, 1961), p. 19; the essay was originally published in 1957.

in reference to America specifically, or to democracy in general, whether those who make this claim aren't a perfect example of those who get their facts about the diversity of American culture right, but draw "a completely wrong conclusion!"

To begin, let us make sure that, descriptively, we get our facts right about American culture. First, the world's boundaries continue to shrink. Made possible by cable and wireless communication systems and the progressive advancements in human flight, the global proliferation of information and personal transportation have become so fast today that virtually no part of the planet is any longer remote or isolated. Fueled by international corporations and a vast entertainment industry, world cultures have slowly, almost imperceptibly, become more homogenized, in spite of their retention of certain essential elements of their own national cultural identity.

Secondly, the ever-increasing means and availability of human mobility and resettlement, prompted by forced expatriation or inspired by free choice, have moved, uprooted, and relocated vast ethnic populations throughout the major urban and industrial centers of the civilized world. In some places, these immigrant populations have been welcomed and comfortably assimilated, while in other places, these *auslander* have been forcibly channeled to ghetto-like enclaves or refugee camps, where frequently clashing cultures intermingle.

Thirdly, from the abolition of slavery and the commencement of women's suffrage to the civil rights movement and the feminist revolution, the worthy affirmation of universal human rights, coupled with the two facts previously noted, have led to dramatic progress in the quality of, and respect for, human life and the character of human societies in many parts of the globe (for example, the United Nations, the Geneva Conventions, the Universal Declaration of Human Rights, the Nuremberg Trials, the World Court, the formation of the European Union, the universal condemnation of terrorism, etc.). While surely laudable in itself for the progress in preserving and insuring the inherent human rights brought about by these changes and organizations, we also can observe the way in which claims about the universality of these intrinsic human rights have come into conflict with local and regional mores, laws, and customs. The resulting discord has fueled debates about "nature versus nurture," the national and political imperialism of larger, first-world nations imposing "their beliefs" upon smaller, often third-world nations, and moral and cultural pluralism in general. These debates themselves have spawned the even larger philosophical debates about truth, moral relativism, and tolerance.

While additional cultural facts may be observed, mention of these alone is sufficient for making clear the cultural upheavals that they have wrought over the last century. As the vast diversity of cultures, races, and religions flooded 4$^{th}$ century B.C. Athens and gave rise to the moral relativism of the Sophists, so too, though this time on a global scale, there is a similar contemporary confusion about truth. Sample questions are plentiful: what is truth? Where is it to be found? Isn't truth relative to time, place, and power? How do we know for sure who's correct about what is right or wrong, good or bad, true or false? From the macrocosm of the melting pot that is America to the microcosms of cities like New York, Los Angeles, or Miami, politically correct ways of thinking challenge those who desire to be good, truly democratic, citizens with questions concerning multiculturalism, diversity, and true tolerance.

This cultural analysis is not without its analogue in philosophy. Here, too, the latter part of the twentieth century has witnessed the slow but steady rise to prominence of post-modernism. From its subtle, virtually imperceptible influence on metaphysics and epistemology, to its culturally observed and significant influence on morality and politics, post-modernism has given an intellectual voice to the undercurrent of moral, cultural, and political relativism which ultimately culminates in, and characterizes, post-modern skepticism: if there are only stories, narratives, and perspectives, themselves the products of nurture in specific cultures or individual lives, then "truth" is entirely relativized as acts of community or personal empowerment, where each "unit" finds and expresses its "own voice." As a result, "truths" are no more or less than whatever the individual, group, tribe, or community may say they are.

Of course, logical reasoning and philosophical debate are of little use here. There can be no goal of discovering the truth by philosophical interchange since, for post-modernism, there is *a priori* no possibility of any absolute or universal truths. Rather, by deconstructing narratives, one may hope to gain an increased understanding of another's perspective or world-view. Shared understanding, while genuinely good and worthwhile in itself, will also lead, so this thinking goes, to harmony within any community populated with diverse groups and sub-groups; each segment, while espousing and embracing its own voice, also ought to tolerate and support the many other voices that also have the right to express themselves and be heard. Criticism concerning this cacophony is futile since post-modernism tends to view truth-claims as little more than assertions that oppress the less powerful. Thus, for post-modernism, mutual respect for the kaleidoscope of diversity is itself the highest value; it alone produces the sonorous harmony that communities, of whatever size, need. In place of any pursuit of truth, they would argue, a democratic society ought to embrace that form of political pluralism that gives pride of place to the voice and will of the majority–so long, of course, as everyone has a voice, and the rule of the majority does not violate the canons of political correctness. In this way, truth is abnegated and tolerance rules ... or so this is the conclusion that such thinking would have us believe!

Opposing these claims of post-modernism, however, are those who would argue that the framers of the Declaration of Independence and the U.S. Constitution understood that American democracy is rooted in immutable truths ("We hold these truths"), and that true tolerance and human and political fellowship are impossible without those truths and the inalienable rights that follow from them. Herein lies the tension between tolerance and truth; that is, herein we find the problem of having our cultural and political facts right even as we draw "a completely wrong conclusion" from them! Certainly, as the world shrinks and cultures homogenize, we can and ought to celebrate cultural diversity and all of those differences that constitute "matters of taste" (as opposed to "matters of fact"). However, to go from the affirmation of this panoply of diversity to the post-modern and politically correct claim that, ultimately, there are no universal truths, is simply to draw the wrong conclusion.

Maritain discusses this tension between tolerance and truth in his essay, "Truth and Human Fellowship."[4] In it, he makes the classical philosophical problem clear: the tension is between two real goods–tolerance and truth–neither of which can be ignored or forgotten. Articulated as a question, the problem that this tension conceals is as follows: how is it possible for a democratic society to balance two essential but *seemingly* contradictory goods, both of which are foundational pillars? More specifically, how can the citizens of a pluralist society maintain a mutual respect and tolerance for the various and diverse ideas of their fellow constituents and at the same time hold firmly to the fundamental truths of a healthy democracy, including the essential, inherent dignity of all human persons and their inalienable, universal human rights?

In the course of human history, at different times and places, human societies have suffered from the discernable moral extremes that result when those in power support only one of these two pillars of a good democracy at the expense of the other. As such, at one extreme, there are those who are so dedicated to the ideal of tolerance that they sacrifice any firm commitment to truth, including the foundational truths of democracy. Doing this results in the moral extreme of Relativism, which sees those who affirm the foundational truths of democracy as intolerant fanatics who oppose diversity.

Swing the pendulum to the other extreme and, in order steadfastly to affirm the fundamental truths of an enduring democracy, there are those who sacrifice an open tolerance for all ideas, especially those that might subvert and undermine the moral and political fabric of democracy. This results in the moral extreme of Fanaticism, which sees those who affirm the need for tolerance in a democracy as skeptical relativists who oppose democracy's foundational truths.

The solution to the errors that lie at the heart of these two moral extremes of Relativism and Fanaticism involves what Maritain calls "right thinking" about both the objective order of ideas and the subjective order of persons. When we think rightly in the objective order of ideas, we see that truth ought to reign and errors ought to be

---

[4] Cf. Ibid.

eliminated. The intellect naturally desires to know the truth of things; instinctively, we don't like it when people lie to us, and we quite naturally seek to correct errors when we observe them and can show the reasoning that leads to their correction; two contradictory propositions of ideas cannot both be true. On the other hand, thinking rightly in the subjective order of persons affirms the immutable intrinsic worth and dignity of all human beings, regardless of the truth or falsity of the ideas they may happen to hold.[5]

This right thinking about the objective order of ideas and the subjective order of persons is essential for the proper and successful balancing of the tension between tolerance and truth; shift or confuse that thinking and the moral extremes result. Specifically, in the first case, if one shifts the right thinking about persons to ideas, the following results: instead of saying, correctly, that "all *persons* are to be loved and respected even when they may be in error," one could incorrectly conclude (because of the desire to preserve mutual tolerance) that "all *ideas* are to be tolerated and respected, especially when our ability to know truth may be shrouded in doubt." Should this shift occur, the moral extreme of Relativism is born, and the right desire for truth becomes its casualty.

On the other hand, if one shifts the right thinking about ideas to persons, the opposite error results: instead of saying, correctly, that "only those *ideas* that are true ought to be defended and proclaimed, and those *ideas* that are in error ought to be corrected or eliminated," one could incorrectly conclude (because of the desire to defend truth itself) that only those *persons* who embrace truth have legitimacy while those *persons* who are in error ought to be eliminated. Should this shift occur, the moral extreme of Fanaticism is born, and the right desire for mutual tolerance becomes its casualty.[6]

The prevailing thinking today is that of the moral extreme of Relativism and, together with the philosophical endorsement it receives from post-modernism, it sacrifices the good of those

---

[5] Ibid.

[6] Ibid., p. 22. (N.B.: Maritain refers to this Fanaticism as "Absolutism.")

immutable truths that are at the foundation of democracy. From this perspective, tolerance appears the easier good to attain. For not only is truth itself more difficult to acquire rationally, there are also erroneous misconceptions about it: specifically, one frequently hears the position that, either no one has the truth and it cannot be known, or, if one should claim to have the truth, that person must necessarily be intolerant and impose it on others. And yet, these are misconceptions about the nature of truth; truth is possible, but it is to be won only by hard thinking and sound reasoning. Acquired slowly and through rational investigation, logical reasoning, public discourse and collegial cooperation, we also discover that the more we know, the more we come to understand how much there is yet to know. Humility in the face of truth is essential for its very preservation.

In this regard, Maritain is again insightful. There are two kinds of ignorance, he tells us, "the ignorance of those who know, [and] the ignorance of those who are in the dark."[7] The latter ignorance leads to Relativism when it concludes: "I don't know the truth ... and neither does anyone else." These people are the ones "who think that the primary condition of tolerance ... is not to believe in any truth...."[8] The former type of ignorance is the ignorance of those who can identify what they don't know and who are humble in their ignorance; they are the ones who know "that it is truth, not ignorance, which ... gives us the sense of what remains unknown in our very knowledge."[9]

Moreover, we quite naturally tend to think that Fanaticism is worse than Relativism because of our fear of the violence and harm that it so often brings to individuals, groups, races, or religions. And yet, as Maritain points out, Relativism may become equally heinous should it reach the point where it holds those who disagree with it as "barbarous, childish, or subhuman, and it may happen to treat them as

---

[7] Jacques Maritain, *Reflections on America*, p. 47.

[8] Jacques Maritain, "Truth and Human Fellowship," p. 18.

[9] Ibid., p. 24.

badly as the zealot treats the unbeliever." In this way, Relativism becomes a "fanaticism of doubt."[10]

Regardless of which of these extremes may be prevalent in a democracy at any given time, they are both fatal; for a genuinely healthy democracy, we need both mutual tolerance and a commitment to truth. Thus, the "completely right conclusion" to be drawn from all of the facts about social, political, religious, and cultural diversity now should be perfectly clear: a healthy democracy needs civil discourse where its citizens respect one another with a mutual tolerance for the diversity of ideas, even while they engage in a civilized pursuit of truth, one that realizes and affirms that "no democratic society can live without a common practical belief in those truths which are freedom, justice, law, and the other tenets of democracy;"[11] for indeed, "...without a general, firm, reasoned-out conviction concerning such tenets, democracy cannot survive."[12]

---

[10] Ibid., p. 17.

[11] Ibid., p. 18.

[12] Jacques Maritain, "The Philosopher in Society," *On The Use of Philosophy*, p. 12.

# Yves R. Simon and Aquinas on Willing the Common Good

John A. Cuddeback

In treating the goodness and evil of the interior act of the will, Aquinas makes the following remarkable assertion:

> But a man's will is not right in willing a particular good, unless he refer it to the common good as an end: since even the natural appetite of each part is ordained to the common good of the whole. Now it is the end that supplies the formal reason, as it were, of willing whatever is directed to the end. Consequently, in order that a man will some particular good with a right will, he must will that particular good materially, and the Divine and universal good, formally.[1]

At issue in this quotation is an essential piece, perhaps indeed the central piece, of Aquinas's understanding of the goodness of human willing and action. Goodness of the human will is from the end willed.[2] And within the hierarchy of ends willed, the willing of higher ends is formal with regards to the willing of lower ends. Thus, the foundational proper ordination in the human will is that it will the true ultimate end. In the above text, as in many other texts, Aquinas identifies the ultimate end as the common good.[3] Willing the common good, it seems

---

[1] Thomas Aquinas, *Summa Theologiae* (hereafter cited as *ST*), I-II, q. 19, a. 10, translation of the Fathers of the English Dominican Province (New York: Benziger Brothers, 1947). Of this article, Yves Simon comments: "It is fitting to quote in its entirety the body of this article, in which few seem to have recognized the most precise exposition ever made of the principles commanding the theory of government," *Philosophy of Democratic Government* (Notre Dame, Indiana: University of Notre Dame Press, 1993), p. 40. (This work is cited hereafter as *DG*.)

[2] Thomas Aquinas, *ST* I-II, q. 1, aa. 4 and 6. The emphasis of goodness as from the end willed (*finis operantis*) does not of course preclude goodness from the object of the action itself (*finis operis*), since goodness is *ex integra causa* (*ST* I-II, q. 18, a. 4, ad. 3).

[3] Another key text is Thomas Aquinas, *ST* I- II, q. 90, a. 2.

to me, especially given its foundational place in Aquinas's ethics and moral theology, receives surprisingly little attention.[4]

The political treatises of Yves Simon are an exception. An astute student of Aquinas's political philosophy, and especially of the notion of authority, Simon is acutely aware of the central role of willing the common good. Both those in authority and those acting as individuals within a community should will and intend the common good. Indeed, in both cases, such willing is at the foundation of moral rectitude. The goal of this paper is to shed some light on how an individual person (i.e., a person not acting in the office of authority) should will the common good. An individual's proper willing of the common good includes that he or she: 1) will the common good most of all, 2) be obedient to authority, and 3) will all else on account of the common good. These points should become clear through an examination of Simon's work, especially his treatment of the role of authority in society.

Before turning to Simon, let us note a few points I will take for granted. The common good is a good proper to a community of persons.[5] A community exercises a collective causality—a causality that belongs to it as a whole (even when only a few members actually

---

[4] That the obviously *political* notion of willing the common good has such a central position in Aquinas's ethics should come as no surprise. For Aquinas, politics is the highest part of moral science. See Aquinas, *Commentary on Aristotle's Nicomachean Ethics*, Bk 1, lect. 1, #4-6 on the parts of moral science, and Aquinas, *Commentary on Aristotle's Politics* (*Sententia libri politicorum*), trans. R. Regan (Indianapolis, Indiana: Hackett, 2007), Prologue, on the primacy of politics: "Therefore, if a superior science concerns what is more excellent and complete, politics is necessarily superior and architectonic to all other practical sciences, since politics considers the ultimate end and complete good regarding human affairs" (pp. 2-3).

[5] On the different senses of the term "common good," see Gregory Froelich, "The Equivocal Status of Bonum Commune," *The New Scholasticism* (Winter 1989): 38-57. The common good of a community of persons is "common" not as a genus or species, but as a "common final cause, according as the common good is said to be the common end" (*ST* I- II, q. 90, a. 2, ad. 2).

perform the action),[6] and it has what we call common actions.[7] A mere partnership, as distinguished from a community, has perhaps a "common interest," yet this is nothing more than "a sum of private interests that happen to be interdependent."[8] The common good that we will consider is the common good of a "perfect" or complete society. There is of course a sense in which we can speak of there being a genuine "common good" of smaller communities—notably the family. But as the imperfect is a part of, and for the sake of, the perfect, [9] it is fitting to focus on the complete society, as it is the complete society that has a common good in the more proper sense, as being the more ultimate end. Now, the heavenly city, too, is a complete society, the end of which is the most ultimate common good.[10] But, for this examination of willing the common good, I will focus on willing the common good of the political society, as my concern is to emphasize the general structure of willing the common good.[11]

To begin our consideration of Simon's account of how to will the common good, we must begin with the distinction between what he calls the form and the matter of the common good. He introduces this

---

[6] Yves R. Simon, *DG* 64.

[7] Yves R. Simon, *A General Theory of Authority* (Notre Dame, Indiana: University of Notre Dame Press, 1980), p. 30–cited hereafter as *GT*–and Yves R. Simon, *DG* 64-65.

[8] Ibid., p. 30.

[9] See Thomas Aquinas, *ST* I-II, q. 90, a. 2, and *Commentary on Aristotle's Politics*, lib. 1.1 n. 30 (Bk I, chapter 1, #22, p. 17 in R. Regan's translation).

[10] Thomas Aquinas, *De caritate* 2. Here, Aquinas employs properly political notions to expound his understanding of charity as a virtue. Charity itself is the love of God as the common good of the heavenly Jerusalem.

[11] I realize that the relation between willing the common good of the civil society and willing the most ultimate supernatural common good is of concrete and critical importance in the moral life. The key to this issue, as to many of the most difficult moral issues in the thought of Aquinas, is in the teleological principle that the lower serves and receives its meaning from the higher, to which it is ordered. I address this briefly at the end of this essay.

distinction by pointing to "an opposition between form and content within the object of volition and intention."[12] He states: "I may will and intend what is good without knowing *what the thing is* that is good."[13] He proceeds to explain that a man of good will is daily faced with the problem of determining just what it is "in which the form of goodness resides." Simon then applies these terms to the common good and speaks of the form of the common good and the matter of the common good as two distinguishable objects of volition. In other words, it is one thing to will the "good" of the community, and it is another thing to will that complex order of goods that actually constitutes the good of the community.[14]

Having asserted a distinction between the form and matter of the common good, Simon is prepared to distinguish between the role of authority and that of the private individual. He says:

> So far as community life is concerned, the problem of matter and form within the end can be posed as follows: Is it desirable that the common good be willed and intended, both with regard to matter and with regard to form, by private persons acting in a private capacity?[15]

It is particularly in answering this rich question that Simon teaches us much about the common good and how to will it. Here is a tripartite outline of his answer. First, it is evident in the scholastic tradition, and particularly in Aquinas, that any good person must will the form of the common good. Second, an individual person, acting in his private capacity

---

[12] Yves R. Simon, *GT* 52.

[13] Ibid.; emphasis original.

[14] It seems to me that what Simon is expressing can also be captured by using a distinction that Aquinas makes as regards the willing of happiness: willing the *ratio* versus willing *that in which the ratio is found*. To answer the question whether all humans will the same final end, Aquinas distinguishes between the *ratio* of beatitude, and that in which beatitude is found. All humans agree in desiring the former, since all "desire the fulfillment of their perfection," but not the latter, since different people seek their fulfillment in different things (*ST* I-II, q. 1, a. 7).

[15] Yves R. Simon, *GT* 52-53.

as a member of the society, should *not* will and intend the matter of the common good. Third, it is the role of authority, indeed its "most essential function,"[16] to will and in some sense determine the matter of the common good. Let us look at each of the three points of this answer.

The first point, that a good person must will the common good formally, Simon sees as uncontroversial. To will the common good formally is to will the common flourishing, the good that is proper to the whole society, and to will it above one's private good. Simon explains:

> The private person, inasmuch as he is morally excellent, wills and intends the common good, and subordinates his private wishes to it. He may not know what action the common good demands, but he adheres to the common good formally understood, to the form of the common good, whatever may be the matter in which this form resides....[17]

While Aquinas holds that all persons necessarily agree in intending the *ratio* of beatitude,[18] the fulfillment of perfection, he does not hold that all persons necessarily *intend* the common good, even just in its form or *ratio*. He does hold that there is a natural inclination or a natural love of common goods above the private good of the self;[19] but, as we all know, natural inclinations are not necessarily acted out. Virtue is required in order to live out this natural inclination. Indeed, we can even say that the refusal actually to love the common good more than self is one of the main ways, if not the primary way, to distinguish a bad person from a good person. Simon remarks on the sad condition of society:

> In societies such as the cities and states of our experience, where selfishness and ignorance prevail, persons have to be constantly directed and often coerced toward the common good.

---

[16] Ibid., p. 57, and *DG* 59.

[17] Ibid., p. 55.

[18] See Thomas Aquinas, *ST* I-II, q. 1, a.7, ad. 1, where Aquinas explains that even in sinning a person does not turn away from "the intention of the last end."

[19] See Thomas Aquinas, *ST* I, q. 60, a. 5c and ad. 5.

> Men of ill will seek their own advantage and ignore the good of all....[20]

Certainly, Simon does us a great service in bringing before us a bedrock truth of our tradition that can often seem to have been forgotten: a good person, by definition, is one who intends the common good above his or her private good.

The second point in his answer to the above question is that an individual person, acting in a private capacity as a member of society, should *not* will and intend the matter of the common good. Simon begins by arguing the other side: the virtuous person, if truly virtuous, wills the form and matter of the common good. Now, since virtue guarantees that a person wills the form of the common good, should it not also guarantee that he or she wills the matter of the common good? Simon comments: "It almost irresistibly seems that a disposition concerned with the form of the common good but not with its matter is just about half a virtue."[21]

In order to refute this position, Simon notes that we must distinguish between two capacities in society. Often referred to as "public" and "private" capacities, Simon prefers to call them "common" and "particular." These capacities must not be confounded, for the primary reason that *they are both necessary for the common good.* Now the common capacity "is defined by a relation to the common good considered not only in its form but also in its matter or content."[22] The particular capacity, on the other hand, does not have such a relation to the matter of the common good; if it did, it would cease to be a particular capacity. Thus, since the common good itself requires both capacities to be exercised, it is important that the particular capacity not be compromised by a direct relation to the matter of the common one.

An analogy from the military life is in order. In war, a commanding officer is ordered to hold a certain position at all costs. The officer, as a

---

[20] Yves R. Simon, *GT* 51.

[21] Ibid., p. 58.

[22] Ibid., p. 57.

good soldier, intends the common good of the army and of the nation, which right now means victory in war. But he has a particular capacity in this effort, namely, the holding of this position. He intends to hold this position, precisely because he intends victory in war. Simon aptly states: "Thus the particular good—holding the place—is willed because of the common good, on the ground of the common good, under a determination supplied by the common good."[23] Now, the next point is as important as it is obvious: the officer must concern himself with the particular good and not with the question of overall strategy. Were he to concern himself with overall strategy, it would be prejudicial both to his maintaining the position and to the overall strategy itself, or in other words, the material common good of the army.

The point of this analogy is clear. The common good demands that particular goods be given "particular" attention. The formal willing of the common good by a virtuous person requires that he or she attend to his or her own particular capacity,[24] and not to the content itself of the common good. This very point is made even more dramatically when Aquinas argues that the wife of the condemned man should will that his life be spared. In other words, her will that he be spared is precisely what her formal willing of the common good demands, even though the material common good requires that he be executed.[25]

Now Simon's third point: authority's "most essential function" is to will and in some sense determine the matter of the common good. This is at the heart of Simon's understanding of authority. One of the great

---

[23] Yves R. Simon, *DG* 43.

[24] Simon distinguishes two kinds of particularity: particularity in subject, and particularity in function. He explains the distinction at *DG* 55-57 and *GT* 60-61. Particularity in subject is the particularity that belongs to a "part" of society as such, the best examples being an individual person, or a family. Particularity in function is the particularity of what is concerned with a certain aspect of a whole, as for instance the army is concerned with the security of the whole nation. "Autonomy" is an excellence that especially attaches to particularity in subject (*GT* 64). The advantage of specialization is an excellence that attaches to particularity in function (*GT* 62).

[25] See Thomas Aquinas, *ST* I-II, q. 19, a. 10, and Yves R. Simon, *DG* 42.

contributions of Simon's treatment of authority is the masterful way he shows that the function of authority is not merely "substitutional;" in other words, its role in human affairs is not ultimately grounded in the defects—intellectual, moral, or other–of human persons. What he calls the paternal function of authority is substitutional; it is rooted in the temporary incapacity of those subject to it and it aims at its own disappearance.[26] What he calls the "essential function" of authority is its causation of "united action" when the means to the common good are not uniquely determined.[27] But he reserves the phrase "most essential function" to that before us now: its role in the intention of the common good. He defends his use of the phrase "most essential" by noting that this function of authority "concerns the most fundamental act of social life"—the intention of the common good.[28]

So how does Simon describe the relation between authority and the intention of the common good? Authority intends, in addition to the form, the matter or content of the common good. The argument that authority intends the matter of the common good is very simple. Simon takes it as evident that there must be some principle that intends the matter of the common good. He states:

> It is obvious that the common good has to be intended not only formally but also materially; if it is established that it should not be intended materially by particular persons, it follows that a nonparticular reason and will ought to be constituted; otherwise the common good, materially considered, would not be intended at all.[29]

---

[26] Yves R. Simon, *DG* 15.

[27] See Yves R. Simon *GT* 41-50, where he argues that this role for authority is not rooted in the imperfection of those under the authority. See, especially, *GT* 49: "Given a community on its way to its common good, and given, on the part of this community, the degree of excellence which entails the possibility of attaining the good in a diversity of ways, authority has an indispensable role to play, and this role originates entirely in plenitude and accomplishment."

[28] Yves R. Simon, *DG* 59.

[29] Ibid., p. 56.

Simon is convinced that the common good of society simply requires that authority order the parts in view of the common flourishing. This implies that authority must make determinations[30] regarding just what constitutes the common good. These determinations are expressed, among other ways, in law.[31] The significance of this point in Simon's view becomes clear in the final paragraph of his masterful chapter "General Theory of Government" in *Philosophy of Democratic Government*:

> Finally, let us again call attention to the illusion that the good will of each, if it were complete and enlightened, would suffice to guarantee the intention of the common good. This illusion is stubborn because it is hard to master the operation of the principles which, at the bottom of the question, seem to conflict but actually condition and supplement each other. The common good demands that particular persons should do full justice to the goodness of the particular good; but, if such is the case, an over-all direction toward the common good is necessary.[32]

We have completed, then, Simon's tripartite answer to his own question of whether it is desirable that private persons will the common good both with regard to matter and to form. The first point of my thesis has been directly treated: an individual's proper willing of the common good implies willing the form of the common good, and this above one's own private good. The second point, too, can now readily be clarified: right willing of the common good requires obedience to authority, which determines the matter of the common good. We can put it this way: for the individual to have the right relation to the common good, it is not sufficient that he or she will the common good formally, and his or her particular good materially.[33] The "something more" that is needed is precisely obedience to authority, and acceptance of its direction concerning the matter of the common good. Simon explains:

---

[30] Yves R. Simon, *GT* 146.

[31] Ibid., p. 55.

[32] Ibid., pp. 70-71.

[33] Ibid., pp. 144-45.

> But what relation will obtain between those in charge of the common good and those whose duty it is to intend, in a material sense, particular goods? Clearly, the very principle of the primacy of the common good demands that the intentions of the latter be subordinated to the intentions of the former. The primacy of the common good demands that those in charge of particular goods should obey those in charge of the common good. It is, in the last analysis, as simple as that.[34]

Here, we gain insight into the beautiful and indispensable virtue of obedience. In obedience, a person's actions and pursuits are given form and direction by the concrete demands of the common good, as determined by authority. And the disposition to obey authority is a necessary expression of the person's willing of the common good, just as surely as the dictates of authority are an expression of the authority's willing of the common good.

Authority's determination of the matter of the common good provides the context for a person's pursuit of good in the private capacity. Simon does not envision the role of authority as simply providing certain boundaries to the private capacity—as though the high command simply arranged things so that subordinate officers might pursue their own affairs. Since the private capacity is itself for the sake of the common good, its very structure is essentially conditioned and determined by the common good itself. Simon refers to this point when he says of the officer, "Thus the particular good—holding the place—is willed because of the common good, on the ground of the common good, *under a determination supplied by the common good*."[35] That the private capacity receives an essential determination from the matter of the common good does not compromise the private-ness of this capacity. Rather, it preserves its place in serving the common good.

Is there an antimony, then, in holding that a person should not will the matter of the common good, but that he or she should be directed

---

[34] Yves R. Simon, *DG* 56-57.

[35] Ibid, p. 43; emphasis added.

by authority's determination of the matter of the common good? There is not. The good person wills the form of the common good, and thus pursues his or her particular capacity precisely within that intention. Simon explains that it is thanks to authority that "the man of good will who wants to do the thing that the common good demands actually knows what that thing is and does it."[36] In other words, the particular capacity itself takes shape in the context of some understanding of the matter of the common good, as determined by authority. Here, the particular capacity is most itself—as integrated into the complex order of goods that constitutes the common flourishing of the community.[37]

We would do well to recall the reason why Simon holds that an individual person should not will the matter of the common good. The reason is *not* that the common good will simply "happen" when each person wills and acts for his particular good. Rather, the common good itself requires the excellence of the particular capacities, which excellence requires the particular attention of individuals.[38] And such particular attention can only be properly given by individuals who do not seek to determine the matter of the common good themselves, but who are obedient to the determinations of authority. In sum, the common good is best achieved if individuals will the common good most of all, and thus obediently receive direction in the exercise of their private capacities.

The third and final point of my thesis regarding how to will the common good–that one should will all else on account of the common good–hearkens back to the opening quotation of this paper:

---

[36] Yves R. Simon, *GT* 145.

[37] Given the role of authority, it goes without saying that any significant failure in its determining the matter of the common good has serious repercussions, both for the common good itself and the individuals who will it. We can consider Simon's sober words: "When the private person has to emerge above his capacity and substitute for nonexistent public persons, an awe-inspiring solitude makes him realize that the structure of society has broken down" (*DG* 44).

[38] See Yves R. Simon, *GT* 64-65.

> But a man's will is not right in willing a particular good, unless he refer it to the common good as an end: since even the natural appetite of each part is ordained to the common good of the whole. Now it is the end that supplies the formal reason, as it were, of willing whatever is directed to the end. Consequently, in order that a man will some particular good with a right will, he must will that particular good materially, and the Divine and universal good, formally.[39]

It seems to me that here we have the most significant and challenging aspect of the proper willing of the common good. It is not enough that the common good be willed as higher than other goods; the common good should also be the reason for willing other goods: i.e., the goods that are ordered to it.[40] This point is of course closely connected to our last considerations above. If a person wills particular goods precisely because he or she wills the common good, he or she will have every reason to be attentive to the material determinations of authority.

As I noted earlier, my point in this paper is to address the universal structure of how to will the common good, without giving special attention to the issue of different levels of common good. In the above quotation, Aquinas is speaking of the ultimate common good: the divine good itself. The central point, that the end supplies the formal reason of willing whatever is directed to the end, is a fundamental teleological principle that first of all obtains and is observable in the natural, political realm. For Aquinas, the common good of the civil

---

[39] Thomas Aquinas, *ST* I-II, q. 19, a. 10.

[40] We might consider again the words of Simon regarding the military officer: "Thus the particular good—holding the place—is willed *because of the common good*, on the ground of the common good, under a determination supplied by the common good" (*DG* 43); emphasis added.

society is the highest end of human action in the natural order,[41] and as such it supplies the formal reason for willing other human goods.[42]

This point is especially highlighted in Aquinas's understanding of what he calls general or legal justice. General justice is a virtue that "directs man to the common good," by referring the acts of other virtues to the common good.[43] In a striking article, Aquinas says that this virtue is a "general virtue" not by predication, but rather "virtually," as "a universal cause is general in relation to all its effects." He proceeds to explain:

> Now it is in the latter sense that, according to what has been said, legal justice is said to be a general virtue, in as much, to wit, as it directs the acts of the other virtues to its own end, and this is to move all the other virtues by its command; for just as charity may be called a general virtue in so far as it directs the acts of all the virtues to the Divine good, so too is legal justice, in so far as it directs the acts of all the virtues to the common good.[44]

The comparison to charity is of particular significance; general justice is the natural analogate for charity. Now, for Aquinas, since charity is what orders one to the ultimate, supernatural end, and things ordered to the end are "not said to be good except in relation to the end," no "true virtue" is possible without charity.[45] He thus also asserts:

> Now it is evident, in accordance with what has been said (a.7), that it is charity which directs the acts of all other virtues to the last end, and which, consequently, also gives the form to all

---

[41] See Thomas Aquinas, *Commentary on Aristotle's Politics*, Prologue: "...since politics considers the ultimate and complete good regarding human affairs" (paragraph 7 in the Latin; Regan, pp. 2-3).

[42] See Yves R. Simon, *The Tradition of Natural Law* (New York: Fordham University. Press, 1992), p. 105: "The end of the moral virtues resides in the common good of the temporal society." (This work is cited hereafter as *TNL*.)

[43] Thomas Aquinas, *ST* II-II, q. 58, a. 5.

[44] Ibid., a. 6.

[45] Thomas Aquinas, *ST* II-II, q. 23, a. 7.

> other acts of virtue: and it is precisely in this sense that charity is called the form of the virtues....[46]

Aquinas's treatment of general justice as a natural analogate for charity highlights our third point about willing the common good: willing the common good, which is the ultimate end, either in the natural or supernatural order, provides the reason and thus gives form to the willing of more particular goods. This is why general justice, the virtue of willing the (natural) common good and referring other goods to it, is called both the highest of all moral virtues,[47] and the cause of all other moral virtues.[48]

Given that the common good should provide the reason for willing the goods that are subordinate to it, it is important that we advert to the apparent problem of having more than one common good as a "final end." With characteristic clarity, Simon comments, "Let it also be remarked that an end may be final in a genuine sense and yet be contained within an order which is not, itself, final."[49] Aquinas directly addresses the issue of the two ends when he addresses whether there can be any true virtue without charity. If virtue be directed to a "particular good," such as the welfare of the state, while not further directed to the supernatural end by charity, it is true virtue, albeit imperfect.[50]Thus, even the common good of the civil society is a "particular good" in relation to the ultimate, supernatural common good. There is no contradiction or disorder but rather harmony and perfect order in the moral agent who wills goods according to their place in the teleological hierarchy. That a person wills particular natural goods both for the sake of the common good of society, and then also more deeply for the sake of the divine common good, is a reality that is perhaps only fully understood by those who do it.

---

[46] Ibid., a. 8.

[47] Ibid., a. 12.

[48] Ibid., a. 6.

[49] Yves R. Simon, *TNL* 100.

[50] Thomas Aquinas, *ST* II-II, q. 23, a. 7.

In conclusion, Simon has done us a great service in helping us to understand how to will the common good. The metaphysical relation of the common good to the particular goods that come under it is the reality to which the rightly ordered human will responds. Thus, the end "supplies the formal reason, as it were, of willing whatever is directed to the end,"[51] precisely because "the end is the rule of whatever is ordained to the end."[52] The good human will wills the common good, the final end, most of all, and so it wills particular goods as conditioned by the direction of authority regarding the matter of the common good. It seems that this understanding of willing of the common good grounds Aquinas's judgment regarding the hierarchy of virtues. Among the moral virtues, which are lower than the theological and intellectual virtues, Aquinas puts justice first.[53] If we look within the priority of justice, we find that more specifically he puts legal justice first, since it concerns the common good.[54] At the same time, he does not hesitate to say that obedience, a part of justice,[55] "whereby we contemn our own will for God's sake, is more praiseworthy than the other moral virtues...."[56]

---

[51] Thomas Aquinas, I-II, q. 19, a. 10.

[52] Thomas Aquinas, *ST* I-II, Prologue: "ex fine enim oportet accipere rationes eorum quae ordinantur ad finem."

[53] Thomas Aquinas, *ST* I-II, q. 66, a.4.

[54] Thomas Aquinas, *ST* II-II, q. 58, a. 12. See, also, *ST* II-II, q. 161, a. 5, where he asks whether humility is the greatest: "Therefore after the theological virtues, after the intellectual virtues which regard reason itself, and after justice, especially legal justice, humility stands before all others."

[55] Thomas Aquinas, *ST* II-II, q. 104, a.2, ad. 2.

[56] Ibid., a. 3.

# JOHN STUART MILL'S DEONTOLOGICAL HEDONISM

Francis Slade

*Thought freed from the senses, as if original, and freed from the Common things; thus the opposite of Dante who saw agape with eros as a common thing in Beatrice's eyes.*[1]

Alternatively, the title for these remarks concerning John Stuart Mill's moral doctrine could have been *Doin' Right Ain't Got No End*, a statement made by one of the characters in Clint Eastwood's film, *The Outlaw Josey Wales.*[2] Why that is so I hope will become evident in the substance of this paper. The direction in which I am headed can be gathered from an entry in Nietzsche's *Daybreak* (*Morgenröte*) entitled *Fashions in Morality* (#131):

> How the overall moral judgments have shifted! The great men of antique morality, Epictetus for instance, knew nothing of the now normal glorification of thinking of others, of living for others; in the light of our moral fashion they would have to be called downright immoral, for they strove with all their might for their ego and against feeling with others (that is to say, with the sufferings and moral frailties of others). [3]

John Stuart Mill's moral doctrine as it illustrates this shift in the "overall moral judgments" is the focus of my attention. My remarks fall under five headings: 1. The Context of Mill's Moral Doctrine; 2. Socratic Dissatisfaction; 3.The Disinterested and Benevolent Spectator; 4. Minding Other People's Business: Caring and Ruling; 5. The New Holiness.

---

[1] R. P. Blackmur, "San Giovanni in Venere," in *A Primer of Ignorance*, ed. Joseph Frank (New York: Harcourt, 1967), p. 176.

[2] The character who makes the statement is "The Redlegs Captain," not otherwise identified, who leads a relentless pursuit of Josey Wales, the outlaw.

[3] Friedrich Nietzsche, *Daybreak*, trans. R. J. Hollingdale (Cambridge: Cambridge University Press, 1982), p. 131.

## I The Context of Mill's Moral Doctrine

In a talk given at Kenyon College in 1947, entitled "Manners, Morals, and the Novel," the literary critic Lionel Trilling made this observation:

> [T]he moral passions are even more willful and imperious and impatient than the self-seeking passions. All history is at one in telling us that their tendency is to be not only liberating but also restrictive.... [W]e must be aware of the dangers which lie in our most generous wishes. Some paradox of our nature leads us, when once we have made our fellow men the objects of our enlightened interest, to go on to make them the objects of our pity, then of our wisdom, ultimately of our coercion.[4]

John Stuart Mill's moral doctrine exemplifies "the dangers of our most generous wishes;" it teaches us to make our fellow men the objects of our enlightened interest, our pity, our wisdom, and our coercion. The "dangers" make us wonder about the "generosity" of the wishes. Mill's moral passion is an instance of what Nietzsche has described as "the preaching of altruistic morality in the service of individual egoism."[5] Trilling's distinction between what he calls "moral passions" and "self-seeking passions" is endemic to modern moral philosophy and is the core of Mill's own doctrine. The morality Mill preaches requires the dissociation of the self into a self of moral passion, to stay with Trilling's terms, and a self of self-seeking passion, for both of which dissatisfaction is constitutive, because in each case "end" in the sense of *telos* is not. Since what gives unity to the self is the end towards which it moves, a movement for which at least since Plato the word *eros* has been appropriated, Mill's doctrine has no place for *eros*. *Eros* signifies that we

---

[4] From Lionel Trilling, "Manners. Morals, and the Novel," in *The Liberal Imagination* (New York: Doubleday Anchor Books, 1953), p. 214, reprinted, with an introduction by Louis Menand (New York: New York Review of Books, 2008), p. 221. This essay also appears in Lionel Trilling, *The Moral Obligation to be Intelligent, Selected Essays,* ed. Leon Wiesenteil, (Farrar, Straus, Giroux: New York, 2003). The passage quoted is on page 118.

[5] Friedrich Nietzsche, *The Will to Power*, ed. Walter Kaufmann (New York: Random House, 1967), #784, p. 412. "One of the most common lies of the nineteenth century," he adds.

are constituted by something other than ourselves. The non-erotic Love of Humanity asserts precisely the opposite.

Mill uses several terms as names to designate his moral doctrine, among them, most obviously, of course, "Utilitarianism." In addition, he speaks of it, and not infrequently, as "that real, though purely human religion that sometimes calls itself the Religion of Humanity and sometimes that of duty."[6] "Religion of Humanity" is Auguste Comte's term. Mill's moral doctrine is in fact a version of what Comte calls the "Religion of Humanity." The canonized version of Mill as the philosopher of unfettered liberty, "the champion of heretics, apostates, blasphemers" does not emphasize this.[7] Mill did. In *Utilitarianism*, speaking of Comte's *Traité de politique positive*, Mill says:

> I think it has superabundantly shown the possibility of giving to the service of humanity... both the psychological power and the social efficacy of a religion, making it take hold of human life, and color all thought, feeling, and action in a manner of which the greatest ascendancy ever exercised by any religion may be but a type and foretaste[.][8]

Mill wished to see his moral doctrine, which he summarizes here under the heading "the service of humanity," given "the psychological power and social efficacy of a religion." Psychological power and social efficacy constitute what Mill calls "the temporal usefulness of religion."[9] He believed that, taught as a religion, his revised utilitarianism would possess this power and this efficacy to an eminent degree:

---

[6] John Stuart Mill, *Theism*, in *Three Essays on Religion* (Amherst, New York: Prometheus Books, 1998), pp. 255-56, reprints of John Stuart Mill, *Nature, The Utility of Religion, and Theism* (London: Longmans, 1874), pp. 255-56.

[7] Isaiah Berlin, "John Stuart Mill and the Ends of Life" in *Four Essays on Liberty* (New York: Oxford University Press, 1969), p. 179. The canonized version tends to separate the essay *On Liberty* from the context of Mill's work as a whole.

[8] John Stuart Mill, *Utilitarianism*, ed. Oskar Piest, The Library of Liberal Arts (Indianapolis, Indiana: Bobbs-Merrill, 1957), chapter 3, p. 42.

[9] John Stuart Mill, *The Utility of Religion*, in *Three Essays*, p. 76.

> If we now suppose this feeling of unity [with all mankind] to be taught as a religion... I think no one who can realize this conception will feel any misgiving about the sufficiency of the ultimate sanction for the happiness morality.[10]

Of his moral doctrine, Mill says: "It is not only entitled to be called a religion: it is a better religion than any of those that are ordinarily called by that title."[11] And why is this? Because "in the first place it is disinterested," i.e. "it does not tempt... [one] to regard the performance of... [one's] duties to others, mainly as a means to... [one's] own personal salvation.... What now goes by the name of religion operates mainly through the feelings of self-interest... This is the radical inferiority of the best supernatural religions compared to the Religion of Humanity."[12]

Mill entertained the hope that the cultus of Philanthropy would supplant what he called "the inferior religions of history." One might be tempted to regard this as merely Mill's personal aberration did we not know that in fact the Religion of Humanity, "one of the fantasies of the saeculum rationalisticum,"[13] has to a large extent supplanted Christianity and has become the established public religion of the West, "the natural religion of modern democratic society," it has been called.[14] That Comte regarded Mill as a close collaborator is evident from Comte's remark about "my eminent friend, John Stuart Mill, who is," Comte says, "in fact fully associated with the immediate establishment of the new philosophy."[15] Mill confirms what Comte says

---

[10] John Stuart Mill, *Utilitarianism*, chapter 2, p. 42.

[11] John Stuart Mill, *The Utility of Religion*, p. 110.

[12] Ibid., pp. 110-11.

[13] I borrow the term from Michael Oakeshott, *Hobbes on Civil Association* (Indianapolis, Indiana: Liberty Fund, 1975), pp. 75-76.

[14] Pierre Manent, *Cours familier de philosophie politique* (Paris: Fayard, 2001), p. 206.

[15] The statement occurs in his *Discours sur L'Esprit Positif*, where Comte speaks of Mill as "mon ami éminent, John Stuart Mill, ainsi pleinement associé à la fondation directe de la nouvelle philosophie," *Oeuvres Choisies d' Auguste Comte*, ed. Henri Gouhier (Paris: Aubier, 1948), p. 192.

regarding the role of his *ami eminent*: "I had contributed more than anyone else to make his speculations known in England."[16] Comte is quite clear about what *la nouvelle philosophie* portends: "While the Protestants and the Deists have always attacked religion in the name of God, we, on the contrary, ought finally to get rid of God in the name of religion."[17] Although Mill dissented from the manner in which Comte institutionalized the Religion of Humanity, he fully endorsed the reform of religion on the basis of the altruistic morality proposed by Comte:

> We... not only hold that M. Comte was justified in the attempt to develop his philosophy into a religion, and had realized the essential conditions of one, but that all other religions are made better in proportion as, in their practical result, they are brought to coincide with that which he aimed at constructing.[18]

Both Comte and Mill intend the subversion of Christianity through its transformation and replacement by the Religion of Humanity.[19] In *Daybreak* (*Morgenröte*), speaking of what he calls "the echo of Christianity in morality," Nietzsche describes how the move is made:

> That men today feel the sympathetic, disinterested, generally useful social actions to be the moral actions–this is perhaps the most general effect and conversion which Christianity has produced in Europe: although it was not its intention nor contained in its teaching. But it was the residuum of Christian states of mind left when the very much antithetical... fundamental belief... in the absolute importance of eternal

---

[16] John Stuart Mill, *Autobiography of John Stuart Mill* (New York: Columbia University Press, 1960), p. 194.

[17] "Tandis que les protestants et les déistes ont toujours attaqué la religion au nom de Dieu, nous devons, au contraire, écarter finalement Dieu au nom de la religion," Auguste Comte, *Correspondance inédite*, 2, 107. See Henri de Lubac, S.J., *Le Drame de L'Humanisme Athée*, 3e édition, (Paris: Éditions Spes, 1945), p.178.

[18] John Stuart Mill, *Auguste Comte and Positivism* (Ann Arbor, Michigan: University of Michigan Press, 1965), p. 137.

[19] John Stuart Mill, *Utilitarianism*, chapter 3, p. 42.

> personal salvation, together with the dogmas upon which it rested, gradually retreated and the subsidiary belief in 'love,' in 'love of one's neighbor,' in concert with the tremendous practical effect of ecclesiastical charity, was thereby pushed into the foreground. The more one liberated oneself from the dogmas, the more one sought as it were a justification of this liberation in a cult of philanthropy: not to fall short of the Christian ideal in this, but where possible to outdo it, was a secret spur with all French freethinkers from Voltaire up to Auguste Comte: the latter did in fact, with his moral formula *vivre pour autrui*, outchristian Christianity.... In... England [it was] John Stuart Mill who gave the widest currency to the teaching of the sympathetic affects and of pity or the advantage of others as the principle of behavior.[20]

Nietzsche neatly summarizes this in an aphoristic sentence in *Twilight of the Idols* (*Götzen-Dämmerung)*: "After every little emancipation from theology, one must rehabilitate oneself by showing in a veritably awe-inspiring manner what a moral fanatic one is."[21] The core of the moral fanaticism of this "outchristianed Christianity" is a self that experiences itself as sublime, that can, as Kant puts it, "make palpable to itself the sublimity of its own vocation as superior to nature."[22] Morally, disinterestedness is the assertion of that superiority to nature. Disinterest is moral sublimity.[23] Profiled against the understanding of morality, the morality of the good, that it was intended it should replace, what distinguishes the moral doctrine expounded by Mill and Comte comes clearly into view.

---

[20] Friedrich Nietzsche, *Daybreak*, #132, p. 82.

[21] Friedrich Nietzsche, *Twilight of the Idols* in *The Portable Nietzsche*, trans. Walter Kaufmann (New York: Viking Press, 1954), p. 515.

[22] Immanuel Kant, *Critique of the Power of Judgment*, trans. Paul Guyer (Cambridge: Cambridge University Press, 2000), §28, p. 145.

[23] Alain Besançon, *La Falsification du Bien* (Paris: Julliard, 1985), pp. 47, 92–96, 104; *The Falsification of the Good*, (London: The Claridge Press, 1994), pp. 33, 64–65, 73. Cf. Alain Besançon, *Trois Tentations dans L'Église* (Paris: Calmann-Lévy, 1996), pp. 105–15.

## II Socratic Dissatisfaction

"It is better to be a human being dissatisfied than a pig satisfied. Better to be Socrates dissatisfied than a fool satisfied. And if the fool, or the pig, are of a different opinion, it is because they only know their side of the question." This is John Stuart Mill's gloss in the second chapter of *Utilitarianism*[24] of that passage in Plato's *Republic*, Book II (372c–373e), where Glaucon, interrupting Socrates' account of the "first city,"[25] accuses Socrates of having failed to provide properly for the inhabitants of this city, not even, Glaucon says, having "given them a relish for their meal, making them feast on dry bread." Socrates acknowledges Glaucon's objection, saying that he had "forgotten" about the need for a relish to the meal. Glaucon then objects to the rude simplicities of life in what he calls "a city of pigs" and what Socrates will call "the true and healthy city." "Now I understand," Socrates says, "the question which you would have me consider is, not only how a city, but how a luxurious city comes into being."[26]

---

[24] John Stuart Mill, *Utilitarianism*, chapter 2, p. 14.

[25] Aristotle, commenting on the *Republic* in *Politics*, Bk. IV, 1291a18-20, calls it the "first city," formed, as Aristotle observes, "only for the sake of necessaries and not for the sake of what is noble."

[26] Plato, *Republic,* trans. Benjamin Jowett (New York: Vintage Press, 1991), Bk. II, 372–73 (pp. 64-65): "They will feed on barley meal and flour of wheat, baking cakes of the meal, and kneading loaves of the flour. These they will serve up on mats of reeds or on clean leaves, and themselves reclining on rude beds of yew or myrtle-boughs. They and their children will feast, drinking of the wine which they have made, wearing garlands on their heads, and singing the praises of the gods, enjoying one another's company. Interrupting, Glaucon said, You call it feasting when you have given them only dry bread for their meal; you have given them a meal without relish. True, I said, I had forgotten–of course their meal must have relish–salt, and olives, and cheese, and they will boil roots and herbs such as country people prepare. For a dessert we shall give them figs, and peas, and beans; and they will roast myrtle-berries and acorns at the fire, drinking wine in moderation.... Socrates, he said, if you were founding a city of pigs, would you feed them any differently? But what would you have me give them, Glaucon? I replied. Why, he said, you should give them the ordinary conveniences of life. People who are to be comfortable are accustomed to lie

Mill believes that dissatisfaction is superior to satisfaction. The rhetorical flourish about Socrates' dissatisfaction and the satisfaction of fools and pigs is meant to assert that. But if Socrates is dissatisfied, it is not because he believes, as Mill does, that dissatisfaction is superior to satisfaction. In the passage at hand, it is not Socrates who expresses dissatisfaction; it is Glaucon, dissatisfied with the satisfaction of the inhabitants of Socrates' "first city." In their satisfaction, Glaucon thinks, they are indistinguishable from "a city of pigs," i.e. nothing sets them apart as human beings. Mill asserts that fools and pigs are satisfied, and therefore fools and pigs, by virtue of the manner in which they hold the opinion that satisfaction is superior to dissatisfaction: they know only "their side of the question." Their side of the question is the superiority of satisfaction to dissatisfaction, i.e. the reality of ends and their ontological priority to our desires. This knowing "only their side of the question" is Mill's swipe, in his attempt to appropriate Socrates for his side of the question, at pre-modern philosophy, which teaches the reality of ends and their ontological priority. But while fools do, pigs do not have opinions, yet they do have a side of the question. They don't, for instance, make an issue of the absence of a relish for their meal; their meal quite naturally satisfies them. Mill's implication here is that man, understanding himself in terms of a supposed teleology of nature, cannot effectively distinguish himself from the pig; his side of the question, nature as end/*telos*, the superiority of satisfaction to dissatisfaction, makes him a fool. In commenting on the exchange between Glaucon and Socrates, Mill takes no note either of Socrates' forgetfulness or of what Socrates calls "the luxurious city," both important items in considering how Socratic dissatisfaction differs from that of Mill.

The luxurious city differs from the city of pigs in this: the existence of the luxurious city requires that some have asked the question, "What is the best kind of life?" And in the luxurious city they have answered this question by saying, "more of, and refinements of, what we enjoyed

---

on sofas, and dine off tables, and they should have sauces and sweets in the modern style. Now I understand, I said, the question which you would have me consider is, not only how a city, but how a luxurious city comes into being."

in the city of pigs." The luxurious city is a city of men, not of pigs, for pigs, unlike men, are not concerned with luxury, because they do not seek an answer to the question, "What is the best way of life for us?" The pigs do not need luxury because, being pigs, they are not concerned to seek out what is the best life. What they have as pigs satisfies them. For the pig the life of the pig is the only possible life and, as such, an eminently satisfactory one. For the pig the only possible life is the best life. There is good reason for pigs not to be dissatisfied. For being healthy pigs, they are satisfied as what they are. The pig is not an erotic animal.

Luxury is a sign that human beings seek not mere life, but the best kind of life. Men are concerned with the relishes and refinements of meals; pigs are not. When Glaucon breaks into Socrates' account of the first city, saying, "You have given them a meal without relish!" and calls it "a city of pigs," his interruption reveals that he is concerned with the right way to live. By implication he has introduced the question of what is the best kind of life. Pigs would not notice the absence of relish. Noticing the absence of relish will lead to the presence of philosophy. In the circumstances, it is the introduction to philosophy. To be a complete human being one must ask the question about the best life. To reflect on the question and its meaning is the beginning of philosophy. The answer to the question, as the *Republic* shows, is the philosophic life. What takes place in the *Republic*–its action–is the initiation of that life.[27]

The luxury of the luxurious city is evidence that it is a human city, not a city of pigs. Luxury is sought as the answer to the question, "What thing is most eminently satisfying? What brings completion, fulfillment, wholeness?" Luxury testifies to the fact that human beings ask questions and that even if they lead the simple life, the life opposed to the luxurious life, they do so because they believe that it answers the question, "What is the best kind of life?" This is why Socrates can say, referring to his first city, "[I]n my opinion the true and healthy city is the one that I have described." This is his considered judgment

[27] With the *Dialogues*, we must remember that we are dealing with poetry, which imitates action.

concerning politics in the light of what really constitutes satisfaction,[28] making clear the Socratic ranking of the political life in comparison with philosophy. Just as Socrates' forgetfulness about the pleasures of the table points toward the primary concern of the *Republic*, philosophy as the pursuit of the truly satisfying, so his "true and healthy city" points to the diminishment of politics and the life of the city in the light of what is most eminently satisfying. The desire for bodily pleasures and the desire for the public honors of the political life recede from view as desirable ends and a deeper dissatisfaction appears as wisdom kindles the *eros* for itself. It is not that these loved and lovable things are not instances of good; it is only that there are better instances. Mill takes no note of Socrates' forgetfulness nor of the luxurious city because Mill is unable to recognize that the dissatisfaction of the Socratic and erotic self–which is the self in pursuit of satisfaction, that is, of completion, fulfillment, perfection, wholeness–differs profoundly from the dissatisfaction which is the essence of his moral doctrine. "The aim of *eros*," Diotima tells Socrates in the *Symposium*, "is the everlasting possession of the good"[29]: "All then is full, possessing and possess'd,/ No craving void left aching in the breast."[30] Mill cannot recognize the erotic self of Socrates because for him there is no everlasting possession of the good, the ontological status of ends having been denied. What takes its place is benevolence without end, the everlasting pursuit of pleasure on behalf of others. *Doin' right ain't got no end,* as the Redlegs Captain in Clint Eastwood's film *The Outlaw Josey Wales* says, for right is not done for the sake of an end as *telos,* and there is no end as *termination* in the pursuit of pleasure and the diminishment of pain on behalf of others.

## III The Disinterested and Benevolent Spectator

Mill's moral doctrine is *Altruism*, a term that designates his teaching more accurately than the term he favors, *utilitarianism* with its

---

[28] Plato, *Republic* 373a.

[29] Ibid, 207a2–3.

[30] Alexander Pope, "Eloisa to Abelard," in *The Complete Poetical Works of Pope*, ed. Henry W. Boynton (Boston: Houghton Mifflin, 1903), p. 111, lines 93–94.

"nebulous comprehensiveness" as it has been called.[31] *Altruism*–literally "otherism"–is a term invented by Auguste Comte to designate the core teaching of his *Religion of Humanity*: *vivre pour autrui*, "live for others." Altruism is an instance of that peculiarly modern union, the marriage between hedonism and moral obligation,[32] which has several philosophical variants, including John Rawls' "deontological liberalism."[33] The occupant of what Rawls calls "the original position," who is behind "a veil of ignorance," bears a strong resemblance to Mill's disinterested and benevolent spectator. Mill, professing to be a hedonist, teaches that "[p]leasure and freedom from pain are the only things desirable as ends; and that all desirable things are desirable either for pleasure inherent in themselves or as means to the promotion of pleasure and the prevention of pain."[34] Happiness, then, means pleasure and the absence of pain; unhappiness is pain and the privation of pleasure.[35] The rightness of an action lies in its tendency to produce pleasure, its wrongness in its tendency to produce pain. Here, however, Mill enters a *caveat*: not the pleasure or pain of the agent, as previous versions of philosophical hedonism had taught, but the pleasure or pain of others. This is a very significant departure from philosophic hedonism–I am thinking of Epicurus and Lucretius–for

---

[31] Maurice Cowling, *Mill and Liberalism*, 2nd edition (Cambridge: Cambridge University Press, 1990), p. 27.

[32] "[L]e principal caractère du positivisme. Il consiste à résumer enfin, dans une même formule, la loi du devoir et celle du bonheur, jusqu'alors proclamées inconciliables par toutes les doctrines[.]... Voilà comment le bonheur coincidera nécessairement avec le devoir": Auguste Comte, *Catéchisme Positiviste* (Paris: Librairie Garnier Frères, n.d.), pp. 279–80.

[33] "I suppose with utilitarianism that the good is defined as the satisfaction of rational desire"; "The principles of right... impose restrictions on what are reasonable conceptions of one's good": John Rawls, *A Theory of Justice* (Cambridge, Massachusetts: Harvard University Press, 1971), pp. 30, 31. "Deontological liberalism accepts an essentially utilitarian account of the good, however its theory of rights may differ": Michael J. Sandel, *Liberalism and the Limits of Justice* (New York: Cambridge University Press, 1982), p. 165.

[34] John Stuart Mill, *Utilitarianism*, chapter 2, p. 10.

[35] Ibid.

which philosophy is itself the greatest pleasure and for that reason constitutive of happiness: *Happy [Felix] is he who has been able to know the causes of things.*[36] Mill's deontologized hedonism instrumentalizes philosophy; it is the servant of "doin' right," *vivre pour autrui.* Philosophy is to be understood and practiced as the promotion of right, not the enjoyment of the good.

> I must again repeat what the assailants of utilitarianism seldom have the justice to acknowledge, that the happiness which forms the utilitarian standard of what is right in conduct is not the agent's own happiness but that of all concerned. As between his own happiness and that of others, utilitarianism requires him to be as strictly impartial as a disinterested and benevolent spectator.[37]

Pleasure is the good, but actions are right only insofar as they are taken to promote pleasure and diminish pain as another's good.

*Not the agent's own happiness, but that of all concerned.* It is in this–what he calls its "disinterestedness"–that Mill thinks the moral superiority of the doctrine of altruism consists, and on this basis he proposes it as morally obligatory. "*Of all concerned*" means others as distinguished from myself and myself seen as indistinguishable from the others so far as "the good" is concerned. Moral rightness does not consist in my seeking my "good," but the good of the community. Mill says, "[T]he interests of mankind collectively, or at least indiscriminately, must be in the mind of the agent when conscientiously deciding on the morality of the act."[38] The "morality of the act" means the obligation to promote the pleasures of others and to diminish their pains, whatever the pain to oneself as distinguishable from the others. Mill's moral agent is *the agent as disinterested and benevolent spectator.* Thus defined, the agent must apprehend itself as two discontinuous selves: a self distinguishable from other selves, seeking pleasure as its good–the

---

[36] Virgil, *Georgics*, Bk. II, line 490. The context of this line makes clear that "Felix" designates the Epicurean philosopher.

[37] John Stuart Mill, *Utilitarianism*, chapter 2, p. 10.

[38] Ibid., chapter 5, p. 65.

"self-seeking self"–and a self which sees itself as indistinguishable from other selves, preferring the good of "all concerned" whatever the pain to itself. Mill is not being original here. The requirement for some form of this distinction is systemic in modern moral and political philosophy, as the instances of Hobbes, Rousseau, and Kant demonstrate. Mill is simply repeating and restating it in his own terms.

The moral agent is not only *disinterested* and *benevolent*, most importantly it is *spectator*. In seeing itself as indistinguishable from the others, the moral agent sets itself apart, distinguishes itself, as spectator. To be disinterested and benevolent, to be a moral agent in Mill's sense, requires that I be a spectator, that I see myself, i.e., distinguish myself, as indistinguishable from others. To do this, to see myself as indistinguishable from the others, I must distinguish myself from myself as distinguished from others. This self seeing itself as indistinguishable is a self effected through thought, and the word to be underlined here is *effected*, for this self has no author but its own act, the act of thought from which it proceeds. It is a self effecting itself through thought, not a self discovering itself through the object of thought, not a self evoked by the Good. It does not come to light as a potentiality of the human person. The moral agent as a disinterested and benevolent spectator is generated by thinking to be discontinuous with a self thought of as continuous with desire. The act by which thought creates a self discontinuous with desire also creates the thought of a self continuous with desire, a self-seeking self, the self of desire. In order to think of itself, the disinterested and benevolent spectator requires a conceptual foil, the self of desire. The self of desire, no less than the self which is the disinterested and benevolent spectator, is something effected by thought. As thoughts, they are inseparable; neither thought exists without the other. To think myself as disinterested and benevolent requires that I also think myself as interested and self-regarding desire. I could not recognize myself as the disinterested and benevolent spectator, if I did not entertain the possibility of thinking of myself as another opposed self, a self of interested self-regarding desire. These are conceptually constructed, or ideal, selves. Neither self is just *myself,* for neither coincides with the reality I am. And neither is what we have called, speaking of Socrates and Glaucon, an erotic self.

Disinterestedness means indifference to an end or aim proper to myself as a determinate kind of being, i.e., as self-seeking. Disinterestedness is indifference to my specific identity as a human being and to that being being mine. Altruism negates the will to be myself as an actual instance of realized humanness. Mill is explicit that it means indifference to my specific identity as a human being. The utilitarian standard, he says, is an existence as exempt as possible from pain, and as rich as possible in enjoyments both in point of quality and quantity "secured to all mankind; and not to them only, but so far as the nature of things admits, to the whole sentient creation."[39] If there is not an end constitutive of my identity, it is not clear what I am. As distinctness vanishes, I merge into "the whole sentient creation," ceasing to exercise the will to be myself as a human being, to stand out in my essence.[40] "Man is finished," Nietzsche said, "when he becomes altruistic."[41]

Mill's moral doctrine depends upon the opposition between the disinterested self and its foil the self-interested self, both of which are possible only on the presupposition that ends are irrelevant. The disinterested self is a self without ends, for to recognize dependence upon an end for completeness is recognition of incompleteness, and the disinterested self is always complete, being self-constituted as a whole by the act of thought which creates it. Thus its sublimity. Being without an end, it is not a self constituted through *eros* pursuing the whole. Unlike what Maritain says of "the soul when it loves," that it "aspires toward what it is not, as to another self,"[42] this disinterested self is not actualized by the Good. Doing right, the disinterested self endlessly asserts itself as other than the self-interested self of desire, asserting its completeness and superiority to nature.

---

[39] Ibid, chapter 2, p. 16.

[40] See Friedrich Nietzsche, *Twilight of the Idols*, trans. R. J. Hollingdale (Baltimore: Penguin Books, 1968), p. 91.

[41] Ibid., p. 87.

[42] Jacques Maritain, "Action and Contemplation" in *Scholasticism and Politics*, ed. Mortimer J. Adler, 2nd ed. (London: Geoffrey Bles: Centenary Press, 1945), p. 136.

The self-interested self, the self of desire, the foil of the disinterested self, is the incomplete self, necessarily incomplete and unable to be completed. If there are no ends, there is desire, but it is loveless desire, not the desire of *eros*, which is the pursuit of wholeness, completion, fulfillment. Self-interest is understood to be prescribed by desire, not by the objects of desire, that is, by ontologically prior ends. The self of desire is moved by its purposes–which it calls "ends"–prompted by its desires. Unlike eros, which is created by what is loved,[43] the end/*telos*–desire produces the object of desire. Ends understood as purposes are hypotheses of desire and are relevant only to the one whose posited purposes they are. The self of desire can only conceive of "felicity" as, in Hobbes' succinct formulation, "a continual progress of the desire from one object to another," and not as "the repose of a mind satisfied."[44] The desiring self, always unable to be satisfied, can never be whole. Once ends lose their ontological priority, *eros* understood as the pursuit of wholeness, has no place. Speaking of the 17th Century Archbishop of Cambrai, Fénelon, whose doctrine of "pure love" supposes a radical opposition between the disinterested love of God and love of self in formulations strikingly similar to those of Mill and Comte's altruism, Henri Gouhier writes: "Pure love is not an *eros* which has found its end; it annihilates every trace of *eros*."[45]

## IV Minding Other People's Business: Caring and Ruling

Altruistic virtue is disinterestedness, or indifference to the good as my good. In the *Republic*, the case against justice argued by Glaucon and Adeimantus is that it is "another's good," not one's own.[46] To answer their argument, Socrates argues that justice, being the right order of the soul, makes me good, for it is the right order of the soul that is constitutive of my own fulfillment and perfection as a human being.

---

[43] Plato, *Symposium* 204c4–6.

[44] Thomas Hobbes, *Leviathan*, ed. Michael Oakeshott (Oxford: Basil Blackwell, 1949), pp. 63-64.

[45] "Le pur amour n'est pas un éros qui a trouvé sa fin: il anéantit tout éros": Henri Gouhier, *Fénelon philosophe* (Paris: Vrin, 1977), quoted in Alain Besançon, *Trois Tentations*, p. 108.

[46] See the beginning of *Republic* Bk. II, 357a–357e.

Political and moral philosophy as originally conceived–Socrates, Plato, and Aristotle–teaches that the best life is the philosophic life, not the life lived *pour autrui*. The life lived *pour autrui* is the political life. The political life is the life devoted to ruling. Rule is exercised on the basis of an asserted and recognized claim to superiority, the claim to being the best at serving the good of the city, i.e. the good of others, and therefore entitled to rule in preference to others. "Disinterestedness," or altruistic virtue, is such a claim. Ruling is "minding other people's business." In the *Republic*, Socrates shows that "justice is minding your own business and not being a busy-body,"[47] i.e. it means seeking one's fulfillment, completion, perfection as a fully realized human being. The justice of ruling depends upon its subsumption within the right order of the soul. That order places primacy in knowledge of the highest things: "For it would be strange to think that the art of politics... is the best knowledge, since man is not the best thing in the world."[48] If ruling were the best life, philosophy would be impossible. For that would imply that ruling, managing human beings, was the highest human activity and man the best thing in the world. In the exchange with Glaucon about the need for a relish for the meal, Socrates has forgotten about the pleasures of food in the light of other objects of desire that have kindled in him the eros for wisdom.

Glaucon is dissatisfied, disappointed because there's not a relish for the meal, something that Socrates had "forgotten about."[49] Glaucon compares those who are unconcerned with relishes for meals to pigs. Glaucon recognizes and directs attention to the difference between man and the other animals: pigs are concerned with food, not with pleasure per se. It is because Glaucon recognizes and acknowledges this difference that Socrates is able to show Glaucon how to become satisfied as a human being through the pursuit of philosophy. The concern with pleasure per se, i.e. as the Good, is distinctly human and separates man from the other animals. The other animals seek food and offspring, but they are neither epicures nor voluptuaries. Epicures and

---

[47] Plato, *Republic* 433a1–434a2.

[48] Aristotle, *Nicomachean Ethics*, VI, 7 (1141a20 ff.).

[49] Plato, *Republic* 372c.

voluptuaries seek the Good and, therefore, seek pleasure, i.e. they seek pleasure not simply as pleasure, but as the Good, as what completes, fulfills, perfects. Animals are not hedonists; human beings are. That there are epicures and voluptuaries testifies to the existence of the Good and so to the difference between man and the other animals. This difference is constituted by man's apprehension of the Good. Without this apprehension, man would not view pleasure as the Good. He would simply enjoy it as the pigs do, for there would be no appearance of the Good. To be an epicure or a voluptuary is to have an opinion about what the Good is. It is this apprehension that is the ground of Socrates' dissatisfaction. Philosophy is Socratic dissatisfaction, the existence of philosophy testimony to the actuality of the Good.

For Mill, there is no resting in the end/*telos* achieved. Dissatisfaction, not coming to completion in perfection and fulfillment, is the essence of Mill's morality. Mill's moral paradigm is the life of ceaseless activity in benefiting others, the life of philanthropy. "Benefiting" in Mill's scheme can only mean relieving the pain of others and producing pleasure for them. Mill's moral universe implies an elite which enjoys the privilege of caring for others, rulers who, because they are rulers, instance the highest moral ideal. But such a moral universe necessarily implies that the largest number of human beings will be those who need to be taken care of, who suffer various kinds of pain and are deprived of many pleasures: the victims. Mill's moral universe must be filled with victims who call forth the activity of the moral elite as rulers. The moral elite is a caring elite. "Caring" is the paradigm of what it means to be good. Jacques Maritain's lucid description of transitive activity makes clear what grounds the accuracy of Nietzsche's judgment of "altruism as the most mendacious form of egoism:"[50]

> Transitive activity is that which one being exercises upon another, the so-called patient, in order to act upon it.... The Greeks were right in saying that in this activity, the action in which the agent and the patient intercommunicate is accomplished in the patient, *actio in passio*, and being common to

[50] Friedrich Nietzsche, *The Will to Power*, Bk. I: *European Nihilism*, #62, p. 42.

> both, makes the agent (notwithstanding its being as such the nobler of the two) dependent on the patient, in which alone it obtains perfection. The Agent is itself *in actu* and attains its perfection only by acting on another than itself, and in the instant of this action. Transitive action is a mendicant action, which achieves itself in another being, and is essentially in need of another being. On the other hand, while the agent's perfection is also, in fact, that of the patient, the agent as such does not seek the patient's good, but its own.... Hence its 'egotism.' People who exercise philanthropy as a transitive activity need the poor to help if they want to be helpful, sinners to preach to if they want to be preachers, victims whose wrongs they can redress. They need *patients*.[51]

"Doin' right ain't got no end." For Mill's altruism doing right is not an end (*telos*) and is endless, interminable. That the many can be satisfied is indicative of their inferiority to the elite, whose superiority is attested by their unsatisfiable dissatisfaction. It is a necessary assumption for the altruistic morality that the many on whose behalf the caring elite is active can be satisfied by the things that satisfy pigs. Mill's city, ruled by a caring elite, is a "city of pigs."

In the essay, *The Utility of Religion*, Mill makes a singularly revealing comment:

> [I]n a higher, and, above all, a happier condition of human life, not annihilation but immortality may be the burdensome idea;... that human nature... would find comfort and not sadness in the thought that it is not chained through eternity to a conscious existence which it cannot be assured it will always wish to preserve.[52]

Nothing could make clearer what happens to thinking, and therefore to philosophy in a doctrine such as Mill's–in which thinking is purely instrumental, not an end-in-itself–than the contrast between this passage

---

[51] Jacques Maritain, "Action and Contemplation," *Scholasticism and Politics* (London: Geoffrey Bles: The Centenary Press, 2nd edition, 1945), p. 136.

[52] John Stuart Mill, *The Utility of Religion*, p. 122.

from *The Utility of Religion* and Socrates' speech in Plato's *Apology* 40e4–41c5:

> But if death is a journey to another place, and there, as men say, all the dead abide, what good, my friends and judges, can be greater than this?... What would not a man give if he might converse with Orpheus and Musaeus and Hesiod and Homer? If this be true let me die again and again... Above all, I shall then be able to continue my search into true and false knowledge; as in this world, so also in the next; and I shall find out who is wise, and who pretends to be wise, and is not.... It would be an unspeakable happiness to converse with them and to be with them and to examine them.[53]

"*Eros*," Diotima told Socrates, "is desire for everlasting possession of the good." Altruism necessarily requires an instrumentalized reason, but the life lived for the sake of philosophical inquiry, the Socratic life, is an end in itself. The exercise of instrumentalized reason provides no reason to live.

Mill's version of a dissatisfied Socrates is a Socrates who has undergone metamorphosis. It is not the Socrates whom Alcibiades observed on the Athenian expedition to Potidaea during the Peloponnesian War. "One morning he was thinking about something," Alcibiades says in the *Symposium*. "He would not give it up, but continued thinking from early dawn until noon. There he stood fixed in thought. The rumor ran through the army that Socrates had been standing and thinking ever since break of day.... He stood there until the following morning."[54] That Socrates poses a problem for philosophical modernity becomes evident in the reservations expressed about him by Montaigne: "These humours soaring to transcendency terrify me as do great unapproachable heights; and for me nothing in the life of Socrates is so awkward to digest as his

[53] Plato, *Euthyphro, Apology Crito*, trans. F.J. Church, rev. Robert D. Cumming, The Library of Liberal Arts Press, 2nd Edition (Indianapolis, Indiana: Bobbs-Merrill, 1956).

[54] Plato, *Symposium* 220.

ecstasies.... "[55] Mill had explicitly identified Socrates with his moral teaching in the opening paragraph of *Utilitarianism* saying, "the youth Socrates listened to the old Protagoras and asserted... the theory of utilitarianism."[56] Mill chooses Socrates as the emblem of dissatisfaction, identifying Socrates with his own moral teaching, thereby identifying Socratic dissatisfaction, which is erotic, with the dissatisfaction fueled by the *altruism* Mill teaches, which is not. This identification is a confusion. It joins together things different as if they were the same, and, here, it is intentional. Mill knows that what he is doing is not philosophy in the Socratic sense. "Philosophy," as Robert Sokolowski has said, "explains by distinguishing; it "consists in making distinctions, in showing how one thing is necessarily not another, in thereby bringing out what that thing necessarily is."[57] Philosophy in the Socratic sense aims at understanding the being of things through displaying the differences among them, and it rests in this essentially contemplative activity enjoyed for its own sake. Mill, on the contrary, assimilates things that are different and makes them the same.

Mill is engaged not so much in trying to understand something, as he is in trying to persuade us to believe something. Mill's procedure aims to produce unanimity of belief, like-mindedness about the way to live, not philosophical understanding. This is a political aim, not a philosophical one. "From the winter of 1821, when I first read Bentham," Mill writes in his autobiography, "I had what truly might be called an object in life; to be a reformer in the world. My conception of my own happiness was entirely identified with this object."[58] Mill is engaged in producing a change in religion and, as Machiavelli has

---

[55] "Ces humeurs transcendantes m'effrayent, comme les lieux hautains et inaccessibles; et rien ne m'est à digerer fascheux en la vie de Socrate que ses ecstases et ses demoneries": Montaigne, *Essais*, III., 13 (near end). The English is from Michel de Montaigne, *The Complete Essays*, trans. M.A. Screech, Penguin Classics (London: Penguin Books, 1991), p. 1268.

[56] John Stuart Mill, *Utilitarianism*, chapter 1, p. 3.

[57] Robert Sokolowski, "The Method of Philosophy: Making Distinctions," in *The Review of Metaphysics* (March 1998): 516.

[58] John Stuart Mill, *Autobiography*, Chapter V, p. 93.

observed, "[W]hen a new sect–that is a new religion–emerges, its first concern is to extinguish the old to give itself reputation."[59] Taking over symbols of the old order and infusing into them a new content is the ordinary means of the suppression of an existing religion. It is not to be confused with philosophy. Comte is very specific about the role of a caring elite:

> The dedication of the strong to the weak can be assured only by the occurrence of an order of the strong which has obtained social ascendancy by means of its zeal for the weak and the consequent veneration freely accorded them by the weak. It is thus that the priesthood [of the Religion of Humanity] becomes the soul of the true Sociocracy.[60]

Mill approaches vehemence in his repudiation of Comte's organization of the Religion of Humanity. Nevertheless, the difference between them regarding that religion is perhaps best described as a difference in political style. In what is essential Mill does not differ: "I agreed with him [Comte] that the moral and intellectual ascendancy, once exercised by priests, must in time pass into the hands of the philosophers...."[61] Although the means differ by which their rule is to be effected, for both Mill and Comte philosophers rule. Unlike the philosophers in Socrates' best city set forth in the *Republic*, neither Mill's nor Comte's philosophers have to be compelled to rule.

## V The New Holiness

Auguste Comte's *Catéchisme Postiviste* teaches that for those who practice the Religion of Humanity "religion must above all dispose us

---

[59] Niccolò Machiavelli, *Discourses on Livy*, II. 5. 1, trans. Harvey C. Mansfield and Nathan Tarcov (Chicago: University of Chicago Press, 1996), p. 139.

[60] "On ne peut assurer le dévouement des forts aux faibles que par l'avénement d'une classe des forts qui ne puisse obtenir d'ascendent social qu'en se dévouant aux faibles, d'après leur libre vénération. C'est ainsi que le sacerdoce devient l'ame de la vraie sociocratie": Auguste Comte, *Catéchisme*, pp. 306–307.

[61] John Stuart Mill, *Autobiography* (1944), p. 148.

and teach us to live for others."[62] Practically every form of Christianity has been significantly penetrated by the moral doctrine of altruism and has adopted the procedure described by the German term, *die Gleichschaltung*, "correct alignment," or, more familiarly and concretely, "political correctness," attempting to harmonize their teaching with it by means of a shift that has been characterized as "from orthodoxy to orthopraxis:"[63] "henceforth and forever God is only present in and as one's neighbor."[64] Alain Besançon has labeled this shift "la nouvelle sainteté,"[65] "the new holiness," in which one proposes to practice their religion in terms of what St. Ignatius Loyola, a contemplative even in the midst of action, called *effusio ad exteriora*, the pouring oneself out toward external things.

The works of mercy in Christianity are eschatological signs: not works of "this world," but signs of the new creation brought into existence through the life, death, resurrection, and ascension of Jesus Christ. They signify the very opposite of "philanthropy," or the "religion of humanity." They are not concerned with building the city of man, but are evidences of the presence of the city of God. As the works of mercy performed by Christ related in the Gospels, which as a Christian one is to imitate, their doing, their being done, is evidence that a new world has been created, brought into existence through the Incarnation of the Second Person of the Trinity. This was the testimony of Mother Teresa of Calcutta. It is portrayed and taught in the great painting by Rubens, *The Miracles of St. Ignatius Loyola*. In Rubens's painting the saint, vested in a chasuble for the celebration of Mass, is presented in a state of ecstatic contemplation surrounded by those for

---

[62] "*La religion doit surtout nous disposer et nous enseigner à vivre pour autrui*": Auguste Comte, *Catéchisme*, pp. 306–307.

[63] This is Thomas Sheehan's description in "Revolution in Catholicism," *The New York Review of Books*, June 14, 1984, p. 38.

[64] Thomas Sheehan, as quoted by Paul Mankowski, S.J., "Atheistic Catholics," in *Faith, Moral Reasoning, and Contemporary American Life Lecture Series 1991- 93* (Brighton, Massachusetts: The Cambridge Center for the Study of Faith and Culture, 1994), p. 95.

[65] Alain Besançon, *Trois Tentations*, p. 133.

whom cures have been effected through his intercession. This painting portrays and teaches the wonderful union of *eros* and *agape*. Although the contemplation of the philosophers is to be distinguished from the contemplation of the saints–the former being "what the energies of human nature left to themselves can achieve," the latter a divinely infused gift–nevertheless, "supernatural contemplation achieves and fulfills a natural aspiration to contemplation which is consubstantial to man."[66] We could not receive the divine gift if we were not naturally ordered to contemplative activity. "Grace elevates and perfects, it does not destroy, nature."

[66] Jacques Maritain, "Action and Contemplation," pp. 141-42.

## MARITAIN AND THE PROBLEM OF CHRISTIAN PHILOSOPHY

Matthew S. Pugh

Toward the end of "The Philosopher in Society" Jacques Maritain makes the following provocative claim:

> Philosophy, especially moral and political philosophy, can perform its moral and political function in our modern society especially as regards the need of democratic society for a genuine rational establishment of its common basic tenets, only if it keeps vital continuity with the spirit of the Judaeo-Christian tradition and with the wisdom of the Gospel, in other words, if it is a work and effort of human reason intent on the most exacting requirements of philosophical method and principles, equipped with all the weapons and information of contemporary science, and guided by the light of the supreme truths of which Christian faith makes us aware.[1]

Now it should be clear from this quote that what Maritain has in mind by philosophy is Christian philosophy, a controversial notion that for him best describes the complex relation between philosophy and Christian theology. And it must also be clear from the quote above that in Maritain's view rationally establishing the common basic tenets and values of democratic society presupposes a recognition of the truths of revelation. The quote makes it clear, in other words, that, for Maritain, the moral philosophy needed to undergird democratic society must in some sense rest upon the foundation of revealed theology. Moral philosophy presupposes moral theology, reason presupposes faith. Is "Christian philosophy," then, for Maritain, just another name for Christian theology? Is moral philosophy ultimately reducible to moral theology, and if so, does this not make a purely rational establishment of the basic tenets and values of democracy impossible?

---

[1] Jacques Maritain, *On the Use of Philosophy* (Princeton, New Jersey: Princeton University Press, 1961), p. 13; my emphasis.

Certainly Maritain rejected the position held by some of his colleagues,[2] who maintained that there can be no real relation between philosophy and theology, that philosophy and theology describe two formally distinct orders. Philosophy operates under the light of natural reason, they said, while theology operates under the supernatural light of revelation. In their view, the premises of the arguments which philosophy uses are taken from reason and observation, while the premises (or at least one of the premises) of the arguments which theology uses are given to reason by revelation. For these philosophers, any use of theological premises in philosophical argumentation turns philosophy into theology. Consequently, the notion of Christian philosophy is a contradiction, like 'square circle.'

But Maritain also rejected the position of those who held that the orders of philosophy and theology do not constitute two formally distinct orders.[3] In this view, there can be no real distinction between philosophy and theology. Philosophy, correctly understood, is simply a part of theology. This is the position most often identified with Augustine, who believed that philosophy is simply faith seeking understanding. With Augustine, the advocates of this view believe that the intellect has been so wounded by sin as to require God's grace (through His divine illumination) not only to have the Beatific Vision, but even to apprehend the most basic rational truths.

Lying between these two extreme views of Christian philosophy, however, was the view of Etienne Gilson.[4] For the early Gilson,

---

[2] Cf. Émile Bréhier's *Histoire de la philosophie: tome I, l'antiquite et le moyen age* (Paris: Presses Universitaires de France, 1943).

[3] Cf. P. Mandonnet, *Des ecrits authentiques de St. Thomas* (Fribourg: St. Paul, 1910). See also M. Blondel's *Le Problem de la Philosophie Catholique* (Paris: Presses Universitaires de France, 1944).

[4] Etienne Gilson, "What is Christian Philosophy?" in *A Gilson Reader*, ed. A. Pegis (Garden City, New York: Hanover House,1957), pp. 278-97. Cf. *The Spirit of Medieval Philosophy* (Gifford Lectures 1931-32), trans. A.H.C. Downes (London: Sheed & Ward, 1936/repr. 1950); *Reason and Revelation in the Middle Ages* (New York: Charles Scribner's Sons, 1950), Part III; and *The Philosopher and Theology*, trans. C. Gilson (New York: Random House, 1962), pp. 92-93.

philosophy and theology constitute two formally distinct orders. Yet, historically, theology has intrinsically entered into philosophy in its moments of discovery, though it has remained extrinsic to philosophy in its moments of proof. According to Gilson, for example, theology has made positive contributions to philosophy by giving to it the revelation of creation *ex nihilo*, and God as the "I am." Here faith is simply an auxiliary to reason, pointing out to reason certain naturally knowable truths of which it might not otherwise have been aware. Faith helps reason discover rational, natural truths, but it cannot help reason prove these truths. Later, Gilson broadened his notion of theology to include philosophy. Insofar as theology uses philosophy, philosophy becomes a part of theology. In this case, philosophy becomes the handmaid of theology by presupposing the truths of revelation, and then attempting to prove them rationally. For the later Gilson, philosophy is completely bent to a theological end.

Maritain, of course, outlined a position very close to the early Gilson.[5] In agreement with Gilson, he said that, in terms of their natures, philosophy and theology are absolutely distinct, constituting two distinct formal orders. Yet he added that in terms of the state of the subject in which they inhere, if the subject happens to be a believer, the believer's philosophical, or intellectual, *habitus* may be aided by a higher theological *habitus*, such as faith. In terms of its state, then, philosophy may receive the guidance of theology without ceasing to be philosophy.

Now, as we shall see, Maritain's position certainly has many strengths, but it also, unfortunately, has a weakness that ultimately keeps it from serving the social and political function that Maritain intended for it, *vis á vis* the rational establishment of the basic tenets and values for democratic society. But in order to make this clear, and then discover a possible remedy that will enable Christian philosophy

---

[5] Jacques Maritain, *An Essay on Christian Philosophy*, trans. Edward H. Flannery (New York: Philosophical Library, 1955). For a good overview of the whole debate, see M. Nedoncelle, *Is There a Christian Philosophy?* trans. I. Trethowan (New York: Hawthorne, 1960), pp. 85-99.

to function as Maritain intended, we must first examine in more detail Maritain's understanding of Christian philosophy.

## I Maritain's Understanding of Christian Philosophy

Maritain's understanding of Christian philosophy is most fully developed in his marvelous work *An Essay on Christian Philosophy.*[6] There, he says that if we wish to make sense of the notion of Christian philosophy, and avoid the two extremes of theologism and rationalism which have arisen in some Catholic philosophical circles in reaction to the very notion of Christian philosophy, we must distinguish "the nature of philosophy, or what it is in itself, from the state in which philosophy exists in real fact, historically in the human subject, and which pertains to its concrete conditions of existence and exercise."[7] Given that the operation proper to a science is specified by the object proper to that operation, it is the proper object of a science's proper operation that determines a science's nature, or essence. Since the proper object of philosophy's operation is the whole order of intelligible being, that is, the whole domain of objects that lie within reach of the human intellect, philosophy is wholly rational in nature. Nothing of faith enters into philosophy because there is nothing in its domain that transcends reason; philosophy bases its conclusions entirely on the evidence of the senses and intrinsic rational criteria. It is philosophy's nature, therefore, to be essentially rational in regard to its object, its principles, and its methods.[8]

Furthermore, philosophy's nature, like all natures, is reached through the process of formal abstraction (*abstractio formalis*), which abstracts from philosophy's nature, or essence, all of those individuating or existential features that mask its intelligibility. Yet no nature actually exists in pure abstraction, and so, when considering philosophy, the state in which philosophy exists must also be taken into account. Thus, if philosophy is to be understood in its entirety, it must be viewed from the standpoint of both its nature and its concrete

---

[6] Jacques Maritain, op. cit.

[7] Ibid., pp. 11-12.

[8] Ibid., p. 15.

state, i.e. from the standpoint of both its essence and the historical conditions of the subject in which it inheres.

Now the Christian, relying on revelation, believes philosophy's state is that of a nature inhering in a subject (namely, man's intellect) as elevated by grace, for he believes (again by revelation) that man is destined for a supernatural end; an end that man's reason is wholly incapable of reaching through its own powers. Maritain thus avers that in terms of its nature philosophy is entirely rational, but in terms of its state it exists in a subject dependent on that which issues from faith. 'Christian philosophy' therefore identifies a unique discipline that exists in a peculiar tension between a nature wholly rational and self-sufficient, and a state in which its subject is dependent upon a higher and rationally inaccessible order.

Of course, if the above description of the state of philosophy is correct, then philosophy's Christian state has altered the practice of philosophy in a number of important ways; and this is a claim which the history of philosophy in fact confirms. For example, historically Christian revelation has contributed data to philosophy which have entered into it so intrinsically as to change the very way in which philosophy views its own subject matter. These data have been of both natural and supernatural kind. There are certain data, for instance, of strictly natural kind (that is, that are wholly accessible to reason), but included in revelation, that have aided philosophy primarily in its moments of discovery, though they have also aided philosophy in its moments of proof. In agreement with Gilson, Maritain identifies three notions of special merit in this regard: creation, God as Self-Subsisting Being, and sin.[9] Although reason *could* have discovered these ideas strictly through its own means, their inclusion in the data of revelation has given them a prominence that has caused philosophy to re-examine its subject matter in their light, and thereby brought to reason's attention certain natural truths that it might not otherwise have discovered.

But Christian revelation has also contributed supernatural data to philosophy, and these have likewise entered into philosophy in an

---

[9] Ibid., pp. 18-19.

intrinsic way, though again primarily in terms of philosophy's moments of discovery. For Maritain, philosophy would not have been able to discover the metaphysical problem of the human person without the dogmas of the Trinity and the Incarnation. The latter dogma also gives to philosophy its "ontological pivotal center."[10] In this case, metaphysics tests it natural claims in the light of the supernatural data of revelation–data which is said to 'complete' reason. These contributions, of course, are objective contributions. Yet revelation also gives subjective super-natural contributions to philosophy. The virtue of faith, for example, strengthens reason in regard to what it can know through its own powers, namely, that God exists. Also, the theological contemplative *habitus* clarifies the natural philosophical *habitus*. In regard to man's true end, faith sharpens the natural mystical desire for God, pointing out to reason that the Beatific Vision of God is indeed man's true end, and that reason itself cannot attain this end. Finally, faith elevates man's intellect so that it might in fact attain that end, and even strengthens reason's natural operation, aiding that operation insofar as grace helps to bring man's appetites under the control of reason. In short, Christian revelation has historically contributed both objectively to the content of philosophy, and subjectively to the condition of the believer's intellect, and in so doing has thereby significantly altered philosophy's state.

Nevertheless, though revelation has certainly contributed to philosophy in an intrinsic way by aiding philosophy in its moments of discovery, these contributions have been fundamentally extrinsic in regard to philosophy's moments of proof. As Maritain says, "Thus once again do we arrive at Mr. Gilson's conclusions: 'Though this relationship is intrinsic, the two orders (reason and revelation) remain distinct.'"[11] For Maritain, then, philosophy and theology are formally distinct though intrinsically related, yet intrinsically related only in regard to philosophy's moments of discovery, not its moments of proof.

However, Maritain rather strikingly makes an exception to this rule when it comes to moral philosophy. And this is striking because even

---

[10] Ibid., p. 24.

[11] Ibid., p. 30.

though Maritain admits that theology has a light, and a method, that differ entirely from those of philosophy, he claims that moral philosophy is necessarily sub-alternated to theology. Now this exception creates a real problem, for the notion of Christian philosophy works only insofar as the two orders of philosophy and theology remain formally distinct, that is, works only as long as the supernatural data of revelation do not enter into philosophy's moments of proof. But if the data of revelation enter even into philosophy's moments of proof, that is, are used as premises (which by their very nature are inaccessible to reason) in its arguments, then philosophy collapses into theology, and the two orders become one. Simply put, because moral philosophy has as its proper object "that universe of man and human things envisaged in their moral dynamism *and in relation to their proper end*,"[12] in order to become proportioned to its proper object which clearly lies in the supernatural order, moral philosophy must become super-elevated, or sub-alternated, to theology. It must, in other words, become a philosophy that borrows its most basic and important principle from theology. Hence, in the case of moral philosophy, philosophy and theology share a common domain. For Maritain, consequently, ethics is not a purely philosophic discipline. It must, in order to deal adequately with its subject matter, and particularly with the finality of that subject matter, use the data of revelation.

Of course, Maritain was not unaware of the problem created by his notion of Christian philosophy, especially as this bears on the status of moral philosophy *vis á vis* moral theology, and this is why he goes to great lengths to clarify his position on this question in the second part of the lengthy appendix to *An Essay on Christian Philosophy*,[13] where he specifically addresses the problem of the relation of moral philosophy to theology. In that appendix, Maritain clearly states that moral philosophy cannot exist in separation from theology, precisely because human conduct cannot exist in isolation from its concrete historical situation. Considered in abstraction, or by itself, moral philosophy is incomplete. In order to be complete, it must have knowledge of man's

---

[12] Ibid., p. 38.

[13] Ibid., pp. 61-100.

true end, as well as the actual conditions of man's existence. But that knowledge only comes to moral philosophy through revelation. As Maritain says: "All the great ethical systems which are ignorant of the ways of grace, however rich in partial truths they may be, are bound to be deficient."[14]

In point of fact, then, moral philosophy and theology seem to cover the same domain. But it does not follow from this fact that moral philosophy therefore becomes theology, for, as Maritain is quick to point out, the Scholastic philosophers understood that the domain of a science is restricted to either its material object, or to its formal object, that is, to its object as viewed either from the standpoint of its materiality, or from the standpoint of that which makes it be the kind of thing that it is. A science's domain does not, however, include the formal object viewed from the standpoint of that which determines it as an *object of knowledge* and that makes it the properly specific object of a science, i.e. that makes it the truly specifying object of the science in question. Thus, two sciences can have the same domain, materially and formally, but still be specifically distinct. For instance, moral philosophy and moral theology have the same domain, or field, materially and formally considered, namely, human acts, but nevertheless have specifically distinct proper formal objects specifying distinct kinds of knowledge. In effect, the same formal domain can give rise to more than one specifically distinct scientific *habitus.*

To further clarify his point, Maritain turns to the works of Cajetan and John of St. Thomas,[15] and in particular to their application of this principle to the problem of how theology is related to the science of the blessed. They begin with the notion that every science considers its object from two perspectives–from the formal perspective of the *object as thing*, or kind, and from the formal perspective of the *object as object.* From the perspective of *object as thing*, or kind, the *habitus* in question knows those properties of the object that formally determine the subject matter of the science, e.g. *being* in metaphysics, *quantity* in mathematics, and *mutable being* in natural philosophy. From the

[14] Ibid., p. 64.

[15] Ibid., pp. 66-76.

perspective of the *object as object*, however, the *habitus* in question knows the object from the standpoint of its immateriality, or degree of abstraction from matter. There is, then, corresponding to these degrees of immateriality, lights or media of varying degrees under which the object in question is viewed. This means that the unity and diversity of the sciences is actually determined by the purity of the lights under which their formal objects are viewed. Thus, although there is in theology only one formal perspective (the divine light of revelation), by which its object as object–or as object of knowledge–is viewed, nevertheless, because this unity is generic rather than specific, the *habitus* of theology can be divided into three: (1) the divine evident light, corresponding to the science of the blessed; (2) the divine revealing light, corresponding to theology as commonly understood; and (3) the divine non-evident light, corresponding to faith. Since the formal object of theology taken as a whole is God considered in His Deity, this is what constitutes the actual formal unity of the science. Yet, because this formal object can be viewed from different perspectives as an object of knowledge, and can consequently be the subject of different *habitus*, theology properly considered, insofar as it studies God from the standpoint of His revealability, is specifically distinct from the science of the blessed.

Applying these same insights to the problem of the proper relation of moral philosophy to moral theology, we see that these two sciences have the same formal object and the same formal reason, or light, under which they view their object as thing, namely, human acts insofar as they conform to, or can be conformed to, the proper ends of human life. But they have different proper objects insofar as they view their formal object, as object of knowledge, under different lights. In other words, moral philosophy and moral theology have the same formal object, or domain, and the same formal reason, because man has one true ultimate end to which he is ordained–the Beatific Vision of God. Yet these same sciences view their object, as an object of knowledge, under different intelligible lights, or specific *habitus*. Thus, moral philosophy views its formal object under the light or *habitus* of what can be ordered or regulated by reason. Moral theology, on the other hand, views its formal object as object under the light or *habitus* of what is divinely revealable.

For Maritain, then, these two lights suffice to keep moral philosophy and moral theology specifically distinct. Moral philosophy reflects on human actions according to what they are in themselves, or according to their natures, and takes its reasons from the proper causes of things, while moral theology views these only insofar as they refer to God, Who is considered first in the order of knowledge. In a sense, philosophy ascends from creatures to God, while theology descends from God to creatures. Moral theology, in effect, considers human acts as these are referable to a God who reveals Himself to man.

In sum, moral philosophy considers human action as directed to God as final end and regulable by reason, that is, under the light of reason, while moral theology views these actions as ordered to God under the formal viewpoint of revelation. Although both moral philosophy and moral theology view human acts in reference to a supernatural final end (the Beatific Vision), the lights under which that end is viewed are entirely different. The first views it under the practical light of human reason, the second under the light of revelation.

Nevertheless, Maritain says quite clearly that though moral philosophy is specifically distinct from moral theology, moral philosophy is only completed when elevated or sub-alternated to theology. Moral philosophy must be sub-alternated to theology precisely because it has the same formal object as moral theology; if it is to view that object, it must become properly proportioned to it, and this can only occur through a human but elevated light. However, if moral philosophy must be sub-alternated to theology, does this not threaten to collapse moral philosophy into moral theology? Maritain does not think so, although, as we shall see, his defense is inadequate.

Of course, Maritain says that moral philosophy is sub-alternated to moral theology in a rather special way–moral philosophy, he says, is sub-alternated to moral theology as regards the latter's principles, but not as regards its subject matter.[16] Were moral philosophy sub-alternated to theology in regard to its subject matter, it would take the latter from theology and then simply add to it some accidental difference from its own object materially considered, in the same way,

---

[16] Ibid., pp. 82-89.

for example, that acoustics borrows its subject matter from arithmetic, but adds *sounding* to it, so that its proper subject matter (its formal object) becomes *sounding* number, or optics borrows its subject matter from geometry, and adds *visual* to it, so that its subject matter (its formal object) becomes *visual* line. As such, these sciences are formally mathematical and materially physical; hence they are called *scientiae media.*

Moral philosophy, however, does not take its subject matter from theology, but it does take from theology principles which complete its own purely natural first principles. Unlike the *scientiae media*, moral philosophy is formally philosophical–it is not a formally theological and materially philosophical discipline. In other words, moral philosophy does not simply borrow its subject from theology and then add an accidental material difference to it. Moral philosophy's subject matter is its own, even though it has the same domain as moral theology, namely, human acts. What makes the two sciences specifically distinct are the different lights under which that domain is viewed.

Typically, though, even in sciences sub-alternated to a higher science as regards principles alone, the sub-alternated science is said to resolve its conclusions in its own principles through the mediation of the sub-alternating, or superior science. Thus, the *habitus* of the proximate principles of the sub-alternated science is in fact the higher *habitus* of the sub-alternating science. Yet here, however, Maritain is quick to point out that though moral philosophy (as sub-alternated to theology) receives its completing principles from moral theology, moral philosophy does not resolve its naturally evident conclusions directly in the light of revelation and faith, nor does it resolve them indirectly in naturally evident first principles by the intermediary of theology. Moral philosophy, rather, resolves its natural conclusions in naturally evident first principles and the light of practical reason, even though these naturally evident first principles are completed by principles taken from theology. Revelation simply offers to practical reason certain data which it could not uncover through its own powers–data which it then uses for its own purposes. Unlike moral theology, moral philosophy is oriented toward the natural world, and it is in the natural world that it resolves its conclusions. Moral philosophy uncovers its naturally evident first principles by its own power, and it resolves its conclusions in these by its own power. Here, then, the light or *habitus*–which knows the first principles of practical reason and by which it resolves its conclusions–is the *habitus* of philosophy; theology simply offers that light by which these natural principles are perfected and completed. The *habitus* of theology does not replace the *habitus* of philosophy–it simply complements it. In sum, for Maritain, moral philosophy does not need the light of theology either to resolve its conclusions or to take possession of its natural first principles, nor does it need the light of theology to resolve its conclusions in those natural first principles. Yet moral philosophy does need moral theology in order to complete, or perfect, its own first principles.

**II Critique**

All of this makes it quite clear that Maritain's notion of Christian philosophy is a complex and sophisticated notion, but it is also quite clear that it fails to meet the challenge of those critics who wish to safeguard the autonomy of moral philosophy. For, insofar as moral philosophy needs moral theology for the completion of its own natural principles, the data of revelation enter into moral philosophy, not simply in an intrinsic way, but in so deep a way as to destroy the very autonomy of the philosophy that Maritain is at pains to preserve. Like any sub-alternated science, moral philosophy must accept on faith the truth of the principles which it takes from the higher science of moral theology. Moral philosophy is not able to see of its own accord, either the principles of theology (actually, its conclusions), nor those first principles of theology in which those conclusions are resolved. This, by itself, is enough to destroy the autonomy of ethics for many secular and non-secular philosophers alike. Simply put, if philosophy admits into its arguments the data of revelation, and uses these as premises in its arguments, then philosophy is no longer philosophy, no longer purely rational. It has in fact become some species of theology.

Now, as we have seen, the most important notion that moral philosophy borrows from theology is the doctrine of man's ultimate end. And because in practical philosophy ends play the role of principles, the doctrine of man's ultimate end is the most important, and indeed the genuinely first principle of moral philosophy, and should therefore according to Maritain "dominate all of moral philosophy."[17] The first principle of practical reason, for example, only makes sense on Maritain's reading if viewed in the context of the doctrine of man's ultimate end: in fact this is how it must be viewed if philosophy is to take into account not only its nature, but also its concrete existential state.

We must point out, however, that this position is based on a presupposition that need not, and I dare say must not, go unchallenged if we wish to establish a truly workable notion of Christian philosophy. The presupposition in question asserts that man's desire for the Beatific Vision of God, man's true ultimate end, is a purely *natural* desire. It asserts, in effect, that man has a purely natural desire for a supernatural end. Of course, if this assertion is true, then moral philosophy is indeed dependent on theology for the justification and completion of its principles.

Historically, of course, this position had generally come to be accepted by many Catholic theologians for a number of apparently good reasons. Foremost among these was the desire to reject a conception of man's supernatural destiny that appeared to be overly extrinsic or juxtaposed to man's nature. More specifically, there was a desire to reject Cajetan's concept of obediential potency (a creature has a purely passive capacity for supernatural elevation so long as this is not repugnant to its nature), in favor of a much more dynamic and positive concept of obediential potency. For theologians such as Henri de Lubac,[18] for example, man's supernatural end or destiny must resonate very deeply with man's natural being. These theologians sought to show that grace establishes a kind of continuity between man's intellect and his supernatural end. Secondly, their reading of Aquinas supported, or so they believed, the notion of a positive, natural exigency in man's natural being for a supernatural end. Thus, the later Scholastic doctrine of a hypothetical state of pure nature was an aberration stemming from a misunderstanding of Thomas on this very

[17] Ibid., p. 96.

[18] Henri de Lubac, *The Mystery of the Supernatural*, trans. Rosemary Sheed (New York: Herder and Herder, 1967).

point. There never has been, nor could there have been, they said, such a state of pure nature. Man has been destined from the very beginning for a supernatural end–an end that is, furthermore, entirely gratuitous insofar as it is God's free gift to man through creation. Karl Rahner even went so far as to speak of a supernatural existential intrinsic, yet somehow super-added, to man's being: a pre-requisite for grace manifested in the form of man's natural desire for the Beatific Vision of God.[19] Man's being is such that it is inconceivable apart from this supernatural destiny. In sum, they believed that though man has a natural exigency for the Beatific Vision, this exigency does not obligate God in any way.

Nevertheless, those Scholastics who rejected the doctrine of a natural desire for the Beatific Vision had their own good reasons for doing so as well. Most importantly, the idea of a natural desire for the Beatific Vision seemed to compromise the gratuity of man's final end, turning it into something due man's nature. The problem becomes obvious immediately–if man's desire for the Beatific Vision is natural; if, as Thomas clearly says, it is impossible for a natural desire to be in vain; and if man's end necessitates that man's nature be elevated by grace, then nature places a demand on God that God is obligated to satisfy. Put another way, if man's destiny is an exigency of nature, then the supernatural order would seem to be reduced to the natural order, and the supernatural would simply become a perfection of nature within the order of nature, i.e. the supernatural order would be collapsed into the natural order.

Yet the Scholastics in question found an even more compelling reason to reject the doctrine of a natural desire for the Beatific Vision of God. If grace is an exigency of human nature, then its loss would thoroughly corrupt human nature–a position which the Church did not and could not accept.[20] Indeed, it was precisely a concern to safeguard the fundamental goodness of man's nature that ultimately led some

---

[19] Karl Rahner, "Concerning the Relationship between Nature and Grace," *Theological Investigations*, v. 1, trans. Cornelius Ernst, O.P. (Baltimore, Maryland: Helicon, 1961), pp. 295-317.

[20] Pope Pius XII, *Humani Generis* (Boston: St. Paul Editions, 1950).

Scholastics to postulate the doctrine of the hypothetical state of pure nature. That is, in order to safeguard the goodness of man's being even after the Fall, it was necessary to say that God could have created man in a state of pure nature wherein he would possess all of the physical and spiritual realities necessary to man, including a physical body and rational soul, with a purely natural end properly proportioned to his natural capacities. Such an end would consist of the love of God above all things as author of nature, and the purely philosophical contemplation of His being as First Cause.

Though it is true that the Scholastic philosophers who rejected the doctrine of a natural desire for the Beatific Vision disagreed on the finer points at issue in that complex debate, they all agreed that the desire for the Beatific Vision is not natural in the sense of being an exigency of nature–it is rather, dependent upon grace, or supernatural in origin. Thus any 'natural' desire for God must be understood to be consequent on the intellect's knowledge of the existence of the Beatific Vision as man's actual end, (which can only be known to man if given to him in the form of a datum of revelation–and, even then, the desire elicited by this act of reason enlightened by revelation need not necessarily become a desire for the Beatific Vision as such–it might simply become a desire for God as First Cause),[21] or be relegated to a lesser kind of desire, wherein the desire is prior to revelation and hence purely natural, but nevertheless is not a desire for the Beatific Vision, being instead a desire to know God as First Cause and elicited by an act of the intellect which knows that God is.[22]

Certainly, this is a position that is perfectly consistent with Aquinas's position, even though there appear to be some passages in Thomas's works, such as *Summa Theologiae* I-II, q. 3, a. 8, that seem to point to the contrary. In that passage Thomas discusses the nature of man's beatitude, which he says consists in seeing God's essence. His discussion begins with a recognition of an apparently natural desire for the Beatific Vision. He says that so long as there is something for man to desire, he cannot be happy. Furthermore, the perfection of every

---

[21] This was Cajetan's position, for example.

[22] This was Sylvester of Ferrara's position.

power is judged from its object. Since man's soul is rational, and since reason is its highest power, the perfection of reason, and hence the soul, is attained when the intellect knows the essence of a thing. But in knowing the essence of an effect the act of knowledge is not complete unless the intellect also knows the essence of the cause; knowledge of the simple existence of the cause is not sufficient, even if that knowledge comes via the effect. In knowing the essence of the effect, then, the intellect automatically desires to know the essence of the cause. Thus, if knowing the essence of a created effect leads to a knowledge of the existence of God, its uncreated cause, the intellect will naturally desire to know the essence of that cause. In other words, only a direct knowledge of God's essence will ultimately satisfy the intellect's natural desire.

Evidently, then, Aquinas certainly seems to be claiming in *ST* I-II, q. 3, a. 8 that there is in man, prior to revelation (though not prior to the intellect's knowledge of God's existence), a natural desire for the Vision of God. Yet, when this article is placed in its proper context, and read in the light of Thomas's principle that claims priority for the intellect over the will, we see that this is in fact not the case.

According to Thomas, the will or rational appetite depends on the intellect by nature; as the rational appetite, the will is rooted in the intellect, since it is that appetite of the soul which follows what the intellect apprehends as good. (In this respect, the intellect can be likened to a mover which is not moved, while the will can be likened to a moved mover.) Nevertheless, as two distinct powers, the intellect and the will have two distinct ends. The intellect's proper end is knowledge, while the will's proper end is happiness. Yet the will cannot be moved towards happiness until the idea of happiness is present in the intellect. Since Thomas believes that happiness consists in the Vision of God, and since that Vision is withheld from man in this life, the will is not moved of necessity (that is, naturally) to desire the Vision of God. Consequently, the good that the will naturally and of necessity desires is happiness in general, and since no particular thing appears to the will to be good in every respect, the will does not naturally identify any particular thing with happiness in general. Thus, although the will necessarily desires happiness, it does not necessarily desire the Vision of God as its happiness. At best, the desire for God is included in the desire for happiness in general only in a very obscure and confused way. We have no explicit desire for the Vision of God, and Thomas does not say that the will by its very nature desires such a vision.

Furthermore, although *ST* I-II, q. a. 8 might seem explicitly to recognize the existence of a natural desire in the intellect for the Vision of God, this desire must again be viewed in the context of the relation of the will to the intellect. When so viewed, we see that this "desire" is not what it appears to be. Thomas gives us the key in *ST* I, q. 82. a. 4, where he explains how the will moves the intellect. Among an order of active powers, that power which regards the universal end moves those powers which regard particular ends. But the object of the will is the good and the end in general, while the other powers have as their objects some good suitable to their proper operations, as the knowledge of truth is the end proper to the intellect. Hence the will moves all the powers to their respective ends, including the intellect. In other words, the will desires, in addition to its own goodness or happiness, the good of all the powers of the soul, including the intellect. The will naturally moves the intellect to complete its act of cognition. In this case, the will naturally moves the intellect to seek completion in the Vision of God. The will here acts as an agent that alters what is altered, or impels what is impelled. Thus, the natural desire that Thomas is talking about in *ST* I-II, q. 3, a. 8 is simply the result of the will's willing the intellect to complete its act of cognition. This is why Thomas refers to the desire in question as a desire for perfection, or completion.

Nevertheless, this desire is not to be confused with the will's genuine desire for the Vision of God, and here is where the intellect truly takes priority over the will for Thomas. In the first case (wherein the will moves the intellect to complete its act of cognition), the intellect does not know God as He is in Himself (there the intellect simply desires to know more about God). In the second case (wherein the will desires the Vision of God), it does so precisely because the intellect has actually seen God as He is in Himself, or has been given knowledge through revelation that this is in fact our true end, and an end that will one day be actually realized. Here, the will is moved by what is actually in the intellect. Since the Beatific Vision cannot be actually present in the intellect in this life (except perhaps in the most advanced states of mystical ecstasy, which of course can only be given to us by God), there can be no innate tendency or natural desire in either will or intellect for the Vision of God. The intellect does naturally desire to know God's essence after it has learned of His existence; however, since God's mode of being transcends creation and thus the created intellect's mode of being (which knows only those objects naturally proportioned to that created mode of being), the intellect can have no knowledge through its own power that such a desire will ever be satisfied. Thus, the only natural desire for God that the intellect has in this life is the desire, vague and confused though it be, to know more about God. The genuine Vision of God, in other words, is not the terminative end of the intellect's natural desire for God. What appears to be the intellect's natural desire for the Vision of God, then, is not the genuine desire for the Vision of God, the true Beatific Vision.

In addition, because God cannot be seen as He is in Himself in this life, the will enjoys a freedom of both specification and exercise in regards to the Vision of God. Not only are we free to act or not to act in regard to the Vision of God, but we are also free to reject this end. Hence, the will enjoys a freedom that it does not have in regard to happiness in general (which appears to be good in every respect). In the case of happiness in general, we are free to act or not to act in regard to it, but, if we act, the act cannot be one of rejection. In short, what appears to be the intellect's natural desire for the Vision of God must be distinguished from the will's genuine desire for Beatitude.

If we have a desire for the Beatific Vision, then, this desire must be a supernatural desire. And this is exactly what Aquinas says in *De Veritate*, q. 27, a. 2.[23] This means that in our concrete state of existence, insofar as we have a desire for the Beatific Vision, the natural desire for God (the intellect's desire to know the essence of God, as well as the will's desire that the intellect complete its act of cognition) has had super-added to it the supernatural gift of the will's desire for beatitude, that is, the desire for the anticipated beatitude that would come from the Beatific Vision itself. This is a gift that was conferred on us in our

[23] Thomas Aquinas, *De Veritate*, q. 27, a. 2, trans. Robert W. Schmidt (Chicago: Regnery, 1954), p. 315.

second elevation in Christ,[24] which restored to us not only the supernatural gifts of our elevation in the First Adam, but also the preternatural gifts of the first Adam.[25] In our prelapsarian state we had neither the Beatific Vision, nor the desire for the Beatific Vision[26]–the second cannot be had apart from the first, or apart from our elevation in Christ, which the First Adam did not have. And this also means that the loss of those gifts through sin did not so corrupt man's nature as to make our intellect incapable of apprehending first principles, or knowing God in natural philosophical contemplation. Nevertheless, though a purely philosophical knowledge of God is possible in our present state, this knowledge is incomplete short of grace.

Yet, if there is no natural desire in man for the Beatific Vision of God, then God surely could have created man in a state of pure nature with a purely natural and terminative end. This end, as noted before, would consist of the purely philosophical contemplation of God as First Cause and author of all creation. It would, in essence, be what Aristotle meant by the intuitive contemplation of the Unmoved Mover. Yet its perfection would be realized only in death, when the encumbrances of the body fall away and the path cleared for the intellect's pure

---

[24] There are numerous passages (too many to reference here) in both Scripture and from tradition that confirm this notion. For example, cf. St. Leo the Great, "What fell in the first Adam, is raised up in the second" (*Sermon* 12.1; PL 54: 168); also *Ephesians* 1.4 and 1.6. In short, these passages state that Adam had *gratia Dei*, but not *gratia Christi*.

[25] The preternatural refers to the supernatural gifts which surpass the nature of some particular kind of creature (like man) but not others (like the angels), as opposed to the absolutely or simply supernatural, which surpasses the nature of every kind of creature. Adam's immortality and right ordering among the parts of his soul were preternatural gifts. In addition, the preternatural does **not** elevate a creature to a share in God's life. Hence, Adam did not have the Beatific Vision. The restoration of man in Christ (his second elevation) thus did not, strictly speaking, restore man's desire for the Beatific Vision. It was restored only in the sense that man was destined for this end from the very beginning, but, again, strictly speaking, this desire actually exits in man only from the time of Christ.

[26] Cf. Thomas Aquinas, *Summa Theologiae* I, q. 94, a. 1 ad 3.

contemplation of God–a contemplation taking place *through* the soul and in a kind of natural mysticism, wherein the soul understands God's immensity as being present to it as a cause is present to its effects.[27] Realizing this end would comprise perfect natural beatitude; prior to death, only imperfect natural beatitude is possible in the state of pure nature.

In sum, man in his present state of being has only one true ultimate end–the Beatific Vision of God. This has been our destiny from the very beginning, insofar as it has been a part of God's plan, from the very beginning. Yet the desire for the Beatific Vision of God is a supernatural desire, and it is a desire that was given to man by God in man's second elevation in Christ. Hence, in his present concrete state of being, man is inconceivable apart from grace, but this does not mean that man in his essence is inconceivable apart from grace, nor does it mean that God could not have created man in a state of pure nature, with a purely natural end. Indeed, such a possibility is the only way to truly protect the gratuity of the Beatific Vision, to keep the order of nature separate from the order of supernature, and to preserve the goodness of man's being, even after the Fall.

But most importantly for our purposes, it is also the only way to preserve the autonomy of moral philosophy, for once we know that man could have existed in a state of pure nature with a purely natural end, we can, in essence, construct a purely rational moral philosophy which has God (though not the Beatific Vision of God), as its natural and terminative end. We can, in other words, construct a moral philosophy whose first principles are in no way dependent on theology, either for their completion or their justification. In this moral philosophy, God is indeed man's final end, but the end is purely natural, and thus purely rational, given that the end in question is in this case entirely knowable by us through the natural intellect. Here, nothing more is needed for the completion of the first principle of practical reason than reason's understanding that the first principle of practical

---

[27] Cf. Jacques Maritain's "Natural Mystical Experience and the Void," in *Challenges and Renewals*, ed. Joseph W. Evans and Leo R. Ward (New York: Meridian Books, 1966), pp. 76-106.

reason's underlying metaphysical principle–all things by nature desire the good–is grounded in an even more basic metaphysical principle (all natures exist for some end), which in turn culminates in an ultimate First Cause/Final End. There is nothing here that transcends the nature of reason, nothing that goes beyond natural metaphysics.

**III Conclusion**

Maritain's notion of Christian philosophy, then, ultimately works only if it has added to it the correction which eliminates any conceptual dependence on the natural desire for the Beatific Vision of God. In this corrected version of Maritain's understanding of Christian philosophy, moral philosophy rests upon a purely rational foundation needing no completion by theology. Here, man's ultimate end–and hence the ultimate principle that grounds the first principle of practical reason–is indeed God, but God as known through reason alone. This does not mean, however, that moral theology provides no guidance for moral philosophy. Theology may indeed enter into philosophy in terms of its moments of discovery, but it must remain extrinsic to philosophy in terms of its moments of proof. No revealed (supernatural) truth is used in philosophy's arguments, either in its premises or its conclusions. Yet revealed truths can provide guidance to philosophy by pointing out to reason certain natural truths of which it might not otherwise have been aware. And this is exactly how moral theology functions when it points out to moral philosophy that the desire for the Beatific Vision of God that we do have in our concrete state of existence is a supernatural desire for the vision of God. Reason's attention is thereby drawn, in spite of our existential state, to the real possibility of a purely natural, and hence rational, end for man. Thus, a purely natural, rational truth that reason could have discovered on its own is simply made more evident to reason by the light of moral theology. Reason is made to see, in other words, that there is an end that is perfectly completive, and perfectly attainable, for reason, and that might have been the one end for which we exist.

Finally, this corrected version of Maritain's Christian philosophy has the added advantage of making a strictly rational establishment of the basic tenets and values of democracy possible. For it provides the rational completion needed for a moral philosophy grounded in a natural teleology, and therefore requiring a natural end. So completed, the moral philosophy that must be the foundation for democracy becomes rationally self-enclosed, making no appeal to truths beyond reason's grasp. In short, only a Christian philosophy that safeguards the real autonomy of philosophy can provide for democracy a genuine rational foundation, for the basic tenets and values of democracy are only established in a truly rational way if the moral philosophy justifying those tenets and values is itself free of non-rational presuppositions.

# A Controversy Reconsidered

## Ralph C. Nelson

It is usually said by historians of the topic that the subject of Christian philosophy in contemporary thought was initiated by an essay written by the noted historian of philosophy Émile Bréhier, appearing in *Revue de métaphysique et de moral* in 1931,[1] entitled "Is there a Christian Philosophy?" The answer, according to Bréhier, was negative.

In one way or another this provoked a number of responses in what has been called "the debate of 1931"[2] concerning the meaning and validity of Christian philosophy. For our purposes the most significant statements in reply, if you will, were by Etienne Gilson in *The Spirit of Medieval Philosophy*, and by Jacques Maritain in *Christian Philosophy*, with further elaborations and answers to critics in *Science and Wisdom.* If Gilson, on the one hand, argued that on the theoretical side of philosophy there was indeed a significant biblical influence on metaphysics–the metaphysics of *Exodus*–it was Maritain's contention that only a moral philosophy subalternated to faith and theology could produce what he called a moral philosophy adequately considered, that is, adequate to its object. This is what he means by Christian philosophy. If Maritain confines his claim to practical philosophy, Gilson seems to confine his to theoretical. I should add that the name of Maurice Blondel is also mentioned in this context.[3]

I want to argue that Maritain's treatment of the issues confronting moral philosophy underwent a development in which the role of

---

[1] Émile Bréhier, "Y a-t-il une philosophie chrétienne?" *Revue de métaphysique et de moral* 38 (avril juin 1931), pp. 133-62.

[2] Henry Bars, *Maritain en notre temps* (Paris: Bernard Grasset, 1959), p. 211. Father Bars also wrote "A propos du *Paysan de la Garonne*," *Revue Thomiste* (Janvier-Mars 1968): 89-100. The long introduction to Father Joseph Owens's *Towards a Christian Philosophy* (Washington: The Catholic University of America Press, 1990), pp. 1-59, gives a good idea of the state of the question at that time.

[3] Ibid., p. 209.

philosophy at first dependent on theology, in part at least, expands and becomes of assistance to theology. If this expansion meant that philosophy has become a sophisticated instrument at the behest of faith, Maritain would simply have become a theologian, given the age-old concept of philosophy as handmaiden to theology. But Maritain, as we shall see, insists even when dealing with Christology or Ecclesiology that he does so as a philosopher. But how does he move from the initial position in which moral philosophy is subalternated to theology to the final position in which he stresses that philosophy has something to offer theology? And how to deal with texts that appeared in the interim in which he concentrates on the problems of moral philosophy and its history in *An Introduction to the Basic Problems of Moral Philosophy*[4] and in *Moral Philosophy*?[5] How does all this hang together?

I shall proceed in three stages: first, the elaboration of the concept of moral philosophy adequately considered; secondly, the works dealing with moral philosophy in itself and in its history; and third, and last, the new role for moral philosophy, if not philosophy altogether, announced in *The Peasant of the Garonne*,[6] and exemplified in *The Grace and Humanity of Jesus*.[7]

Those of us of an older generation remember those days in which Thomism, textbook or otherwise, was widely taught in Catholic institutions. Some will say that died with the Second Vatican Council. In any case, there was a diversity of approaches to Thomism, which included the use of the two *Summas* to identify Aquinas's main philosophical principles and positions, as well as an approach based on

---

[4] Jacques Maritain, *An Introduction to the Basic Problems of Moral Philosophy*, trans. Cornelia N. Borgerhoff (Albany, New York: Magi Books, 1990).

[5] Jacques Maritain, *Moral Philosophy: An Historical and Critical Survey of the Great Systems*, trans. under the direction of Joseph W. Evans (New York: Charles Scribner's Sons, 1964).

[6] Jacques Maritain, *The Peasant of the Garonne: An Old Layman Questions Himself about the Present Time*, trans. Michael Cuddihy and Elizabeth Hughes (New York: Holt, Rinehart, and Winston, 1968).

[7] Jacques Maritain, *On the Grace and Humanity of Jesus*, trans. Joseph W. Evans (London: Burns and Oates, 1969).

the assumption that the genuine philosophical thought of Aquinas did not exist in a pure state in theological treatises, but in his commentaries on the works of Aristotle. The impression was given that the commentaries were not just interpretive works, but were an exposition of Thomas's own ideas. And no doubt other approaches were also employed.

Now Maritain had written a number of works in which he attempted to explain Thomas's philosophy and, just prior to his first presentation of Christian philosophy, he had published a study of Thomas Aquinas anticipating some aspects of moral philosophy adequately considered.[8] We are prepared for further elucidation.

The key distinction used by Maritain in his little treatise on Christian philosophy is that between nature and state in regard to philosophy. The question of the nature or definition of philosophy is one matter. Its state is another. So Christian philosophy involves "those utterly distinctive conditions of existence and exercise into which Christianity has ushered the thinking subject."[9] Philosophy includes a number of *habitus* specified according to their distinctive objects. However, the order of exercise, the conditions as he says, have to be taken into account: philosophy as exercised by the Christian. In fact, there are two ways in which Christianity affects moral philosophy: "by providing objective data, and by supplying certain subjective reinforcements."[10] The former concerns what has been revealed by God and particularly, in regard to moral philosophy, "the ultimate end of man."[11] The latter concerns the virtues infused as well as acquired and how they are "interconnected in exercise," for, "without charity, they have no real connection, they are not bound together in one strong

---

[8] Jacques Maritain, *St. Thomas Aquinas*, trans. Joseph W. Evans and Peter O'Reilly (New York: Meridian Books, 1958), p. 126.

[9] Ralph Nelson, "Moral Philosophy Adequately Considered," in Joseph W. Evans, ed., *Jacques Maritain: The Man and His Achievement* (New York: Sheed and Ward, 1963), p. 139.

[10] Ibid., p. 140.

[11] Ibid., p. 142.

organism, because they are only *connected in statu virtutus*."[12] This is described as "the synergic union."

The relative autonomy of philosophy is assured because moral philosophy does not need theology "in a radical or originative way."[13] It is "completive and perfective."[14] In short, "only theology knows the true state of man, and it is not possible to direct human actions if one is in ignorance of their conditions of exercise."[15] In *Science and Wisdom*, this is spoken of as philosophy in faith.[16]

At the risk of some simplification, it can be fairly stated that the critics of Maritain's notion of moral philosophy adequately considered found no place for a third alternative between moral philosophy, on the one hand, and moral theology, on the other. There is nothing in between. For them, a moral philosophy subalternated to theology was purely and simply theology. This does not mean that they were defenders of a pure moral philosophy.

The case of Yves Simon in this regard is significant. When he first treated the concept of a subalternated moral philosophy in his *Critique of Moral Knowledge*,[17] in 1934, he stated the notion as follows: "No purely natural system of morality can be completely true, because it is essential to moral philosophy to take into account the existential conditions of humanity."[18] He then goes on to say that the idea of moral philosophy adequately considered is "quite new, involved in

---

[12] Ibid., p. 153.

[13] Ibid.

[14] Jacques Maritain, *An Essay on Christian Philosophy*, trans. Edward H. Flannery (New York: Philosophical Library, 1955), p. 89.

[15] Ralph Nelson, "Moral Philosophy Adequately Considered," pp. 150-51.

[16] Jacques Maritain, *Science and Wisdom*, trans. Bernard Wall (London: Geoffrey Bles, 1940), p. 70.

[17] Yves R. Simon, *Critique de la connaissance morale* (Paris: Desclée de Brouwer, 1934). An English translation of this work, by Ralph M. McInerny, has recently been published as *Critique of Moral Knowledge* (New York: Fordham University Press, 2003).

[18] Ibid., p. 121, n. 1.

discussions, and we do not intend to take sides on the issue."[19] He obviously is unwilling at this point to come to a conclusion, in spite of the respect he has for Maritain.

It turned out to be a long time before the question was privately expressed in several letters he exchanged with Maritain shortly before Simon's death in 1961.[20] In one of these, dated February 11, 1961, he says: "I have no doubt that a moral philosophy which is not subordinated to theology cannot be existentially true."[21] Yet, in the same letter, Simon expresses "my remaining doubts concerning the necessity of a moral philosophy adequately taken."[22] He is definitely opposed to granting to moral theology complete possession of the moral field; he still defends a role for moral philosophy. In short, while conceding the validity of Maritain's basic argument, he seems to refuse to give up his reservations. In a letter dated February 22, 1961, Maritain assumes an endorsement when he says: "I am very happy with our agreement over the notion of moral philosophy adequately considered."[23] Indeed, Simon's subsequent letter of March 8, 1961, apparently concurs with Maritain's estimation. And, if this were Simon's last statement on the subject, one might speak of an intellectual conversion. But it is not. For, in the last truly public utterance in regard to this general question of philosophical ethics, Simon insists that he prefers the method of isolation:

> When these positions are clearly formulated, the question remains as to whether it is desirable that philosophical issues be treated in a state of abstraction or in a concrete condition of association with the problems of our super-natural destiny. I would not hesitate to say that it is, to a large extent, a question of calling. I am strongly attracted by the method of isolation

---

[19] Ibid.

[20] Yves R. Simon, *Practical Knowledge*, ed. Robert J. Mulvaney (New York: Fordham University Press, 1991).

[21] Ibid., p. 105.

[22] Ibid., p. 106.

[23] Ibid., p. 108.

> because it furnishes special guaranties of epistemological purity and logical rigor.[24]

I interpret his remark to mean that he wants to pursue a moral philosophy distinct from moral theology or theology *tout court* for reasons of method and argument. However inadequate such an approach may be, he is convinced that it is the only way that the lack of confusion can be assured. This moral philosophy has its shortcomings; it does not present the whole picture, but he accepts it, warts and all.

Some years after his essays on Christian philosophy, philosophy in faith, Maritain once again devotes considerable energy in developing the critical concepts of a moral philosophy, first in *An Introduction to the Basic Problems of Moral Philosophy* and then in the historical treatment of moral philosophy in the lengthy study *Moral Philosophy*. For those who might interpret this new endeavor as a departure from the notion of moral philosophy adequately considered, he is quite clear on his abiding adherence to that conception.[25]

Were one to plan systematically an investigation of moral philosophy, it is obvious that one would follow an order directly opposite to that which Maritain followed. After an historical canvass of the subject, the next step would be doctrinal, that is, the philosopher's own conception of the basic principles of moral philosophy, followed by an assessment of its adequacy. The press of philosophical discussion led him into the initial expression of a Christian philosophy, before having extensively treated moral philosophy as such. Then, having looked into the basic problems of moral philosophy, he undertook the historical and critical examination of the subject. He envisioned a return to the basic problems in a subsequent volume:

> Yet the systematic examination of the fundamental problems of moral philosophy has been left to a second volume which I hope to undertake after the publication of the present [*Moral*

[24] Yves R. Simon, "Jacques Maritain: The Growth of a Christian Philosopher," in *The Man and His Achievement*, p. 23.

[25] Jacques Maritain, *Moral Philosophy*, p. 422. There are numerous references in *Basic Problems of Moral Philosophy*.

> *Philosophy*]. A central fragment of this projected volume has already been offered in outline form–however incomplete–in a few lectures previously published.[26]

We know, of course, that this second volume never appeared.

What is particularly significant in the series of lectures translated as *An Introduction to the Basic Problems of Moral Philosophy* is the way in which Maritain relates moral philosophy to other forms of knowledge. It must be said that the epistemological map of knowledge has been a constant preoccupation of the author. Here, he argues that, in order "to justify the real objective validity of social norms and values....we must have recourse to metaphysics."[27] Whether it be the relation of being and the good, or the distinction between theoretical and practical value judgments, or the analysis of teleology, the understanding of value, the *debitum*, and the analogous meanings of evil, he begins from the metaphysical concept and moves on to the moral. As he emphasizes: "Here again, the best philosophical approach is to begin with the metaphysical or ontological perspective, in order to move on from there to the specifically moral one."[28]

And yet, lest we believe that this recourse to metaphysics in ethical inquiry compromises the study of moral philosophy, he describes the latter as "*autonomous and irreducible*."[29] He wants to say that it indeed is autonomous, but not self-sufficient or independent, for it relies on metaphysical argument.

Another important conception concerns the "natural knowledge" of the natural law.[30] The fundamental knowledge human beings have is "*by the mode of inclination*."[31] Maritain has insisted on this primitive knowledge, sharply contrasted with philosophical knowledge, in a

---

[26] Ibid., p. ix. I have changed the translation, replacing "lessons" by "lectures".

[27] Jacques Maritain, *Basic Problems*, p. 18.

[28] Ibid., p. 183.

[29] Ibid., p. 68.

[30] Ibid., p. 52.

[31] Ibid., p. 62.

number of works, notably in *Creative Intuition in Art and Poetry.*[32] He reiterates his conviction that it is the natural way, the primitive way, the original way human beings came to form value judgments, and even those norms and values stemming from a socialized morality are grafted on to knowledge of this kind. But, once again, it is not philosophical knowledge.

For a number of reasons, Maritain's conception of a moral philosophy based in some sense on metaphysics, and his conception of knowledge "*by the mode of inclination*"[33] are both specifically rejected by "the new natural law theory" that was expressed in the writings of Germain Grisez, John Finnis, and, more recently, Robert George.[34] The advocates of this tendency argue for a different conception of the autonomy of practical reason and moral philosophy, and reject out of hand the very notion of a knowledge by the mode of inclination. Since I am primarily concerned with the exposition of Maritain's moral theory, I point this out here as a possible line of objection to it.

Aware of the way in which various sciences have become a source of moral theories, particularly Darwinian biology, Marxist economics, and Freudian psychology, Maritain places himself in the wake of those French thinkers who were influenced by sociology of the Durkheim School. What he is suggesting is that sociology and anthropology are the most useful sources of information among the social sciences about human beings. Of course, it must be recognized that Durkheim and Lévy-Bruhl fell into the error of making "socialized morality... the

---

[32] Jacques Maritain, *Creative Intuition in Art and Poetry* (Princeton, New Jersey: Princeton University Press, 1977), pp. 117-25.

[33] Jacques Maritain, *Basic Problems*, p. 62.

[34] A seminal essay by Germain G. Grisez, "The First Principle of Practical Reason" in Anthony Kenny, ed., *Aquinas: A Collection of Critical Essays* (Garden City, New York: Doubleday and Company, 1969), pp. 340-82, was followed by John Finnis, *Natural Law and Natural Rights* (Oxford: Clarendon Press, 1980), and Robert P. George, ed., *Natural Law and Moral Inquiry* (Washington: Georgetown University Press, 1998). There are several other works by George.

whole of human morality,"[35] of falling into sociologism. I have argued elsewhere how Maritain may be related to Durkheim and Bergson in a kind of dialectical series,[36] in which Bergson, follower and critic of Durkheim, in turn is subject to criticism.

Finally, in this lecture series, described later as an outline, Maritain returns once more to the conception of a moral philosophy adequately considered.[37] The reasons for continuing to uphold this conception are as before, objective data–such as the notion of the ultimate end of human life, known from theology–and those subjective reinforcements, the infused virtues. If anything, he broadens the conception, no longer speaking of just Christian philosophy, but stressing "that moral philosophy has no chance of being adequate to its object unless it attaches itself to one or another of the religious traditions of humanity."[38] He does not, however, examine the difficulties of say a Muslim philosophy, or any kind other than the Christian. The reliance in any case is on "the concrete existential state of human nature."[39] He attacks once again the notion of a separate philosophy, an idea he had introduced many years before in an essay on Descartes, when he said the latter wanted to philosophize in complete separation from theology.[40]

If the *Introduction* largely passed unobserved when it was first published, *Moral Philosophy* was severely criticized because it had very little to say about certain important contributors to moral philosophy and gave the impression that the British had little to offer to the

---

[35] Jacques Maritain, *Basic Problems*, p. 13.

[36] Ralph Nelson, "Maritain and the Continuation of Bergson," *Maritain Studies* 6 (June 1990): 107-28.

[37] Jacques Maritain, *Basic Problems of Moral Philosophy*, pp. 97, 98, 107, 113, 115, 118-19, 130, n. 5, 139, 140, 154, 196, 214, and 215.

[38] Ibid., p. 113.

[39] Ibid., p. 139.

[40] Jacques Maritain, *The Dream of Descartes*, trans. Mabelle L. Andison (New York: The Philosophical Library, 1944), p. 74.

subject.[41] One thinks of the moral writings of Henry B. Veatch that involved him in a constant dialogue with leading British ethicists. Even though Maritain had clearly announced that his purpose was "doctrinal in order, not historical,"[42] the historical chronicle following easily led to misunderstanding. The only English speaking philosopher examined was Dewey, though his Hegelian background was made much of. Nothing was said of Max Scheler's important contribution to moral philosophy, although Sartre's moral thought is discussed. Maritain's allusion to "great systems"[43] explains why so much space is assigned to a detailed exposition of Hegel and Comte. The overall impression is that this is very much a continental European perspective on moral philosophy and Maritain is hardly the first to see Dewey's work evolving, as much as Marx's and Kierkegaard's, out of the massive system of Hegel.

In the statement of aims, it is pointed out that "our task is philosophical, not theological," that moral philosophy, authentic moral philosophy, "has yet to be developed."[44] This explains why Maritain plays down the teleological approach to ethics, which we identify with Aristotle, and takes an analysis of moral obligation as a suitable starting point in the course of commenting on Bergson's *The Two Sources of Morality and Religion.*

Let us summarize by saying that the primary purpose of the work is to present "the method proper to moral philosophy as an authentically philosophic discipline."[45] Moral philosophy, or moral science, is distinguished from the natural knowledge of natural law, affective connaturality. Then the secondary purpose appears to be sketching out that super-moral knowledge that comes from faith and theology.

---

[41] If Vernon Bourke has almost nothing good to say about the treatise in his review in *The Modern Schoolman* 43 (November 1965): 81-82, James Collins is extremely favorable to it in his account in *The Critic* 23 (August 1964): 69-70.

[42] Jacques Maritain, *Moral Philosophy*, p. ix.

[43] Ibid.

[44] Ibid.

[45] Ibid., p. x.

Christianity played an enormous role in the development of moral knowledge, and much is said about the Christian moral experience, but in the great modern systems, such as those of Hegel and Comte, religion, particularly Christian religion, is either transcended in Hegel's absolute knowledge, or becomes outmoded in Comtean positivism. Only Kierkegaard and Bergson are mentioned among modern philosophers as instances in which Christian revelation continues to be relevant. And while Maritain makes only one reference to the conception of moral philosophy adequately considered in this *magnum opus*,[46] he too joins them as a Christian philosopher.

Once more, as at the outset, he announces a second volume "given over to the doctrinal examination of the great problems [which] must constitute the normal conclusion of the long historico-critical introduction that has been the object of the present volume."[47] It never appeared, and so *The Introduction* remains as a kind of sketch of this proposed work.

And now we come to the third stage of this exposition. I am not at all convinced that the course taken by Maritain could have been foreseen from what he says in *Moral Philosophy*. It is expressed in *The Peasant of the Garonne* for the first time and illustrated in the study *The Grace and Humanity of Jesus*.[48] Henceforth, for his remaining years, it will predominate. After having mentioned Christian philosophy ("and faith can enter the domain of reason bringing along the help of a light and truth which are superior, and which elevate reason in its own order")–he prefers to call it "philosophy of faith"[49]–he examines the condition of theology and is concerned about certain tendencies, though he asserts "the superior rights of faith and of the queen of sacred knowledge."[50] A new note enters in as he expands the task of Christian

---

[46] Ibid., p. 422.

[47] Ibid., p. 449.

[48] Perhaps the practice preceded the declaration in *The Sin of the Angel*, trans. William Rossner, S.J. (Westminster, Maryland: Newman Press, 1959).

[49] Jacques Maritain, *Peasant*, p. 142.

[50] Ibid., p. 164.

philosophy: "If it is sufficiently versed in theology," Christian philosophy "may happen–with no intention, of course, settling the matter definitely–to become interested in questions which, by themselves, fall within the province of the theologian."[51] But he will view such questions from a philosophical perspective. There is a risk involved, he says, and I suppose this means he may be accused of doing theology, or going beyond his own competence. With the assistance of faith, Christian philosophy is authorized "to concern itself in its own way with matters belonging to theology."[52] In this way, "philosophy can eventually be of service to theology, since, by its own nature, it is more available for a work of research and discovery. At this point the *ancilla* becomes research-worker."[53] The earlier definition of Christian philosophy depended on the aid received from theology; the extended definition concerns what philosophy can do for theology. If the philosopher presents the theologian with the research hypothesis, does this not mean that the philosopher acts as a kind of research assistant and hence falls into that instrumental role traditionally assigned to the philosopher by theology? Is not the autonomy of philosophy compromised by this new task?[54] In any case, this bears on the future role of the Christian philosopher. Maritain thinks the philosopher has more freedom in these matters, has an advantage in dealing with dialogue between rival opinions, and melds with an increased role for the laity.

I said that *On the Grace and Humanity of Jesus* illustrates or exemplifies this new role of Christian philosophy. It also shows the risks involved in that role, as witness the criticism that the concepts are archaic and cumbersome–symptomatic of the reaction against Thomism–or that Maritain ignores theologians who have made a contribution to Christology.[55] During this period, Maritain deals with angelology,[56]

---

[51] Ibid.

[52] Ibid.

[53] Ibid.

[54] Ibid., p. 163.

[55] I refer to the review by Father Bruce Vawter, C.M., in *The Critic* 27 (June 1969): 76.

Christology, and ecclesiology: that is, with subject matter known by faith, not by philosophical experience. Of course, it is true that Plato and Aristotle had something to say about intellectual substances, but what we know about the angels comes from Sacred Scripture, along with the extensive interpretations of Aquinas and others. Maritain always insisted that he approaches these matters from a philosophical perspective: "Shall I hesitate to make this exposition because I will appear to be treading on the flower-beds of the theologians, I who am not a theologian, but a mere philosopher?"[57] He proceeds to point out that his perspective is that of a Christian philosopher. He then repeats verbatim what he has said about the research-worker and the offering of hypotheses of research in *The Peasant of the Garonne*. And in his book on the Church Maritain proposes "to enter, yes, onto the proper terrain of the *sacra doctrina* in order to make there itself an effort of reason and to propose there eventually to the competent doctors new views."[58] The philosopher can do this because he is free of the responsibilities of the theologian. It is rather puzzling, then, when he tells us "this book has nothing to do either with a treatise of ecclesiology,"[59] a term which seems best to signify its genre. So by now we are accustomed to these declarations that he is doing philosophical work–"I who am not a theologian"–while dealing with theological matters.[60] Among his contributions are the distinction between the person and the personnel of the Church, and the use made of the distinction between proper and instrumental causes.

---

[56] This is not a term Maritain used, but it has gained a certain currency today. Michel Serres says, "Perhaps what I was writing all along was an angelology": Micheal Serres with Bruno Latour, *Conversations on Science, Culture, and Time*, trans. Roxanne Lapidus (Ann Arbor, Michigan: University of Michigan Press, 1995), p. 118.

[57] Jacques Maritain, *Grace and Humanity*, p. 11. Later (p. 111, n. 43), he says: "I who am not an exegete but a philosopher."

[58] Jacques Maritain, *On the Church of Christ: The Person of the Church and Her Personnel*, trans. Joseph W. Evans (Notre Dame, Indiana: University of Notre Dame Press, 1973), pp. v-vi.

[59] Ibid., p. vi.

[60] Ibid., p. 203. See other remarks on pp. 14, 35, 117, and 174.

The culmination of the task of research worker for theology is found in that long section of *Untrammeled Approaches* dealing with theological matters, although the essay on intuitivity is only marginally theological.[61] Here, Maritain deals with such topics as our nature wounded by sin and its effect on theoretical intellect, theological knowledge, exegesis, the substitute for theology among the simple, the sacrifice of the Mass, the Church of Heaven, the priesthood and the laity. But for our concern in this paper, the most pertinent passages are expressed in his discussion of theological knowledge. He speaks of "the application of his philosophical reflection to the more lofty questions treated by that knowledge superior to his own which is called theology."[62] Yet, far from being reduced to a servant, philosophy is actually set free. A philosopher, he goes on, "should take on as the object of his reflection matters which of themselves depend on the science of theology."[63] But this can only occur if he educates himself through the teachings of theology. As a research worker, he is subject to the control of theology, requiring a certain docility on his part. And his strongest statement:

> There could be no Christian philosophy that is not led eventually to raise its eyes toward theology, and to propose *tentatively* its own views on matters whose *knowledge* (Christian philosophy knows this) depends, not on philosophy, but on a superior wisdom to which the *opus theologicum* is dedicated.[64]

So that it may be said that theology is the destination of Christian philosophy.

Now, despite Maritain's frequent references to himself as a philosopher, who is also a research worker in theological matters, his good friend Cardinal Journet, who had access to most of the pieces in

---

[61] Jacques Maritain, *Untrammeled Approaches*, trans. Bernard Doering (Notre Dame, Indiana: University of Notre Dame Press, 1997). Chapter fourteen deals with intuitivity and only refers to theology in a footnote (p. 345, n. 49).

[62] Ibid., p. 266.

[63] Ibid., p. 267.

[64] Ibid., p. 269.

the theology section of *Untrammeled Approaches* (these having appeared previously in *Revue Thomiste* and *Nova et Vetera*) waves aside that characterization: "But I regard him as being in his own way the most penetrating theologian of our time."[65] High praise indeed, however problematic it renders the whole project of Maritain, first spelled out in *The Peasant of the Garonne*.

By way of a conclusion, I return to the manner in which Yves R. Simon distinguished two callings between which the philosopher who is a Christian must choose, mindful of the inadequacies of the philosophical approach. True to his calling, Simon, to my knowledge, had written only one article in which theology is discussed at any length.[66] His comments on method at the end of his life are consonant with his writings throughout his life. True to his calling, Maritain the Christian philosopher had undertaken a journey that eventually led him to theological matters, however emphatic he was that he was only doing so as a philosopher.

---

[65] Charles Journet, "Jacques Maritain Theologian," *The New Scholasticism* 46.1 (Winter 1972): 32.

[66] Yves R. Simon, "The Rationality of the Christian Faith," in Anthony O. Simon, ed., *Philosopher at Work* (Lanham, Maryland: Rowman and Littlefield, 1999), pp. 41-55.

# A GOOD SHEPHERD? THOMAS AQUINAS ON THE NAMES OF GOD IN THE *SUMMA THEOLOGIAE* (I, Q. 13, AA. 1-7)

Timothy Valentine, S.J.

The door opened to the hospital room of a 70-year-old man recovering from a heart attack, and a 22-year-old chaplain wearing a Roman collar entered. The young man was a seminarian learning how to administer "pastoral" care to Catholic patients, among whom was the heart attack victim. The older man, named Pete, sporting a black beret, reacted with a combination of amusement and mild disdain when his visitor offered to pray with him. The seminarian began by reciting the text of Psalm 23: "The Lord is my shepherd; there is nothing I shall want..." The response was immediate and contentious: "Now hold it right there. Why in the world would I ever address God as a shepherd? Does that mean that I'm a sheep? Just think what a shepherd does! He makes sure those stupid, dirty creatures are fattened up so that he can deliver them safely to some butcher, who kills them, guts them, and carves them for others to eat. No thank you–I have no intention of praying to such a God."

The startled trainee, who had previously not found this particular religious image problematic, compounded what was already an unfortunate situation by suggesting, perhaps somewhat presumptuously, that God is not just "any old shepherd," but rather the "*Good* Shepherd" who loves and saves his people. This attempt to justify divine imagery failed even more miserably than the first. Pete, it turned out, was a writer whose novel had been made into a relatively successful, if somewhat maudlin, Hollywood film. He understood the power and purposes of language, and was not going to let some kid ameliorate his offended aesthetic sensibilities with so much pious speculation. "Good Shepherd, Strong Shepherd, Wise Shepherd: Bah! How do I know that God is good? I don't. I'm sitting in this damned hospital recovering from a life-threatening illness, which God, if he *does* exist, gave me. How is that good? My wife, on the other hand: she is good. She visits me, comforts me, loves me. A Good Shepherd? Don't be absurd. A good wife? That's another story. Now get out."

I mention this embarrassing, if chastening, episode from my own life because it underscores the difficulties of using language to understand God. Pete's negative reaction was due, at least ostensibly, to the limitations of words like "shepherd" and "good," with which I was trying to pray. The first is a metaphor, a word that explains the unknown in terms of the known. The notion of a divine shepherd is drawn from one's knowledge of actual human shepherds, whose motivations (to say nothing of their actions) may be less than impeccable. There must be criteria, then, by which to judge how "shepherd" conveys useful information about God in one sense (that he feeds, protects, and, in the case of Christ, dies for his sheep), but not in another (that he fattens up, leads to slaughter, abandons). The second word refers to a quality found within persons who are good to some extent. We are tempted to believe that the goodness of God (whom we do not experience as we do other human beings) is rooted in imperfect, limited examples of human goodness. Hence, the notion of "God's goodness" is at best limited, and, at worst, meaningless. Indeed, all talk of God is misleading when we overlook what Richard Viladesau calls its "transcendental" basis, because "God is not an 'object' which can be known within the sphere" of ordinary beings.[1]

As Thomas Aquinas states, "Everything is named by us according to our knowledge of it" (*Summa Theologiae*, I, q. 13). Our natural knowledge of God (that he exists, what he is not, how he is the source of all perfection) is dependent upon our knowledge of created things, which we perceive through our bodily senses. Since these are by their very nature limited, they do not allow us to comprehend the infinite God in himself, that is, in his essence (I, q. 12, a. 12). This is not to say, however, that talk of God is without value. In the following pages, I will argue that St. Thomas Aquinas' position is an attempt to preserve the Christian notion of God's transcendence, while demonstrating that language about God is still meaningful.

For the purposes of this essay, I will limit my discussion to the first seven articles of question 13, in section I of the *Summa Theologiae*, i.e., "on the names of God." Other questions concerning God's existence

---

[1] Richard Viladesau, *Answering for Faith* (New York: Paulist Press, 1987), p. 38.

(question 2) and intelligibility (question 12), while important, must be taken for granted.

The essay proceeds as follows. First, I will discuss the ways in which statements about God, both positive and negative, may be considered true. Next, I will present St. Thomas' doctrine of analogy, which distinguishes between various kinds of speech, and how they convey meaningful information about God. Finally, I will explain how words bear primary and secondary meanings, and how these apply to God and to creatures.

Pete's detailed job description of the shepherd hints at something we realize intuitively: we come to know (i.e., we begin to comprehend the essence of) finite creatures because we can perceive them, observe them, analyze them. The same cannot be said of God. Our senses are not aware of any color, taste, smell, feel, or vision of God, precisely because God is incorporeal. Cruel, greedy shepherds notwithstanding, Pete's diatribe implies that the things we say about creatures can be verified. It is as if God, who has no physical components and thus no way of being known directly, must be somehow less than a body.

In the first article of question 13, Thomas disputes the idea that having a body (i.e., any kind of material composition) ought to be the standard of perfection. Indeed, our normal way of speaking hints at the limitations that bodiliness imposes. A creature is either here or there, now or then, this or that, *so* high or wide or tall, and only *so* good or wise or loving. Speech of this sort is entirely inappropriate in the case of God, who by "his" very nature is bound by neither time nor space nor even quality (understood relatively). Thus, when Thomas speaks of God's "simplicity" (I, q. 3, a. 7), he means that God is neither changeable, nor composite, nor created.[2] Creatures are given names that express their dimension, time, observable qualities, etc., all of which indicate their composite mode of being. Copleston writes that God's incorporeality does "not mean that God is less than body, that he lacks the perfection involved in being body, but rather that he is more than body, that he possesses none of the imperfections necessarily

---

[2] Brian Davies, *The Thought of Thomas Aquinas* (Oxford: Clarendon Press, 1992), p. 45.

involved in being a corporeal substance."[3] On the level of finite being, complexity is a sign of greater perfection (I, q. 13, a. 1 ad. 2), and so, for instance, we refer to more complex creatures as "higher" forms of life.

But to say that this is *not* true in the case of God is to affirm the validity of negative statements about God. Language itself (I, q. 13, a. 1 ad. 3) is designed to convey information about substance and quality (nouns), and time (verbs and participles). On the other hand, it is powerless to "define" God, who is not restricted as creatures are, but who is rather their cause. Consequently, the use of apophatic language, such as Dionysius' claim, "Of God there is no name," does not mean that we cannot speak meaningfully about God; it merely implies that words fail to capture the essence of God, i.e., what he is in himself. For Pete, any kind of language one might use to describe God is offensive. And so, when he denied that God is a shepherd, I could have been a bit more tolerant of his reasons for saying so, for there is considerable truth in this denial. If being a shepherd means exploiting one's flock, I should have been the first to acknowledge that God is *not* a shepherd, or at any rate, that he is *unlike* a shepherd in some sense.

Thus, we see that negative statements work somewhat differently than do positive assertions, especially with respect to God. For instance, it is true that human beings are not winged, or four-footed, creatures, but does this provide a lot of meaningful information about them? And yet, we can still compare human beings with birds and horses, for all of these are contingent, material, animate, and sensate creatures. If the only truth I can utter about God is that these words do not apply to him, have I really said very much about God? Indeed, this is more than enough evidence for the troublemaker kid in the back of my religion class to conclude that God does not exist. Hence, Thomas disagrees with the opinion (which he attributes to Moses Maimonides in *Guide to the Perplexed*) that what appears to be a positive statement (e.g., "God is good") is in reality a negative one, that God is not bad. Such a statement, according to Thomas, is simply the "removal" of something from God (I, q. 13, a. 2), just as the statement "God is *in*finite" is the

---

[3] Frederick Copleston, *A History of Philosophy*, vol. 2, part 2 (Garden City, New York: Doubleday, 1962), p. 68.

equivalent of "God is not finite." He also dismisses the argument that "God is good" is just another way of saying that he is the cause of goodness.

Thomas spells out three problems with apophatic God-language in the second article. First, it does not explain why "God is the cause of all good things" is the equivalent of "God is good," but "God is the cause of all bodies" is not interchangeable with "God is a body." Next, it suggests that the word "good" applies to God only in a secondary sense, not as the basis upon which a finite thing is said to be good. Finally, it reduces talk of God (e.g., that he is living) to triviality (that he is not an inert thing).

Instead, Thomas contends that positive assertions about God have value in their own right. When we say that creatures represent him, we do not mean that God is one entity alongside others (as "something of the same species or genus"), but rather that he possesses the perfections in a "super-eminent way." Rather than say that God merely causes goodness, as one element in some longer causal chain, we say, "he diffuses goodness into things,"[4] i.e., he is the ultimate foundation for our saying that anything is good.

Nevertheless, one must distinguish between various forms of positive assertions, namely, those that are said to be literally true, and those that are true, but only in some derived sense. Is God really a shepherd, and is he really good? Thomas disputes the belief that all names applied to God are derived; rather, some can be said of him in a straightforward manner. Ralph McInerny writes that "the limitation of metaphor (an overt simile) is that it tells us what something is like, not what it is."[5] To say that God is a shepherd is to relate the word's ordinary meaning to some new reality, which is like it in some respects, but unlike it in others. Hence, people come to understand what God is like because of their direct knowledge of the human shepherd, but the usefulness of the metaphor breaks down at some point, just as the word "father" can be a problematic term for referring to God for people who

---

[4] Ibid., p. 71.

[5] Ralph McInerny, *A First Glance at St. Thomas: A Handbook for Peeping Thomists* (Notre Dame, Indiana: University of Notre Dame Press, 1990), p. 137.

have a difficult relationship to their own fathers.[6] And so, were one to say that "shepherd" does not exhaustively capture what it means to be God, Thomas would likely concur. He would not agree, however, that such a word is meaningless, for it does point to some divine attribute, e.g., God's power.[7]

But is God really good? Yes, according to Thomas, and in this case, a name can be "properly" said of him (I, q. 13, a. 3). Unlike metaphors, which are inadequate because they say what something is like and unlike, a perfection (e.g., good, wise, etc.) refers to attributes which are absolute, and therefore literally true of God. The word "goodness" is a descriptive word pointing to a signified reality (*res significata*–in this case, the divine substance), and is properly said of God.[8] In other words, God is good by virtue of his being God. On the other hand, finite things are "good," albeit in a deficient way. For instance, a "good shepherd" refers to a different mode of signifying (*modus significandi*) goodness than, say, a "good king." The youthful David may have been a good shepherd, but he was not always a good (i.e., exemplary) king (cf. *2 Samuel* 11:1-27; 24:1-9).

In short, creatures are good but, because of their composite nature, they may vary in their degree of goodness. Working backwards from these, we know something about God (i.e., he is good) "from the perfections which flow from him to creatures" (I, q. 13, a. 3). Hence, we might say that Pete's wife is good, but in a localized, limited way, whereas God is the source of her goodness. By recognizing the goodness of his wife, Pete unwittingly affirms God's goodness.

In the unlikely event that someday Pete might concede the truthfulness of the assertion "God is good," he might still object that it is no different from saying that God is wise, powerful etc., and so to say one is to say them all. He would do this because of God's simplicity. If each of the perfections points to the essence of God who is supremely

---

[6] *Cf.* Erik Erikson, *Young Man Luther: A Study in Psychoanalysis and History* (New York: Norton, 1962), pp. 123-25.

[7] Brian Davies, op. cit., p. 66.

[8] Ibid., p. 65.

one, it appears as if wisdom, goodness, and the others refer to different "parts" of God. Consequently, in order to preserve the unity of God, I would have to admit, "names applied to God are synonymous names" (I, q. 13, a. 4).

Thomas would respond that the problem lies in us, not in God, in whom "the perfections pre-exist unitedly and simply" (I, q. 13, a. 4). Wisdom, goodness, and power all signify one reality, namely, "the divine substance." Nevertheless, our only way of understanding these attributes is through imperfect creatures. Hence, we grasp the meaning of goodness when we contemplate, say, the life of St. Francis of Assisi. In him, goodness is accidental; he did in fact continue preaching to birds, embracing lepers, and giving alms to the poor, but theoretically he could have ditched the scene and become a high-rolling gambler in some medieval version of Las Vegas. Moreover, other perfections, such as power and wisdom, may not apply to Francis at all. One might look to the example of St. Thomas Aquinas to apprehend the meaning of wisdom that one wants to apply to God, *not* St. Francis (whom some consider anti-intellectual).

As we established above, God has no accidents because he is not restricted the way corporeal beings are.[9] St. Francis' accidental goodness and St. Thomas' accidental wisdom therefore point to, but do not encompass, what in God is essential, and so does not fluctuate, namely, his essence. Words like "goodness," "power" and "wisdom" are assorted ways of expressing (*modi significandi*) what is ultimately a single reality (*res significata*). But our talk of "many and diverse aspects" is significant, at least with respect to human knowledge of God. We mean something different when we say "God is good" and "God is wise," because wisdom and goodness are different attributes when observed in creatures. If Pete were to say that "God is a Strong Shepherd" after I declared that "God is a Good Shepherd," I might agree, but I would insist that we mean something different by the two terms.

The thought of extending my conversation with Pete to this point is an exercise in sheer fantasy; if I had attempted to do so in real life, he

---

[9] Frederick Copleston, op. cit., p. 67.

would have sent a tray full of hospital food hurtling in my direction. Still, if cooler heads had prevailed, he might have inquired how I can shift so confidently between the ordinary meaning of words and the special way they apply to God. I would launch into Thomas' doctrine of analogy, which he explains in the fifth article of question 13.

To apply a descriptive word like "good" to two things in exactly the same sense is to use it univocally. Thus, after reading *The Brothers Karamazov* and Pete's tome, analyzing their structure and use of language, and considering their artistic merit, I conclude that the former work is good and the latter is not (although I would not inform the author). This is not what I do, however, when comparing the assertions "God is good" and "Pete's wife is good." If "good" were meant univocally here, then of course God is not good, i.e., in the way that Pete's wife is good. But, when saying that he is not good, we mean that God is more than good in the human sense.[10] We remember that a human being is distinct from his or her nature and existence, and so "good" modifies what this particular human being is here and now. By contrast, essence and existence are the same in God, whose goodness resides, simply and unitedly, with his wisdom and power.[11] Thomas therefore insists that "no name belongs to God in the same sense that it belongs to creatures" (I, q. 13, a. 5), thereby ruling out the possibility that they apply univocally in the case of God.

If "good" does not apply to God and to creatures in a univocal sense, then we must assume that it is used in some other sense. Perhaps the word is used equivocally. Equivocation can be the subject of flexible or strict interpretation. In the former case, equivocal simply means that the term is "predicated of various things under the same name but not in the same sense" (I, q. 13, a. 5). For instance, the word "head" can refer to numerous entities, and most people would agree that I mean something different when I speak of the head of the FBI, the head of a pin, and the head on which Pete's beret sits. These are not entirely unrelated, however, because "head" conveys the meaning of "highest" or "most important," whether in terms of power and prestige (the FBI),

[10] Ibid., p. 115.

[11] Brian Davies, op. cit., p. 66.

an extreme point (the pin), or human endeavor (the seat of Pete's intellectual activity).

On the other hand, a term is said to be "strictly equivocal" when it is used in a completely different sense. This is why we laugh (or cringe) at the anecdote according to which King Arthur commands his two servants: "Bring me my mail!" One delivers a suit of armor, while the other hands him a stack of letters and an L.L. Bean catalogue.[12]

Early on in article 5, Thomas states that, if univocation is the only other possible way of understanding how something can be predicated of God, then "whatever is said of God and of creatures is predicated equivocally." A little later on, however, he makes an important qualification, that "neither are names applied to God and creatures in a purely equivocal sense." If they were, the problem of relevance would arise. Elsewhere (*Summa Contra Gentiles* 1:33:6), Thomas states the predicament succinctly: if names are "said of God and creatures in a purely equivocal way, we understand nothing of God through those names; for the meanings of those names are known to us solely to the extent that they are said of creatures." Pure equivocation undermines the very possibility of saying anything meaningful about God. Accordingly, when I say that "God is a Good Shepherd," Pete might respond, "Fine; God is also a leaky steam pipe; and God is a five-ounce avocado; and God is tenured professor of philosophy; and God is a 'knopke.'" The first three words are no more helpful in understanding anything about God than the fourth, which is entirely artificial. Once terms have been divested of their ordinary associations, gleaned from our experience of actual creatures, they cease to convey useful information, and so Pete's brand of God-talk is no less legitimate than a passage in Scripture. In that case, the project becomes vain, and we rightly ask: Why speak about God at all?

As a solution to the dilemma, Thomas introduces a third alternative: the notion of analogy. Martin D'Arcy calls a term analogous which "is used for what is partly the same and partly different. It stands,

[12] Ralph McInerny, op. cit., p. 138.

therefore, between the univocal and the equivocal."[13] The fact that analogy has one foot planted in both kinds of speaking leads McInerny, citing Aristotle, to call analogy "controlled equivocation."[14]

Thomas explains the metaphysical basis for analogical language (*Summa Contra Gentiles* 1:34:3) by examining the meaning of the word "being" when variously predicated of finite entities and God. For instance, Pete's wife is good; in addition, she *is* (in no particular order) educated, hypochondriacal, a registered Independent, glamorous, patient, and even-tempered. She is all of these things accidentally, as we said above, because the situation could be otherwise. She could very well be bad, uneducated, healthy, Republican, homely, and moody. On another level, existence must be predicated of the woman to the extent that we speak of her as an actual being. Nevertheless, she is a contingent being; there is no reason to believe that she must exist.

When we say that God (who has no accidents) is good, however, we are speaking about his substance, to the effect that goodness is part of what it means to be God. Furthermore, the assertion "God is" does not mean that he happens to exist, but rather that existence itself is of the essence (the "whatness") of God. Thus, we employ language of "being" in different, but related, ways when speaking of ordinary creatures and of God.

At this point, Pete would most likely want to table the discussion by coming down on the side of "realism." That is to say, he sees no reason for my claim that certain things are said more properly of God than of contingent entities. Perhaps in some alternate universe, he maintains, "God is good. But, as everyone agrees, and you yourself admit, we only come to know goodness because we encounter this or that thing which is good, for example, my wife. And so I must conclude that the real meaning of a word like 'good' is the sense in which it applies to a particular good."

---

[13] Martin C. D'Arcy, *St. Thomas Aquinas* (Dublin: Clonmore and Reynolds, 1953), p. 94.

[14] Ralph McInerny, op. cit., p. 138.

It might be helpful to retrace our steps to article 3, wherein Thomas distinguishes between the notions of *res significata* and *modus significandi.* Thomas might agree with Pete about applying a name properly to creatures, but only to the extent that the name "implies corporeal conditions" (I, q. 13, a. 3). This would be the case when we employ metaphors, such as "the arm of the Lord" or "the face of God," or even the image of God as a shepherd. To be sure, God does not have an arm or a face, nor does he look like David the shepherd, precisely because he does not have a body. Still, we know what these expressions are getting at, namely, the divine attributes of power, graciousness and mercy. A name that refers, strictly speaking, to bodiliness is said properly of creatures because it is bound up with creaturely finitude. "Arm," "face," and "shepherd" are merely the "ways of signifying" something about God, and as such, are said properly of contingent reality.

When speaking of goodness, however, we are not referring to corporeal conditions. There is nothing about goodness that requires the existence of a beautiful, patient woman, even though I may have gotten my idea of goodness from the knowledge of such an individual. Goodness points directly to "what is signified" in God, and its association with finite entities does not in any way limit it. According to Thomas, therefore, goodness is an example of a name that can be properly attributed to God. In the case of "being," we mean the perfection of all perfections that "flow from God to creatures." God is not simply our first cause, but rather the one who sustains us in existence.

This brings us to the central idea in article 6, regarding the "primary" and "secondary" meanings of names. Thomas is willing to allow that, in one sense, all names are said primarily of creatures (I, q. 13, a. 6, obj. 1) if, by primary and secondary, we mean the chronological "order of knowledge," for, in fact, "we know creatures before we know God."

A name may apply to God secondarily because he is the cause of attributes like goodness and wisdom in creatures (I, q. 13, a. 6, obj. 3). This is where Thomas employs the "many to one" analogy of health (cf. also *SG* 1:34:2), according to which "health" refers primarily to one being, say, an animal, and only secondarily to its cause (medicine), its preserver (food), and its sign (urine).

Still, Thomas suggests that there are other, more significant criteria by which to judge the primary and secondary applications of a name. True, metaphorical names apply to creatures primarily in the "order of knowledge." Hence, we may think of God as a shepherd in a secondary, derived manner. But this says nothing about what things are in reality, i.e., the "order of nature." If God were merely the cause of goodness in things, then truly goodness is predicated of him in a secondary manner. Thomas contends, however, that "goodness" indicates what God is essentially, whereas creatures, as we discussed above, are good accidentally. In this more profound sense, goodness is predicated primarily of God, and only secondarily of creatures.

Pete might want to make a last ditch effort to diminish the importance of God-talk by making God somehow dependent upon the existence of creatures. He does so by pointing to a name that denotes an affiliation between two realities. "Oh, very well, if you insist: 'The Lord is my Shepherd.' But what if I, or other creatures, do not exist? If there are no sheep, then for whom is God a shepherd–or Lord, for that matter?"

This opens up the question of names implying a temporal relationship between God and creatures (I, q. 13, a. 7). We speak differently about what God is in himself and what he is in relationship to contingent beings. We have already discussed names that point to God's essence (being, goodness, etc.) and are true of him from eternity. But what about other names, like "Lord," which imply a real relation between two things? Thomas lists three kinds of relation. There is the purely logical relationship involving only an idea ("the same is the same as itself"). Next, there is the relationship between two realities that are in a sense "dependent" upon each other to be what they are. Thus, the 70-year-old patient is called the "older man" in relation to the 22-year-old seminarian, but not in relation to his 71-year-old physician. Finally, Thomas proposes the situation in which "a relation in one [entity] may be a reality, while in the other [entity] it is only an idea" (I, q. 13, a. 7). For example, sense perception and science are directed at those things which can either be grasped by the senses, or whose essences can be known by the intellect. Something that cannot be apprehended in either of these ways may in fact be real (in the case of God, he must be real), but its essence would be unknown to the human mind. Consequently, it makes no difference with respect to God's existence that there is a world; God is, with or without creatures. This is what it means to say that a real, though "one-sided" relationship exists between God and finite entities; insofar as creatures exist, they are dependently related to him, but, being independent of them, God's relation to creatures is only in idea.

According to Thomas, the appellation Lord "includes the idea of a servant and vice versa.... Hence God was not Lord until he had a creature subject to himself" (I, q. 13 a. 7, ad. 6). Thomas recognizes that there would no such thing as "Lord," were it not for the existence of a creature, and says so. Nevertheless, for him it is a mistake to think that a name said of God temporally in any way undermines his self-sufficiency.

I have often wondered how my conversation with Pete might have turned out had there not been such an abrupt dismissal. If there were one thing I would have done differently, it would be this. When Pete said, "God is not good," I wish I had had the presence of mind to respond, "You're right. We should not say 'God is good'; we should say, 'God is goodness.'" That is, a word that describes an accidental quality in human beings functions differently when we direct it at God, because it points to the divine essence. In so speaking, I could respond to Pete's misgivings without making God-talk trivial.

In this respect, I believe St. Thomas' treatment of the names of God is of great help to those of us who find ourselves speaking about God, to God, and in the name of God, especially in these troubled times. As my students and I watched helplessly from our window at Fordham University in Lincoln Center as the World Trade Center collapsed, we could not help but invoke the name of God: the Source of all goodness, compassion, wisdom, and love. At that moment, we needed no abstruse justification for the language we used; we knew that what we were saying–"Oh God," "Dear God," "Merciful God"–meant something very important. Our ability to use language is precisely what makes us human. Among the sayings attributed to Confucius, we read, "Without knowing the force of words, it is impossible to know men." In light of the tragedy that occurred at that time, we believers might amend this to read, "Without knowing the force of words, it is impossible to know God."

# CONNATURALITY

## Martin Andic

The highest degree of knowledge is mystical experience involving "knowledge by connaturality," says Jacques Maritain.[1] "We are made connatural to God through charity... [that] lays hold on God as He is really present within us, as a Gift, a Friend, an eternal life companion.... it wins to God immediately as God, in His very deity, in the very... life with which He will beatify us. Charity loves Him in Himself and by Himself."[2] God *is* this charity that makes us share in his life and happiness; he himself must *give* it to us, as a grace; he comes to be within us, hidden in faith, but so that love can touch and taste and judge divine things far more surely than we ever could otherwise; the love that God gives us makes us know in some part *what* God is, and know it in the *way* that God knows it,[3] though never fully in this life;[4] it is what we shall know and see that will bless us. Thus, citing with favor some words of John of the Cross, Maritain says that "As love [God] transforms us into Himself.... In beatitude we shall be deified by intellection.... contemplation is itself a knowledge of love, a 'loving attention to God.'"[5]

---

[1] Jacques Maritain, *Distinguish to Unite, or The Degrees of Knowledge* (New York: Charles Scribner's Sons, 1959), pp. 259-60; cf. 239-40, 253, 287, 293, 338. Other works of Maritain cited here are *Creative Intuition in Art and Poetry*, Bollingen Series 35.1 (New York: Pantheon Books, 1953), and "Love and Friendship," in *Notebooks* (Albany, New York: Magi Books, 1984). These three works will be cited hereafter as *DU*, *CI*, and *LF*. I thank Elizabeth Anscombe and Bernard Doering for helpful conversations directing my attention to this topic and to Maritain's discussions of it.

[2] Jacques Maritain, *DU* 260.

[3] Cf. Søren Kierkegaard, *Journals and Papers*, 7 v., eds. Howard and Edna Hong, (Bloomington, Indiana: Indiana University Press, 1967-1978), 2:1405: "God himself is [to anyone] this: *how* one involves himself with Him... In respect to God, the *how* is *what*"; and 6:6784: "*Everything Depends on 'How.'*"

[4] Jacques Maritain, *DU* 261-63.

[5] Jacques Maritain, *DU* 324.

Maritain takes the phrase "connaturality" from Thomas Aquinas, though, as we shall see, the concept itself has a much older history. As Maritain explains, Thomas uses it to contrast two ways in which we know religious and moral realities. We can judge matters of chastity, for example, with the speculative knowledge of our unaided intellect, or by a certain *connaturality* that comes from loving it and practicing it and embodying it within ourselves. It is an *affinity* and *kinship*, a *congeniality* and *sympathy*, an *assimilation* and *inclination*; it arises from the experience of active charity that is both action and affect, so that we fulfill God's will and taste his joy. It is this way, too, says Thomas, with our affective and experimental knowledge of the things of God himself: we learn them by *suffering*, which joins us to him and *makes us one spirit with* him, so that we judge with wisdom that is the *gift* of the Spirit of God.[6] It is not the fullness of His wisdom, but a share in it that

---

[6] Thomas Aquinas, *Summa Theologiae* (hereafter cited as *ST*), II-II, q. 45, a. 2, ad. 2: "Wisdom implies a certain rightness in judging according to divine norms... through the perfect use of reason or through a certain connaturality [sc. affinity, kinship, congeniality]... Thus in matters of chastity, one who is versed in moral science will come to a right judgment through rational investigation, [while] another who possesses the virtue of chastity will be right through a kind of connaturality. So it is with divine things. A correct judgment made through rational investigation belongs to the wisdom which is an intellectual virtue. But to judge aright through a certain fellowship with them belongs to that wisdom which is the gift of the Holy Spirit. Dionysius says that Hierotheus is perfected in divine things for he *not only learns about them but suffers*. Now this sympathy [*compassio*], or connaturality with divine things, results from charity which unites us to God: *he who is joined to the Lord is one spirit with him.* So then wisdom which is the gift does have its cause in the will, namely charity, but essentially it lies in the intellect, of which the act is to judge rightly."

*ST* II-II, q. 97, a. 2, ad 2: "There are two kinds of knowledge about God's goodness and will. One of these is theoretic, and as to this is it is not lawful to doubt or to test whether God is good or lovely. The other is affective and experimental knowledge of divine goodness and loving-kindness, whereby a person experiences within himself the taste of God's sweetness and the delight in his loving. Dionysius says that *Hierotheus learnt divine things by sympathy*. It is in this way that we are told to prove God's will and taste his sweetness."

we must acquire from Him without our being able to do anything to earn it; God himself must prompt or quicken the love that desires it and that moves the actions that make us like him, and our whole and only action is to consent to what he does in and through us.[7]

Maritain also cites Paul Claudel for the link between connaturality and co-nascence ("connaissance"), and the notion that to know God we must be "born with" Him,[8] which seems to mean that we must be born into God and his life of charity, that we are born for this, and with this. Let us note explicitly here that "nature" means what we are born with, and that "connaissance" means acquaintance and familiarity, and (like Plato's *aisthesis* in the *Theaetetus*) an experience and presence and contact that does *not* always involve full recognition and identification, although it often is preferable to these without experience.[9]

The idea of practical knowledge moved by love that involves transformation and assimilation, so that like is known only by like, is an old one. Plato develops a theory that true and false thought generally are combining things *as* they are or otherwise, so that true thought mirrors being; but he is more interested in living religious and moral

---

*ST* I, q. 64, a 1: "Truth is known in two ways, through grace and through nature. And the knowledge through grace is itself twofold: a purely cognitional knowledge, as when a man is shown divine secrets; and a knowledge quickened by desire and issuing in a love of God. This last, and this only, belongs to the Gift of Wisdom." Cf. *ST* I, q.1, a. 6, ad. 3. Thomas is quoting Dionysius, *The Names of God* 2; cf. *1 Corinthians* 6:17; *Psalms* 34:8; and *Isaiah* 11.2: "And the Spirit of the Lord shall rest upon him, the spirit of wisdom and understanding."

[7] Thomas Aquinas, *ST* I-II, q. 68, a. 1: such *gifts* of the Spirit are so-called "not only because they are infused by God, but also because by them man is disposed to become amenable to the divine inspiration, according to *Isaiah* 50:5: 'The Lord... hath opened my ear, and I do not resist;'" *ST* I-II, q. 55, a. 4, ad. 6: they perfect our actions, so that "God causes them in us, yet not without action on our part, for He works in every will and in every nature."

[8] Jacques Maritain, *DU* 260.

[9] Thus Plato on *aisthesis* (sensation) in *Theaetetus* 151e, 163a-c, 186; *mantike* (intimation, presentiment, divination) in *Charmides* 158e, 169b and *Republic* 6.505e; cf. *Phaedo* 84d-85b.

knowledge and argues that only the pure may know the pure.[10] Similarly Aristotle, while criticizing the idea that like is known by like, speaks of the mind as becoming everything that it knows; yet in his account of moral knowledge he emphasizes that this is practical or productive rather than merely theoretical.[11] It is *empirical* knowledge, of truth that can properly be known only by experience in which we fulfill it and make it known in ourselves and our actions and relationships.[12] If we love and desire the nobility of the wise and good and imitate their example, then what we do is rewarded and clarified by insight. For experience teaches us to see straight; a wise person is a *measure* of what is right and good: as things appear to him to be, so they

---

[10] Plato, *Sophist* 261c-263d, *Timaeus* 35-37c, with Aristotle's comment in *Psychology* 1.3 406b28-31 that Plato's divine artist compounded the soul substance out of the elements and divided it according to the harmonic numbers "so that it may have a connate sensibility for harmony [*hopos aisthesin te sumphuton harmonias echei*], and that the whole may move in movements well attuned." Cf. *Phaedo* 67b, *Phaedrus* 250c, *Theaetetus* 177a, *Republic* 6.484b-d and 501d, and *Letters* 7.343d-344a. See, further, note 16 below.

[11] Aristotle, *Psychology* 1.2 404b8-26, 1.5 409b26-410b9; 3.4 429a14-29, b5-9, b30-430a9; 3.5 430a14, 20; 3.7 430b26; 3.8 431b20-30; *Nicomachean Ethics* (hereafter cited as *NE*) 6.3 1139a9-10: "knowledge presupposes a certain likeness and kinship of subject and object"; 1.2 1094a27-b12; 1.3 1095a: "the end of this kind of study is not knowledge but action"; 2.2 1103b26-28: "we are not studying [merely] to know what goodness is, but to become good, or else there would be no good in studying it"; *Eudemian Ethics* 1.5 and 2.11, and *Metaphysics* 6.1 and 11.7.

[12] Aristotle, *NE* 4.7 1127a24, and b2: a good man "is truthful in his life and in his speech... simply because it is in his character to be that kind of man... a man who loves truth and is truthful when nothing [wrong or right] is at stake will be even more truthful when something is at stake"; 6.2 1139a29: for practical thinking, the goal is "truth in harmony with correct desire." The poet Yeats says that "Man can embody truth, but he cannot know it," sc. we cannot fully know it otherwise, so that with religious and moral truth our best knowledge is embodiment, not theory, life not words. See "Letter to Lady Elizabeth Pelham, 4th January 1939," in *Letters*, ed. Allan Wade (New York: Macmillan, 1955), p. 922.

are.[13] Thus, Aristotle remarks that "we ought to pay as much attention to the sayings and opinions, though they are given without proof, of wise and experienced older men, as we do to truths of which we have proof. For experience has given such men an eye with which they can see correctly."[14]

Thomas follows Aristotle just here when he contrasts the intellectual virtue of wisdom that we acquire by our own efforts with the theological virtue of wisdom that comes down from heaven as the gift of the Spirit to perfect our faith: "Faith assents to divine truth for itself; the gift of wisdom judges things according to divine truth. Hence the gift of wisdom presupposes faith, since [quoting Aristotle] *a man judges well what he already knows*."[15] We may take this good judgment referred to by Aristotle as connatural knowledge, because he remarks that "beginning students can reel off the words they have heard, but they do not yet know the subject. It must grow to be part of them [*sumphunai*, become their nature, as it has with the wise old men] and that takes time."[16]

---

[13] Aristotle, *NE* 9.9 1170a15; 2.1 1103a24-25; 2.6 1106b36; 3.4 1113a29-34; 9.12 1172a10-13; 10.5 1176a16: "in all matters of this sort we consider that to be real and true which appears so to a good man."

[14] Aristotle, *NE* 6.11 1143b10-13. In LF 219-220, Maritain (now 91) quotes this in his own behalf (!) , and goes on to say, "I hope that some of the privileges of the wisdom of great age will be granted to the thoughts expressed here": see *Untrammelled Approaches*, trans. Bernard Doering (Notre Dame, Indiana, University of Notre Dame Press, 1977), note on pp. 219-20.

[15] Thomas Aquinas, *ST* II-II, q. 45, a .1, ad. 2. Aristotle, *NE* 1.3 1094b28. *Isaiah* 11.2.

[16] Aristotle, *NE* 7.3 1147a21-23; cf. Plato, *Letter* 7.341c, 343e-344b. Plato writes that this assimilation should begin in childhood, with a music or cultural education of the emotions and character that makes us feel and love the beauty of right, and feel and hate the ugliness of wrong, so that when reason comes we will know it by our love of, and resemblance to, our harmony (*xumphonian*) and familiarity with it (*Republic* 3.401b-402a). Goodness thus knows itself and evil connaturally, while evil knows *neither* itself nor goodness, neither the evil of evil nor the good of good, and learns only to *do* evil, not to know it as it is (409de, cf. 395bd). In this sense, we have

There is a similar remark in the third century neo-Platonist Porphyry, the friend and editor of Plotinus: "The knowledge [*theoria*] that makes us happy does not consist in piling up reasonings.... Knowledge will do us no good unless it becomes life and nature within us and grows with us.... We mean to return to our true self, and the assimilation [*sumphusis*, connaturality] is to our true self, the intellect [*nous*]; and we aim to live in accord with intellect.... If we could achieve happiness by writing down words, we could do it without thinking about what to eat or what to do. But since we mean to change our life and purify ourselves in our actions as well as our words, we must consider what words and deeds will accomplish this." Both Porphyry and Aristotle think of philosophy as a way of discourse that is part of a way of life, as Pierre Hadot has argued.[17] Words of truth about the ideals we love must *activate* us and *transform* us; unless we fulfill them in existence, they lack full meaning and truth for us, and we betray them. This coming alive in us and becoming our nature and growing with us is connaturality.

Aristotle and Porphyry speak only of growth and return, but the notion of birth is implied insofar as our nature is what we are born with; virtues can become part of our nature. We should also remember Plato's words that love aims at birth in beauty, which seems to be both the birth of *noble excellence* in us through our actions and relationships, and of *ourselves* in noble excellence. Also, speaking of human love, Plato says that love transforms both lover and beloved into the likeness of the god that both follow, so that they learn thereby his way and manner of life.[18]

---

connatural knowledge of good, but not of evil. In maturity, the philosopher seeks this transformative knowledge with passionate love of true being that draws near to and joins with it to reproduce it, or more exactly to let it reproduce itself, in living intelligence and truth: *Republic* 6.490ab; cf. *Republic* 10.603b, and *Symposium* 206b-e, and 212a.

[17] Porphyry, *Abstinence from Animal Food* 1.29. Pierre Hadot, *What is Ancient Philosophy?*, trans. Michael Chase (Cambridge, Massachusetts: Harvard University Press, 2002), pp. 155-59 and 87-90.

[18] See note 16 above, last sentence; cf. *Phaedo* 72a, with Heraclitus DK B 62; *Phaedrus* 252e-253c.

Kierkegaard is another philosopher who speaks of knowledge by assimilation moved by love. Where ethical and religious truth is concerned, he writes, "like is known only by like," by a surrender to the truth *transforming* us into, or into the likeness of, what we know thereby. Truth reveals itself only to those who reveal themselves to it in their love for it:

> Christ says: I will manifest myself to him who loves me. But it is generally true that something manifests itself to the one who loves it; truth manifests itself to the one who loves truth, etc. We usually think that the recipient is inactive and that the object manifesting itself communicates itself to the recipient, but the relationship is this: the recipient is the lover, and then the beloved becomes manifest to him, for he himself is transformed in the likeness of the beloved; the only fundamental basis for understanding is that one himself becomes what he understands and one understands only in proportion to becoming himself that which he understands.
>
> Furthermore, we see here that to love and to know are essentially synonymous, and just as to love signifies that the other becomes manifest [to him], so it naturally means that one becomes manifest oneself. The relationship is so inward (a "to be" or "not to be") that all [mere] protestations and the like about love and loving are neither here nor there.[19]

That is to say, we know justice and charity by *practicing* them, and that is the only way we can know Christ who embodies and fulfills them, and who as God is Charity itself. By practicing them, we become like him, and he knows us as his own, and lets us know him and the Father and their life as our own. Thus the truth about love is known only by love, like only by like.[20]

---

[19] Søren Kierkegaard, *Journals and Papers*, 2.2299; *John* 14.21, 23.

[20] In *Works of Love*, trans. Howard Hong and Edna Hong (Princeton, New Jersey: Princeton University Press, 1995), p. 16, Kierkegaard argues that like is known only by like in the sense that it is only by loving that one knows the reality of love and its presence in other human beings, and only by loving is its presence in oneself made known.

Kierkegaard reflects Thomas's idea that our highest and fullest religious wisdom comes down from heaven as the gift of the Spirit to perfect our faith and the love that seeks it. To need God is a human being's highest perfection, he says, and all that we ourselves can do is to *understand* that we are nothing before him and do nothing to deserve his gift; or rather and more precisely, all that we can do is to be *willing* to understand it.[21] I am citing Kierkegaard here not because he follows Thomas or because Maritain follows him, but because Simone Weil does, and on this crucial point in particular, as we shall see.

Connatural knowledge thus presupposes and is moved by love; in a way it *is* love. Bernard and Augustine said that we will know and enjoy God because we *love* him, while Thomas argues that we will love him because we *know* and enjoy him; William St. Thierry says that love itself *is* our best knowledge.[22] Dante, who means to follow Thomas, clarifies this somewhat, by saying that we know God according to the purity and fullness of our *desire* or consent, our attention and faith; but that we love and enjoy God according to our *knowledge.*[23] The more we love and want to see God and what he sees, the more we can see (this is the connaturality); and the more we see, the more we love and *enjoy*, and go on wanting to see. God responds to our desire: he wants us to *ask* for what he freely gives and has already freely given in prompting our desire; all of our so-called "merit" is grace, and we have only to consent and seek and accept from him, as *his*, what he gives. William would say

---

[21] Søren Kierkegaard, *Eighteen Upbuilding Discourses*, trans. Howard Hong and Edna Hong (Princeton, New Jersey: Princeton University Press, 1990); p. 309, cf. 46, 156, 273, 360.

[22] William St. Thierry, *Exposition on the Song of Songs* 1.24, 64, 76; *The Golden Letter* 1.13.173, 2.3.196, 2.14.249. Similarly, Gregory the Great, *Homilies on the Gospel* 27. Plotinus 5.6.5: "Knowledge [*noein*] is a movement toward the Good in its desire of that good, for desire generates knowledge... and desire [*ephesis*] to see is seeing," 6.7.35.

[23] Dante Alighieri, *Paradise* 28.109-14: "Hence one may see that the most blest condition is based on the act of seeing, not of love, love being the act that follows recognition. They see as they are worthy. They are made to their degrees by grace and their own good will. And so their ranks proceed from grade to grade" (John Ciardi translation).

that Thomas' view and Dante's really imply his, since desire purified by what it seeks and transformed into its likeness is not only connatural knowledge of God, it really is our *best* knowledge of him.[24]

Maritain agrees with William insofar as he says that mystical knowledge by connaturality is the highest degree of knowledge here; but, like Thomas, he will contrast our best knowledge here with the beatific vision hereafter, where what is hidden in faith will be openly revealed; and perhaps William will say this, too.[25] What is partial here will be complete hereafter, as we are more fully transformed by love and become to ourselves nothing but what we love and know. But, even here, so Maritain explains, we already know God in some part and *what* he is and knows, and in the *way* that he knows it: by love.[26]

Simone Weil, for her part, would agree with much of what Maritain is saying about knowledge by connaturality, although she would express it in her own way and sharpen many details. She is writing about a decade after *Distinguer pour unir* was first published in 1932, and while I have no evidence that she read it, there are many details of her work that suggest this. She does not use the word "connatural" in any of its inflections so far as I know, but she has the notion and uses it, as we shall now see.

First, she would say with William that love itself *is* knowledge. "The organ in us through which we see God is love," she writes;[27] "love is the

---

[24] *Philippians* 1.9-10: "I pray that your *love* [for one another] may increase more and more and never stop improving your *knowledge* and deepening your insight, so that you can always discern what is best"; *Ephesians* 3.17: "and then planted in and built on *love*, you may *know* how wide and long and high and deep is the love of Christ that is beyond all knowledge [but *his*], and be filled with the fullness of God"; emphases and bracketed phrases added.

[25] Jacques Maritain, *DU* 262, 323; William St. Thierry, *Golden Letter* 2.17.266-67 and 2.19.275.

[26] Ibid., 262-63.

[27] Simone Weil, *The Notebooks of Simone Weil,* trans. Arthur Wills (London: Routledge, 1956), p. 240. Other works of Simone Weil cited here are *First and Last Notebooks,* trans. Richard Rees (Oxford: Oxford University Press, 1970); *Intimations of Christianity among the Ancient Greeks*, trans. Elisabeth Geissbuhler

soul's looking." It is attention to God, desire, or more precisely consent.[28]

Maritain uses John of the Cross's phrase "loving attentiveness to God" to characterize the union of the soul with God. Weil speaks this way too, but she will underline that it is *God's* attention to us before it is *our* attention to him: God who is love always acts first, and descends to us, and (she repeats, following Kierkegaard) our role is simply to accept and ask for what he offers.[29] Thus, when Maritain says that "We are made connatural to God through charity... [that] loves Him in himself and by Himself," Weil will write that it is the love of God given to us that makes us like him, the same love that constitutes the Trinity of God. He is a love that loves nothing but love and creates nothing else.[30]

For Maritain, through charity God himself comes to be within us "hidden in faith" (in the words of John of St Thomas); for Weil, God is "implicitly" and secretly present in us as the real lover in all our love of our neighbor and friends, the beauty of the world and the sacraments; and He is only explicitly present in us when He has come to us in person, in mystical experience, revealing himself as the true object of our love, as well as its true subject and as love itself; usually he is not someone *whom* or something *that* we see so much as the light *by* which we see everything and everyone; his presence within us is and should be hidden, she says, even and especially from ourselves, from our worldly, materialistic ego who is the prince of this world.[31]

---

(London: Routledge, 1957); *Science, Necessity, and the Love of God*, trans. Richard Rees (Oxford: Oxford University Press, 1968); *Waiting for God,* trans. Emma Craufurd (New York: Putnam, 1951, repr. Harper, 1973); and *Writings*, ed. Eric O. Springsted (Maryknoll, New York: Orbis, 1998). These titles will be cited hereafter respectively as *N*, *F*, *IC*, *SN*, *WG*, and *W*.

[28] Simone Weil, *WG* 212; *N* 527.

[29] Jacques Maritain *DU* 324. Simone Weil, *F* 121; cf. *Psalms* 17.1, 66.19, *Isaiah* 30.18. Simone Weil, *WG* 194-97; cf. *1 John* 3.10, 19. Simone Weil, *WG* 110-11, 129, 133, 220-22.

[30] Ibid., 260. Simone Weil, *IC* 166-67; *WG* 123; *N* 401.

[31] Ibid., 262. Simone Weil, *N* 173; *WG* 137-38, 209-15, 97-98, 150-51, 199, 50; *F* 271.

Our best knowledge of him and what he knows and does, she thinks, is a contact unforeseen by intelligence, an adherence that is love rather than belief; it is experimental rather than merely intellectual, coming from and leading to our fulfillment and embodiment of what we understand, so that we are (or are more fully) opened to grace and undergo a transformation that lights and clarifies us.[32]

We learn especially through suffering, she emphasizes perhaps more than Maritain does; and what we learn is humility and obedience as creatures to our Creator, as servants of the Lord of truth; our only freedom as servants and creatures is to choose to obey his word of love.[33] Thomas quotes Dionysius on learning through suffering, and Maritain cites John of the Cross on hiding oneself so as to enter the hidden place of God; similarly Weil quotes in Spanish the passage in the *Spiritual Canticle* where John says that

> Suffering is... the way... into the thicket of the delicious wisdom of God... and consequently to the purest and highest joy.... the soul which really longs for the divine wisdom longs first of all for the sufferings of the Cross, that it may enter in.... [It] says, "Let us enter into the heart of the thicket, even the anguish of death, that I may see God."

She refers often to these lines in arguing that it is our loving contemplation of Christ, and our imitation of his unconditional love for God despite and because of and through affliction, that opens us to the

---

[32] Simone Weil, *N* 242, 238, 245; *WG* 88, 107, 209; *SN* 93, 133; *WG* 75-77, 98-99, 198-99; *SN* 105; *N* 325, 428–"Knowledge through suffering [is] knowledge through transformation"– 431. Cf. Jacques Maritain, *DU* 293: "This would be the moment to recall that the wisdom of the saints, which judges things divine by the inclination of love or connaturality,... in virtue of the very union with God, not only presupposes faith but charity as well; that it is *experimental*; that it is not only speculative but also *practical*, proceeding *from* union with God, guiding our activity *toward* such a union, regulating human life in accordance with divine rules; and, finally, that it can use discourse and fashion arguments;" emphasis added.

[33] Simone Weil, *F* 344; *IC* 56-59, 186-87, 193-96. *Hebrews* 4.8, *Philippians* 2.8. Aeschylus, *Agamemnon* 177.

secret of divine wisdom and joy.[34] Then we are united to it, so that we let it be our motive and our life: we know it connaturally, as Thomas and Maritain say; as she would put it, we *mediate* it or make it known, showing it to others and drawing them into it.[35]

As for the beatific vision, perfecting our knowledge in the life to come, Maritain would say that this is mostly hidden from us because God's infinity escapes our finitude, and yet faith is the proof of things unseen; in the same spirit, Weil prefers not to speculate at all: we must consent with *all* our soul to everything that God sends, even to the destruction of everything *egoistic* in us, the annihilation of everything that we call "I"; but if there a difference between disappearance into the presence of God and disappearance into the absence of God, we cannot now coherently conceive it. Everything is hidden from us, from the worldly selfish part of us. Only God in us knows. What matters is to love him and desire to obey, that is all.[36]

Thus, as we grow in selfless love and obedience, Weil would say,[37] we know less and less what God does in and through us–we know it less with our materialistic ego, we don't let ourselves take pride in it as if it were our own work worthy of some reward–and in this sense we don't explicitly know our own humility and justice, even as our intention; in another sense, this is just the way that we know humility and justice, by fulfilling them so that they become our nature and life and grow with us. This unselfconsciousness accords with what was said about

---

[34] See note 6 above, and Jacques Maritain, *DU* 262. Simone Weil, *N*, 215; John of The Cross, *Spiritual Canticle*, 2nd redaction, 36.12-13. Simone Weil, *N* 439, 232, 261; *IC* 58-59, 195-96. See also Jacques Maritain, *DU* 366-67.

[35] Simone Weil, *N* 126, 358, 363.

[36] Simone Weil, *WG* 219-20, 225-26; *N* 467-69; *F* 142, 339: "But in these matters everything is impenetrable and unthinkable; it is better to have no opinion at all;" *WG* 90-91.

[37] See note 34, and Simone Weil, *N* 174, 417-18, 434; *F* 213: "the thought that I am giving something freely, simply for love, is false as soon as I think it, sc. with worldly egoism," and 271: "it is perhaps better that the supernatural virtues, faith, charity, should be implicit rather than explicit... The devil has no hold over things that are kept completely secret from oneself."

"connaissance" as acquaintance and contact that does *not* always bring full recognition.

In closing, I will say a few words about Maritain's discussion of connaturality in two other contexts. First, in "Love and Friendship," he writes of the "suitability" and "affinity" of chastity with specifically Christian contemplation,[38] and he goes on to mention a certain simplicity and freedom and intimacy with God that are "connatural" with the chastity of the body;[39] he clearly means that these characterize people who can most truly be said to *know* God in open "mad, boundless love."[40]

He uses the idea without mentioning it when he characterizes the contemplation of the divine passion as "that knowledge of God which is more experience than knowledge and yet supreme knowledge, and which comes about through love and the union of love, and which is miles from the *theoria* of the Greeks and from philosophical speculation or contemplation."[41] Again, this is something Weil could have said.

He uses the idea again when he describes the best conjugal love as genuinely human, spiritual, and personal, in which "each one really

---

[38] Jacques Maritain, *LF* 252.

[39] Ibid., 256.

[40] Ibid., 238 n. Maritain speaks freely of "mad, boundless love" throughout this piece, which first appeared in 1936: see especially *LF* 223-39, 245-51. It is interesting that Weil also brings forward "the madness of love" in her great essay *Are We Struggling for Justice?* (*W* 120-31), published in French in *Preuves* 28 (Juin 1953), then in *Ecrits de Londres* (Paris: Gallimard, 1957). She cites Aeschylus' *Prometheus* 385–"Nothing is better than to love to the point of madness"–and says that "The madness of love, once it has seized a human being, completely transforms the modalities of action and thought. It is akin to the madness of God... in needing man's free consent.... The spirit of justice is... the supreme and perfect flower of the madness of love. It compels one to abandon everything for compassion and, as St Paul says of Christ, to empty oneself... there must sometimes be moments when, from the point of view of earthly reason, only the madness of love is reasonable... when, as today, mankind has become mad from want of love" (*W* 123, 129-30).

[41] Ibid, 239-40.

participates, by virtue of love, in that personal life of the other which is, by nature, the other's incommunicable possession."[42]

This third case throws light on Maritain's puzzling remarks in *Creative Intuition* about poetic experience as "knowledge by connaturality," where he emphasizes union and suffering, and a non-verbal feeling and experience that gives us the world.[43] He intends, I think, the loving sympathy by which I unite myself to other beings and things. In sympathy, I open to you, I forget myself and identify and *feel* your needs as my own, so that I *do* for you what I do for myself. More exactly, my sympathy makes you and I into a *we*, and your needs and my resources become *ours*; and thus I *take part* in your life. When the empathy is mutual, we take part in one another's; we are *in* each other, for each is in the *us* that is in each of us as our new identity. Sympathy so understood is not just a feeling, but an *active* attitude of responsibility and doing what needs to be done; it *transforms* us by uniting us in a larger selfhood or nature; it *reveals* to us that we are not separate, but connected, potentially with everyone and everything; we learn truth that is *not* propositions so much as our nature as members of a community, our experienced fellowship together, the truth of *fidelity* and justice due to fellow creatures; we learn to connect, and that we are social creatures, born for one another. Sympathy gives us the world, the real one that we can experience together.

---

[42] Ibid., 244.

[43] Jacques Maritain, *CI* 115-25, 184-85; but see already *DU* 280-82. The poet's "creative intuition is an obscure grasping of his own Self and of things in a knowledge through union or through connaturality which is born in the spiritual unconscious, and which fructifies only in the work" (*CI* 115); "The soul 'suffers things more than it learns them'" (*CI* 121-22); "[Poetic knowledge is] an obscure knowledge through inclination–born in the preconscious of the spirit–in which the world is known in and through the subjectivity, grasped... [by] an emotion become intentional and intuitive. Such a knowledge is utterly different from what we ordinarily call knowledge, it is more experience than knowledge. It is neither conceptual nor conceptualizable, expressible in signs and images and, finally, only in a work made. But precisely because it is not abstractive nor rational, it has no intelligible boundaries and expands, as it were, to the infinite" (*CI* 184-85).

This is sympathy in practical situations like compassion and married love. In poetic experience, however, there is no question of responding to another's need as our own, but simply of seeing and feeling our community as our own true nature, and enacting it by showing it in a work of art. The Zen writer R. H. Blyth gives a good explanation of this in what he says about the imagination as it was exercised by the poet Wordsworth: it is "the power by which we become so united–or better, by which we realize our original unity with persons, things, [and] situations, so completely–that we perceive them by simple self-consciousness." By this power, Blyth writes, it is "as if the object used [our] eyes to perceive itself," and our voice to name itself. He mentions here the poet's remark that the object of poetry is "truth carried alive into the heart by passion: truth which is its own testimony."[44] This uniting power and truth are compassion (or sympathy) and community. This is our original element, in which we can at last live originally, in our highest ideal.

What I have been calling sympathy is love, or charity; so I can sum up this discussion by saying that connatural knowledge is *love's* knowledge, arising in surrender and transformation and embodiment, and perfected in these. Maritain would emphasize that the *natural* sympathy or connaturality of ethics and poetics give us an analogy of the supernatural connaturality of mystical experience, but that it is only a remote analogy, because, in this highest degree of knowledge, *God himself* changes us into his likeness, giving us religious wisdom as the gift of his own Spirit. Simone Weil, for her part, would say that when the love of God becomes explicit in the soul we will feel and know the passion and *kenosis* of God even in these; but that is to say, when these become for us *super*natural and mystical.[45]

Love's connatural knowledge, of the world and ourselves, of one another and God, then, is *living* knowledge: we have to live it, and we can live by it. I want to add, we don't need a reason to practice it and

---

[44] R. H. Blyth, *Zen in English Literature and Oriental Classics* (Tokyo: Hokuseido Press, 1942), pp. 420-21, 415, 426, 461; Wordsworth, *Lyrical Ballads*, Preface, paragraph 18.

[45] Jacques Maritain, *DU* 278-79, 280-281. Simone Weil, *WG* 137-38, 209, 213-15.

seek it. Reason isn't everything; we have love, too, which is better than reasons. Or, rather, love is the best reason of all, a living reason, and we don't need any other. God doesn't either, for, if Maritain and Weil are right, then it is his love that makes him God, transforming us into his likeness and uniting us to him.

# TIME AND THE HUMAN PERSON

Teresa I. Reed

Jacques Maritain's references to temporality usually concern the distinction between the temporal and the spiritual. In *Integral Humanism*, he says that the temporal and the spiritual must be distinguished as two different "planes of activity." Spiritual activity is essentially directed toward eternal life. Examples of spiritual activity include "liturgical and sacramental life... the work of the virtues or of contemplation... the apostolate or... the works of mercy."[1] Temporal activity, on the other hand, aims at "goods which are not eternal life, but which concern in a general way the things of time, the work of civilization or of culture."[2] Temporal activity may be intellectual, moral, scientific, artistic, social, political, etc., but essentially concerns things of the world. Maritain thus bases the distinction between the spiritual and the temporal on the distinction between eternity and time. In this context, "eternal" does not mean "everlasting for all time;" rather, it means "non-temporal" or "outside of time."[3] The ultimate end of spiritual activity is eternal life, and the end of temporal activity is a good that changes and is subject to time. However, it is important to note that as human activities, both spiritual and temporal activity take place in time despite their different ends.[4] This suggests an intersection between time and eternity. And Maritain does acknowledge a third plane of activity, "the plane of the spiritual in its

---

[1] Jacques Maritain, *Integral Humanism: Temporal and Spiritual Problems of a New Christendom* (1936), trans. Joseph W. Evans (Notre Dame, Indiana: University of Notre Dame Press, 1973), p. 291.

[2] Ibid., p. 292.

[3] It is easy to conflate the two meanings of "eternal," because both the non-temporal and the everlasting are "permanent." Nevertheless, the distinction is important for questions such as the eternity of God, the possible eternity of the universe, and the nature of time.

[4] Some may propose that contemplation is an experience in which time is suspended. However, I would describe contemplation as a relational experience of eternity, in a distinctive form of lived time.

connection with the temporal."[5] Although "the spiritual order is... superior to the temporal order," there is also a "vital union" between the spiritual and the temporal. Activity in this plane of intersection agrees with spiritual activity in having eternal life for its object, but focuses on temporal goods precisely in order to subordinate them to spiritual goods. According to Maritain, such activity includes the "Christian effort of socio-temporal renewal,"[6] which works toward "a relative though real earthly happiness"[7] and the personal growth and relative fulfillment of human beings. This third plane of activity draws attention to the intersection between eternity and time and makes it possible for us to show the relationship between spiritual and temporal activity as well as to explain the difference between them. Because the spiritual and the temporal are two planes of activity of the human person, the nature of the human person provides the link between them.

In this paper, I will follow Maritain in using the term "temporal" to distinguish temporal activity from spiritual activity according to their ends. In order to focus on temporal and spiritual activities as activities, I will distinguish among several different aspects of time: the lived time of human experience, the sacred time of spiritual activity, and the clock time of industrial and post-industrial civilization.[8] Using Maritain's distinction between the person and the material individual, I will demonstrate how the difference between clock time and lived time is related to the difference between the material individual as a part and the human person as a whole, and show how the modern material individual follows the time of the clock. After describing the origins, advantages, and disadvantages of clock time, I will argue that a focus on clock time displaces the lived time of actual human experience and reduces the person to the material individual. I will then show how a

---

[5] Jacques Maritain, op. cit., p. 296.

[6] Ibid., p. 254.

[7] Ibid., p. 137.

[8] Consequently, the adjective "temporal" is reserved for activity directed toward the world as world and cannot be used in this paper for time in general or sacred time in particular.

focus on lived time restores the person as end and as directed toward eternal life, and thereby also restores the sacred time of spiritual activity.

It is possible to distinguish variations with respect to how time is experienced and understood. Maritain was aware of differences in people's understanding of time. For example, in *Integral Humanism*, he observes that the dualism characteristic of modernity created a split between living a "religious" human life and living a "natural" human life:

> For too long during this modern age the Christian world wounded by dualism has obeyed two opposite rhythms, a religious rhythm for the time of the Church and of worship, a naturalist rhythm for the time of the world and of profane life.[9]

He thus points to the difficulty of maintaining an intersection between the spiritual and the temporal, when the temporal is defined by the secular, where holy days yield to the work week and liturgies give way to football games. The very idea of confining religious experience or spiritual activity to an hour or two a week speaks to the primacy of a naturalist and secular view of time. Another variation within the temporal occurs with respect to the use of time for work or for leisure. In *Reflections on America*, Maritain comments on "the American attitude toward time" which includes "a certain horror of any span of time which a man might have at his own disposal in order to *do nothing*."[10] He says:

> The great value and efficacy of standing idle, and lingering over one's dream, is little appreciated in this country.... [F]riendship requires a great waste of time, and much idleness; creative thinking requires a great deal of idleness. So it is that leisure constitutes a serious problem for American life....The question will be to have leisure time occupied in a manner really profitable to man, and not entirely taken up by the kind of

---

[9] Jacques Maritain, op. cit., p. 78.

[10] Jacques Maritain, *Reflections on America* (New York: Gordian Press, 1975), p. 156.

stupefying passivity that is more often than not developed by movies or television.[11]

Maritain thus suggests a use of time which is different from both frenetic activity and stupefying passivity and which allows the development of friendship, creativity, and other distinctively human pursuits. Similarly, in *Leisure, The Basis of Culture*, Josef Pieper points out the vast differences among the busy activity of the work-a-day world, the passivity of simple idleness, and the condition of leisure, which he describes as receptive understanding, effortless relaxation, celebration and the affirmation of reality as a whole.[12] Leisure understood this way is a "time out" from the time of schedules, not just a "break" from work but "the power to step beyond the working world"[13] and to experience spiritual renewal. Thus it is clear that time can be understood and experienced in different ways. Moreover, as Maritain points out, the focus of American culture on scheduled activities tends to leave little room for unscheduled time.

Yet the clock time of schedules, clocks, and calendars differs from the time of lived experience and the time of spiritual activity. I will designate as "lived time" the time of actual human experience in the real world, experience which varies qualitatively according to that which is experienced. Actual human experience is relational, an experience-of something. Any description of lived time focuses on the experience itself, both the experiencing and that which is experienced, i.e., the event through which one lives, and describes the duration of the event in terms of the actual experience. For example, the lived time of intense experiences such as birth and death, joy and sorrow, is uneven, not because of a subjective distortion, but rather because the experiences themselves are relational and not uniform. As a result,

---

[11] Ibid., pp. 156-57.

[12] Josef Pieper, *Leisure, the Basis of Culture*, newly translated by Gerald Malsbury with an introduction by Roger Scruton (South Bend, Indiana: St. Augustine's Press, 1998), pp. 30-34.

[13] Ibid., p. 35.

lived time is not susceptible to precise scheduling.[14] The duration of significant human events tends to expand or to contract in comparison to the clock. When the importance of lived time is acknowledged, the human activities or events take priority over the schedule. Human activities include spiritual activity, and I will call the time of spiritual activity "sacred time." This is a distinctive form of lived time in which human activity is directed toward eternity and opens itself to the presence of God. Like lived experience in general, religious experience overflows any attempt to confine it to a precise schedule. Many people, atheists for example, could acknowledge lived time without acknowledging sacred time. Nevertheless, for those who admit that human beings are directed towards eternal life and have an intrinsic relation to spiritual reality, it is reasonable to consider sacred time to be the lived time of religious experience and spiritual activity.

Some ways of thinking about and of experiencing time rule out sacred time and spiritual activity, and exclude any intersection of the temporal and the spiritual. One such understanding is the "inhuman and materialist" *mythos* of industrial civilization,[15] which emphasizes and depends on systems, schedules, and functions. The system takes precedence over the people who are involved in it. As Maritain says in *Integral Humanism*:

> In the present civilization, everything is referred to a measure which is not human, but external to man: primarily to laws belonging to material production, to the technological domination of nature and to the utilization of all the forces of the world for the fecundity of money.[16]

---

[14] However, the structure of lived time can be described in terms of the horizons of protention and retention. See Edmund Husserl, *On the Phenomenology of the Consciousness of Internal Time (1893-1917)*, revised English trans. John B. Brough (Dordrecht: Kluwer, 1991), and Maurice Merleau-Ponty, *Phenomenology of Perception*, trans. Colin Smith (London: Routledge, 1962), pp. 410-33.

[15] Jacques Maritain, *Reflections on America*, p. 21.

[16] Jacques Maritain, *Integral Humanism*, p. 191.

Nevertheless, Maritain distinguishes between the people who live in a society and "the externally superimposed *structure or ritual of civilization.*" In *Reflections on America*, he expresses hope that the spirit of the American people will overcome "the logic of the structure."[17] Forty-some years later, there are still grounds for hope. However, in our post-industrial civilization, the "logic of the structure" of American culture increasingly dictates the primacy of profit and promotes mindless entertainment. The relentless pursuit of material ends and of the lowest common denominator focuses on the temporal to the exclusion or marginalization of the spiritual.[18] Moreover, the cultural emphasis on schedules and functions presupposes a particular understanding of time that cultivates a material and instrumental view of the human person.

An understanding of time and an understanding of what it is to be human are bound together. Human beings are finite and must decide which activities are most important in their lives. Given the physical and temporal limitations that define human finiteness, the activities dominant in a culture reflect a collective choice about how human beings should live and an implicit view about the nature of the human person. It is necessary, then, to ask about the nature of the person who lives and acts in this world.

In *The Person and the Common Good*, Maritain distinguishes between the person and the individual. The person, considered as a whole, can live a spiritual life directed towards eternity. Thanks to human freedom and the human intellect, the person is capable of both knowledge and love, which transcend the temporal world.[19] However, the individual, considered as the material aspect of the person, belongs only to the temporal world. Maritain describes the material individuality of the person in unflattering terms, as "the detestable ego whose law is *to*

---

[17] Jacques Maritain, *Reflections on America*, pp. 21-23.

[18] Although 90% of Americans say they believe in God, the culture is structured by an economic system that gives primacy to money and material possessions.

[19] Jacques Maritain, *The Person and The Common Good* (1946), trans. John J. Fitzgerald (Notre Dame, Indiana: University of Notre Dame Press, 1966), p. 39.

*grasp* or to absorb for itself."[20] The material individual is best understood as the modern individual, the isolated and self-interested Hobbesian being who competes for survival and advantage in the material world.[21] Maritain's description of the material individual in terms of the modern individual is justified by modernity's emphasis on the material. For example, Hobbes' mechanistic determinism underlies his account of human nature as greedy, grasping, self-interested, ruled by the passions, etc.[22] Hobbes and the later empiricists argued for universal mechanism, and the successes of natural science appeared to contribute to the plausibility of modern empiricism. Contemporary physicalism, along the same lines, concludes that the human being is only the material individual.

A major factor contributing to this view of the human being is the modern understanding of the world in terms of clock time. The modern material individual lives by the modern conception of time, which originated in Western culture with the invention of the mechanical clock. As I have argued elsewhere,[23] the mechanical clock in turn served as a model for and helped to inspire the theory of universal mechanism which, despite its deficiencies, continues to have a tremendous effect

---

[20] Ibid., p. 44.

[21] I believe that Maritain's hylomorphism is not particularly helpful here. Material individuality cannot be identified with animality, for a person focusing his or her life on material individuality still uses the intellect. If the animal body of the person is matter and the rational soul is form, it follows that the animal body of the person cannot be the same as "the detestable ego." The human being does not choose to be embodied, but does choose whether or not to focus on materiality.

[22] Hobbes' famous account of the state of nature occurs in *Leviathan* (1660), chapters XIII-XV (http://oregonstate.edu/instruct/phl302/texts/hobbes/leviathan-contents. html). He gives his mechanistic account of causality in *Concerning Body* (1656), chapter XXV, contained in *Human Nature and De Corpore Politico*, ed. J.C.A. Gaskin (Oxford: Oxford University Press, 1999), pp. 212-30.

[23] Teresa I. Reed, "Time in Relation to Self, World, and God," in *Faith, Scholarship, and Culture in the 21st Century*, eds. Alice Ramos and Marie I. George (Washington, D.C: American Maritain Association, 2002), pp. 166-77.

on people's understanding of the universe and of themselves. The modern conception of time focuses on clock time, to the exclusion of lived time and sacred time.

So far, I have distinguished several understandings of time and sketched an account of modern civilization in relation to time and the human person. In order to demonstrate the connection between clock time and the modern material individual, I will describe the origins, advantages and disadvantages of clock time.

Clock time, the time of schedules, clocks, and calendars, has a firm foundation in reality and human experience. However, clock time also becomes detached from actual human experience. To see this, consider that a clock's purpose is time measurement and that time measurement is really about relations among events. People want to measure two things about events, so they can talk intelligibly with each other about past and present events and make plans for future events. The two things to be measured are "when" and "how long." "When" refers to how an event is related to other events, in the specific sense of its temporal "location" with respect to before and after.[24] (For example: before the Battle of Waterloo; at dawn; after I went on vacation.) "How long" refers to the duration of an event, its relative permanence, how long it lasts. [25] (For example: all morning; for a little while; through the

[24] "Before and after" (or "earlier and later") and "past, present, and future" are equally basic ways in which we describe the location and duration of real events and our experience of them. McTaggart's reduction of the B series (earlier and later) to the A series (past, present, and future) allows him to extend the fixed relations of the past to the whole of time. This extension is illegitimate. McTaggart's argument is a classic case of substituting an abstracted structure (the timeline) for the real events from which it was abstracted in the first place. Of course, his metaphysical idealism does not permit him to make that distinction. For a concise version of McTaggart's argument, reprinted from *Mind* (1908), see "The Unreality of Time," in *Time*, eds. Jonathan Westphal and Carl Levinson (Indianapolis, Indiana: Hackett, 1993), pp. 94-111.

[25] For the realist, duration and passage are features of real events of all kinds. Time exists as a real aspect of real events, including human experiences. Both change and the lack of change can have duration. Augustine's argument

summer.) The "when" and the "how long" of a real event can be observed, lived through experience, theorized about, inferred on the basis of evidence, and/or measured. Measurement requires a comparison to other events.

The two major kinds of time measurement are calendars and clocks, both of which depend on real events. Calendars are based on astronomy, beginning with the "natural" units of the day, lunar month, and solar year.[26] There are various types of calendars (lunar, solar, mixed), and all calendars have conventional elements, but any calendar allows us to compare one event to another, with respect to both "when" and "how long." (For example: in 1995; before last week; on the 10$^{th}$ through the 12$^{th}$ of June; for 5 days.) Similarly, a clock is only a uniform motion machine. The units are conventional but founded upon a real oscillation ("tick"), to which other motions and changes can be compared. The "accuracy" of a clock depends on the uniformity of the oscillation, and the oscillation is most uniform when it has the smallest frequency.[27] A process of abstraction is involved in both kinds of time

---

against duration, that the present time has no length because any given length of time contains a before and an after (*Confessions*, Book 11, chapter XV), actually supports the view that time is continuous. Aristotle (*Physics*, Book VI, chapter 1, 231a21-231b20) successfully shows that time cannot be assembled out of discrete nows, and that the units of time measurement are both conventional and made possible by the continuity of time. "Time itself," as Yves Simon argues, is a concept founded on reality. Yet Simon's discussion of duration is complicated by his failure to distinguish between the two senses of "eternity," outside of time or everlasting for all time. See *The Great Dialogue of Nature and Space*, ed. Gerard J. Dalcourt (South Bend, Indiana: St. Augustine's Press, 2001), chapter VII.

[26] On the calendar, see E. G. Richards, *Mapping Time: The Calendar and its History* (Oxford: Oxford University Press, 1998) and Bonnie Blackburn and Leofranc Holford-Stevens, *The Oxford Companion to the Year* (Oxford: Oxford University Press, 1999).

[27] The most accurate clock, the Cs-133 atomic clock, subdivides the second by defining it as "the duration of 9,192,631,770 periods of the radiation corresponding to the transition between the two hyperfine levels of the ground state of the Cesium-133 atom." This level of accuracy is required for

measurement, as people learn to read a calendar and to "tell time" by a clock. Numbers are attached to centuries, years, months, days, hours, minutes, seconds. Although calendars are given a graphical representation, and thus remain relatively abstract, clocks are actually constructed: a clock is an artifact, a physical, real thing. Whether analog or digital, a clock sets forth not only its own presence but also the presence of clock time itself. "Clock time itself," however, is a being of reason, a concept, an abstraction, based on the process of comparing changes to each other and using one change as a measure for others. A version of the fallacy of misplaced concreteness occurs when people not only apply the abstracted structure to real events, but also forget the real events upon which the structure is based, and then consider the abstracted structure to be more important than the real events that take place within it.

This fallacy is encouraged by the usefulness of clock time. Clock time allows natural science to carry out precise measurements of chemical, physical and biological processes. Precise time-keeping enables navigation to be correct. Clock time permits an industrial economy to reorganize human work by work schedules, multiple shifts, and hourly wages. Transportation, utility, and communication networks rely on closely timed schedules. And, for everyday life, clocks and calendars allow the synchronization of all kinds of human gatherings. These advantages of clock time should not be underestimated. Not only are they convenient, but they also rapidly become indispensable to the functioning of a society.[28]

However, there are also disadvantages arising from a dependence on clock time. Clock time replaces the continuity of lived time with an abstract structure of countable units. This discrete conception of time grants priority to schedules, so that the schedule provides a structure for human events and human events must conform to the schedule.

---

the Global Positioning System and other precision technologies. A quartz crystal clock can measure only thousandths of a second.

[28] Although the disruptions predicted for the Year 2000 fizzled, the predictions drew attention to the nation's infrastructure and its dependence on technological timekeeping.

The impersonal and mechanical functioning of the clock, and related abstractions such as the monetary system, underlie the "logic of the structure" of the industrial and post-industrial societies that make up modern civilization. According to Maritain, modern civilization threatens "not only the earthly happiness of the community" but also "[menaces] the life of the soul, the spiritual destiny of the person."[29] Considering modern civilization in relation to time, the earthly happiness of the community is threatened, because clock time tends to displace the lived time of actual human experience, and the spiritual destiny of the person is menaced, because clock time reduces the person to the material individual.

First, clock time tends to displace the lived time of actual human experience. Lived time, in contrast to clock time, respects the unevenness and non-uniformity of experience. People's experiences of joy, sorrow, creativity, suffering, birth, death, and other significant happenings in their lives differ with respect to actual duration.[30] Any description of lived time focuses on the actual events through which one lives. It is simply inappropriate, a category mistake, to impose a precise schedule on such significant events. Yet a clock-driven culture attempts to do just that, resulting in absurdities such as "personal time," "quality time," specified length-of-stay in a hospital, and so forth. The schedule is rigid, artificial, and impersonal, while the human events that are scheduled are often quite the opposite—flexible, natural, and highly personal. The advantages of the schedule lead people to give priority to the abstracted structures of clock time instead of the real, human and natural events of actual experience. This threatens the earthly happiness of the community as people are torn between what they know to be important and what they can fit into the schedule. Although I think most people are aware of the conflict and

---

[29] Jacques Maritain, *Integral Humanism*, p. 137.

[30] Clock time is objective, but it is not the case that lived time is subjective. Rather, lived time is relational and intersubjective. It is relational because it is always the duration of a real experience of something. It is intersubjective because personal experience does not have to be unique. People have many or most of these experiences in common, so that the common features and structures of experiences can be described phenomenologically.

find it disturbing, there is tremendous social and economic pressure to accept the primacy of the schedule.

When clock time is given priority, human events and activities are reduced to scheduled functions. So, secondly, clock time reduces the human person to the material individual who performs those functions. It becomes very easy to see human beings simply as means to the perpetuation of the structure, particularly when people themselves grant priority to the value of efficiency and think of their own value in terms of their scheduled accomplishments. The dominance of clock time forces human activities into an abstract structure which is dehumanizing because it is reductionist.[31] People are reduced to their material and productive functions, i.e., to material individuals who compete for limited resources and who are valued only insofar as they fit into the "functionalized world." Gabriel Marcel uses the phrase "functionalized world" to describe the society which "equate[s] [an] individual's identity with his or her functions." He says, "The frightful expression, *the use of one's time*, is in this context most significant. Precise amounts of time are allotted for various functions."[32] Similarly, according to Josef Pieper,

> [T]he work-a-day world is the world of the working day, the world of usefulness, of purposeful action, of accomplishment, of the exercising of functions; it is the world of supply and demand, the world of hunger and the satisfaction of hunger. It is a world dominated by one goal: the realization of the "common utility"; it is the world of work, to the extent that work is synonymous with "useful activity."[33]

In that clearly instrumental view of the human being, failure to carry out one's functions means that one becomes useless. Moreover, the human being is considered to be a purely natural phenomenon divisible into

---

[31] People who work on computers are well aware that their productivity can be calculated down to the second.

[32] Gabriel Marcel, "Concrete Approaches to Investigating the Ontological Mystery," in *Gabriel Marcel's Perspectives on the Broken World*, trans. K. R. Hanley (Milwaukee, Wisconsin: Marquette University Press, 1998), p. 173.

[33] Joseph Pieper, *Leisure*, p. 64.

functions. The division of the human being into a collection of functions leads toward a focus on particular and technical problems and away from a sense of the whole person. This produces a fragmentation of personality, according to Marcel.[34] Maritain agrees, for the human being as a collection of vital and social functions is precisely the modern material individual, and material individuality is "inclined to fall" into a dispersion or dissolution of personality.[35] It is very difficult to have a sense of the center of one's being, the whole of one's life and its meaning and purpose, when that life is divided into time slots to be used for separate functions.[36]

So the dominance of clock time produces and reinforces a material, instrumental, and fragmented view of the human being. It also requires people to stuff the most significant events of their lives into time slots, and makes it difficult for people to justify activities that appear to have no useful function (such as philosophy). This menaces the life of the soul and the spiritual destiny of the person, as ultimate questions about the self and the meaning and purpose of human life are replaced by techniques (how-to's) for improving particular functions.

The human person, however, is more than a collection of functions. Resistance to the functionalized world occurs in many ways: family life, vacations, parish work, hobbies, fishing, and so on, can resist the schedule and permit both creativity and wholeness.[37] However, each of these activities can also be turned into a function and sucked back into the relentless whirl of the rat race which is ruled by the clock.[38] It is

---

[34] Gabriel Marcel, op. cit., p. 175.

[35] Jacques Maritain, *The Common Good*, pp. 44-45.

[36] The psychologizing of religion is a tribute to the power of a naturalistic and functional account of the person.

[37] There are also less constructive forms of resistance, such as obscurantism, escapism, passivity, sabotage, etc.

[38] This description evokes Heidegger's description of everyday Da-sein as "falling prey" and being constantly torn away from authenticity into the eddy or whirl(pool) of everydayness. See Martin Heidegger, *Being and Time* (1953), trans. Joan Stambaugh (Albany, New York: State University of New York Press, 1996), §38, pp. 164-68.

necessary to restore an understanding of lived time in order to provide an alternative to the functionalized world.

In contrast to the clock time which gives priority to schedules, the lived time of human events gives priority to human activities. Many of the realities of human experience, by their nature and by their importance, overflow the schedule. As a result, an acknowledgment of lived time entails an openness to activities that are not schedule-driven, activities such as healing; grieving; caring for babies; raising small children; being creative; cultivating a friendship; building a consensus; practicing contemplation; participating in liturgical and sacramental life. To understand such activities, which are event-driven and not schedule-driven, it is necessary to think of them in relation to human development and human fulfillment. In that context, schedules are incidental and subordinate to the activities and processes themselves.

Consequently, instead of emphasizing schedules and functions, an understanding of lived time encourages the person to live as a person and not just as a material individual. Whereas clock time promotes an instrumental view of the human being as a "means only" to accomplish useful functions, lived time is open to the fulfillment of the human being and to the person as end.[39] The lived time of human events acknowledges the relational aspect of experiences, as experiences-of that differ in both duration and significance. (For example: my grief over the loss of a loved one; the healing of the wound on my foot. These are personal experiences of something real and their duration varies.) Lived time brings into focus both what is experienced and who is experiencing. The one who is experiencing cannot be understood as a collection of functions, but must be understood as an acting person. Thus, the modern material individual gives way to the person who is an end and who acts toward ends. As a result, lived time permits the intersection of the temporal and the spiritual in sacred time, the time

---

[39] As John F. Crosby observes, "as subjective person I am not a mere instrumental means for producing results, but am called to realize through my acting entirely non-instrumental meanings that express, among other things, my being as end in myself" *The Selfhood of the Human Person* (Washington, D.C.: The Catholic University of America Press, 1996), p. 113.

of religious experience and spiritual activity in which the person is directed toward the good of eternal life. Moreover, as Maritain points out, temporal activity is subordinate to spiritual activity. Thus, because the ultimate end of the person is eternal life, the lived time of ordinary activity is subordinate to the sacred time of spiritual activity, in its significance for the reality of the human person.

The human person faces a number of dilemmas in contemporary American society, and one of them is how to live with clock time and the structure it places on human activity. Maritain hoped that the American love of freedom and sense of morality would contribute a vital energy toward "overcoming and breaking the logic of the structure."[40] However, the person must acknowledge and cooperate with schedules and functions in order to act in this world. How can lived time in general, and sacred time in particular, be respected in a culture organized by clock time? How can spiritual life be acknowledged, respected, and encouraged in a temporal culture dominated by a material and instrumental view of the person?

I suggest that, first, reflection on different understandings of time can call attention to cultural assumptions about time, schedules, and functions, and make possible a more comprehensive view. Americans can learn from other cultures that seek a better balance between clock time and lived time.[41] It is unreasonable to expect people to give up the advantages of schedules, clocks, and calendars, but it is possible to show the limitations of clock time and to emphasize lived time, which focuses on the depth and quality of human experience. Secondly, since the difference between clock time and lived time is closely related to the difference between the material individual as a part and the human person as a whole, it is necessary to put systems and schedules in perspective by challenging the naturalistic and functional account of the human being and by drawing attention to the ultimate meaning and purpose of human life. Maritain points out that "materialistic

---

[40] Jacques Maritain, *Reflections on America*, p. 23.

[41] See Edward T. Hall, *The Dance of Life: The Other Dimension of Time* (New York; Doubleday Anchor, 1983), and Alfred Gell, *The Anthropology of Time: Cultural Constructions of Temporal Maps and Images* (Oxford: Berg, 1996).

conceptions of the world and life... do not recognize the spiritual and eternal element in man... [and] cannot satisfy the requirements of the person."[42] Of course, the person is in this world and yet not of this world. The person as such transcends the temporal world,[43] and no version of temporal life will be sufficient to satisfy the human soul who finds ultimate happiness in God. Nevertheless, it is worthwhile to advocate an understanding of time that, far from constricting the human person into this world, opens the human person to eternal life.

---

[42] Jacques Maritain, *The Common Good*, pp. 100-01.

[43] Ibid., pp. 69-70.

# Transcending Bodily Existence and Vulnerability

Alice Ramos

## I Introduction

Since 9/11 in New York, Americans have learned in an unexpected and tragic way what it means to be vulnerable and perhaps this experience has allowed our country to come of age, so to speak. While vulnerability and dependence form part of human existence, few philosophical studies throughout the course of history have addressed these aspects of our fragile condition. Western moral philosophy, as Alasdair MacIntyre remarkably advances in *Dependent Rational Animals*, generally depicts moral agents as though they were always rational, healthy, and untroubled. To cite a case in point, MacIntyre refers to Adam Smith who, in his *Theory of Moral Sentiments*, asserts that the "pleasures of wealth and greatness ... strike the imagination as something grand and beautiful," while in instances of illness and old age we are more apt to recognize the false illusions and deception to which such pleasures lead.[1] Rather than embrace a "splenetic philosophy," however, Smith concedes that the illusions about the acquisition of wealth and greatness fostered by the imagination of those in good health and humor are "economically beneficial illusions" and "keep in continual motion the industry of mankind."[2] So, rather than confront the transitory character of extrinsic goods, such as money and fame, and acknowledge the vulnerability and affliction which mark the human condition, we generally prefer to forego such considerations and thus continue to live by imagination and illusion–by that illusion that we are somehow self-sufficient and superior, as Aristotle's *megalopsychos*.[3]

Such a way of understanding ourselves is highly inadequate, since the experience of vulnerability, the capacity to be injured or harmed

---

[1] Alasdair MacIntyre, *Dependent Rational Animals* (Chicago: Open Court, 1999), p. 2.

[2] Ibid.

[3] Ibid.

and to thus feel pain and suffering, can unveil to us a profound and essential dimension of human existence. In an essay titled "Self-Interpreting Animals," Charles Taylor devotes particular consideration to the experience of shame: we may be ashamed of wrong-doing, but shame can also be caused by the lack of certain properties which are essentially attributed to human persons. Because of this lack, I would say that we are vulnerable, afflicted, and thus pained. A man may, for example, be ashamed of his shrill voice or effeminate hands. According to Taylor, "[A] shrill voice is ... something unmanly, betokens hysteria, not something solid, strong, macho, self-contained. It does not radiate a sense of strength, capacity, superiority. Effeminate hands are–effeminate. Both voice and hands clash with what I aspire to be, feel that my dignity demands that I be, as a person, a presence among others."[4] The experience of shame or humiliation thus shows us to have some degrading property, or to be base, dishonorable. The shameful or humiliating also refers to the way we see ourselves and to the way we are seen by others. As Taylor puts it: "Something only offends my dignity because it upsets or challenges the way I present, project or express myself in public space."[5] There is then in this sort of experience of the shameful an aspiration to dignity or excellence, to the quality of being worthy or honorable, but at the same time the experience of reproach and disapproval–disapproval either by others or by oneself. What produces shame or humiliation is opposed to the "grand and beautiful," of which Adam Smith speaks; shame is rather always concerned with the ugly.

The purpose of this paper will be first to consider the experience of vulnerability in reference to the beautiful and the ugly in their external and internal dimensions, and what such an experience can tell us about ourselves and about the meaning of different types of goods. Secondly, I will try to show that the vulnerability which is ours due to our bodily existence is surpassed by a vulnerability freely accepted for the sake of a greater good. This second type of vulnerability requires maturity in freedom and a recognition that fullness of life is not contingent on

---

[4] Charles Taylor, "Self-Interpreting Animals," in *Human Agency and Language* (Cambridge: Cambridge University Press, 1985), p. 53.

[5] Ibid., p. 57.

what might be called "the wisdom of the world." To this type of wisdom, we will contrast "the wisdom of the cross." So, in the third instance, in this paper I will explore what light the Christian framework can shed on human vulnerability and suffering. In this part of the paper, I will take my cue from contemporary thinkers such as John Paul II, Jacques Maritain, and C. S. Lewis, as well as the wisdom of Thomas Aquinas. Lastly, while bodily vulnerability may lead to disapproval by others or even by oneself, just as we are able to distinguish higher goods and higher forms of life, and in fact speak of the highest good and the best life, so we can speak of a different type of approval or disapproval, of the only type of approval or disapproval that ultimately is of any account.

## II Kinds of Goods and Beings, Kinds of Beauty and Ugliness

Although Aristotle does speak of a hierarchy of goods, it is interesting to note how according to him certain aspects of external goods produce a sort of beauty of happiness, since they make a person pleasing in the eyes of others, and to be seen as pleasing belongs to the meaning of beauty. Aquinas comments on this point by saying that to be deprived of certain external goods defiles happiness, since it makes a man somewhat contemptible in the eyes of others; such is the case of the man who lacks nobility, or good offspring, or even bodily beauty. A man is not fully happy who presents an ugly appearance, since by this fact he is made despicable in the eyes of others.[6] While a pleasing appearance is a good thing to possess, we would be mistaken to be so captivated by attractiveness that we would undervalue the qualities of a person who presented an ugly or horrifying appearance. And it is just such a case which MacIntyre presents to us in *Dependent Rational Animals*: a person with a disfigured face is someone from whom we can learn, provided that we are able to separate ourselves from and to stand in judgment of our feelings of dislike or disgust. As MacIntyre says: "What blinds us to our own defects in self-knowledge may also blind us as to qualities of others. So those captivated by appearance and presentation may not be able to identify, let alone understand, examples of the courage and gracefulness of spirit that can be hard-

[6] Thomas Aquinas, *Commentary on Aristotle's Ethics* I, lect. 13, nn. 159, 163.

won responses to afflictions of disfigurement and disablement."[7] Clearly, in this instance, if we separate ourselves from feelings of disgust before a horrifying appearance, we are better able to recognize the limits of attractiveness, of external goods, and the importance of goods of the soul, internal goods, such as the virtues; the person with the disfigured face may thus provide us with the opportunity to learn about our own good and the good of others. Our awareness of the human good is then closely connected to the proper evaluation and alignment of our feelings.

In our contact with those who are vulnerable, we can learn not only to distinguish between external and internal goods, but also to understand ourselves as having demands made on us which are often incompatible with those of desire or feeling. An example of such self-understanding is given by Taylor in the above-mentioned essay. When we come upon someone in trouble, a wounded man, for example, as in the Good Samaritan parable, we may or may not feel any desire to help the man, but we do feel called upon to help him. We feel called upon *qua* rational beings, or moral beings, or creatures made in the image of God, capable of responding as He does, out of love.[8] We are thus "called upon to act. And we are called upon in virtue of being a certain kind of creature. Even though we may not be very sure in virtue of what we are called on, we know that the obligation lies on us, not on animals, stones, or idiots."[9] We are then being called to act out of a higher standpoint, because we recognize that we are a higher sort of being; as such, certain reactions, certain motivations, will not be fitting to us, and we know this because we are capable of judging and discriminating motivations as higher or lower. To this effect, Taylor says:" ... spite, revenge, returning evil for evil, is something we are prone to, but there is a higher way of seeing our relations to others; which is higher not just in producing happier consequences–less strife, pain, bad blood–but also in that it enables us to see ourselves and others more broadly, more objectively, more truly. One is a bigger person, with a broader,

---

[7] Alasdair MacIntyre, op. cit., p. 138.

[8] Charles Taylor, op. cit., p. 58.

[9] Ibid.

more serene vision, when one can act out of this higher standpoint."[10] So, to return to the experience of the person who sees a wounded man lying in the road and has a sense of being called on to help, a sense quite different from the desire to help, the demand made on the person is in virtue of the type of subject that he is, that is, an autonomous moral subject, who can respond to the call of what is truly good or worthy.[11] He is thus capable of acting from a higher standpoint, of seeing his relations to others in a higher way.

As mentioned above, states of vulnerability can lead us to a recognition of different types of goods–lower and higher goods–and also to the realization that we ourselves are a higher type of being, unlike animals or stones, for whom agency cannot be reduced simply to desire or feeling. Now the state of vulnerability which is present in disfigurement in the example given by MacIntyre can give rise to shame, since the person suffering the disfigurement is deprived of a good due to her had she not undergone burns or an illness producing an ugly appearance. But it is important here to distinguish between external and internal ugliness, just as we distinguish two kinds of beauty. On the one hand, there is spiritual beauty, which consists in a due order and abundance of spiritual goods. By contrast, anything that manifests internal disorder or that proceeds from a lack of spiritual good is ugly. On the other hand, there is external beauty, which consists in a well-proportioned body, in its due ordering, and in an abundance of external things which are related to the body, whereas ugliness is associated with disorder of the body or with a lack of temporal things. Just as internal and external beauty delight and give rise to desire, ugliness arouses shame in both its internal and external dimensions. As Aquinas says: "... a person is ashamed of the fact that he is a pauper, or that he has a deformed body, or that he is ignorant, or that he performs disorderly actions. Therefore, since interior ugliness must always be held in contempt, everything that involves shame

---

[10] Ibid., p. 67.

[11] Ibid., p. 73.

arising from this kind of ugliness must be disapproved."[12] Interestingly, as we saw above, it is possible that the person with a disfigured face–disfigurement here being an example of external ugliness–and with a high degree of virtue, that is, spiritual beauty, might still be disapproved, because our disordered feelings would not let us see beyond the immediate appearance. If our feelings were, however, properly aligned, we could, as stated previously, learn from the afflicted person about the human good.

## III Vulnerability, Perfection, and Wisdom

Now, while most of us would not want to be deprived of certain external goods and thus be afflicted or vulnerable, it is possible that for a higher good a person might assume such vulnerability. To this effect, Aquinas provides us with an interesting example: while even holy men will despise the lack, or ugliness, of external things, yet, with a view to perfection and for the sake of Christ, it may be freely assumed by them. Therefore, the man who is ashamed of this sort of ugliness is not to be disapproved, but rather to be greatly praised, should he adopt it because of humility. As Aquinas says, "to beg has a certain shame associated with it on the basis of this second kind of ugliness, for every beggar shows himself as a pauper and sometimes he lowers himself to the man from whom he begs and this pertains to external deficiency. Hence, mendicancy adopted for Christ's sake is not only not to be disapproved, it should be praised greatly."[13] Elsewhere, Aquinas reiterates that mendicancy involves a certain abasement, and that although activity and governance are naturally superior to receptivity and obedience, there are circumstances that may alter this natural ranking: "To suffer," Aquinas says, "is more ignoble than to act, to receive than to give, and to be ruled and to obey than to govern and command; however, on account of the addition of some added circumstance, the appraisal can be reversed."[14] For Aquinas, there may

[12] Thomas Aquinas, *Against the Attackers of the Religious Life*, chap. 7, reply to obj. 9, trans. Vernon J. Bourke, in *The Pocket Aquinas*, ed. V. J. Bourke (New York: Washington Square Press, 1960), p. 268.

[13] Ibid.

[14] Thomas Aquinas, *Summa Contra Gentiles*, III, chap. 135.

be circumstances where sacrificing certain natural goods or enduring certain evils is a way of attaining a greater good. So, virtuous humiliation is not therefore an unthinking acceptance of any deprivation. According to Aquinas, the counsels (which, more generally, could simply be called virtues)–that is, the adoption of voluntary poverty, chastity, and obedience–are not for the weak, but rather for those who, trusting in divine power and providence, freely choose to "cast aside" other things for the sake of the highest Good.[15]

Since the way to the perfect good, as Aristotle called happiness,[16] does not reside in external goods nor in goods of the body, but rather in perfect virtue, in order to arrive at such perfection, Aquinas tells us that a free mind is a necessary condition.[17] For this reason, he counsels voluntary poverty: "that a man's mind, being withdrawn from earthly cares, may be more at liberty to give itself to God;" and elsewhere he says: "poverty frees a man from that which hinders him from being intent on spiritual things." And, "man's greatest good is that he adhere with his mind to God and divine things."[18]

In order therefore to assume the vulnerability implicit in poverty, man's life cannot be seen simply in terms of self-preservation–the preservation of bodily existence. The whole purpose for which the human person, being rational in nature, exists is to contemplate the truth, which is divine activity, and so, to be taken into the life of God, our minds must be free of earthly attachments and creatures. In describing the perfect good, the state of happiness, Aquinas says: "... man's mind will be united to God by one, continual, everlasting operation. But, in the present life, in as far as we fall short of the unity and continuity of that operation, so do we fall short of perfect happiness."[19]

---

[15] Thomas Aquinas, *Summa Theologiae*, III, q. 7, a. 2, ad. 3. See also Thomas S. Hibbs, *Virtue's Splendor* (New York: Fordham University Press, 2001), p. 193.

[16] See Thomas Aquinas, *Summa Theologiae*, I-II, q. 3, a. 2, ad. 2.

[17] Thomas Aquinas, *Summa Contra Gentiles*, III, chap. 132.

[18] Ibid, chap. 130.

[19] Thomas Aquinas, *Summa Theologiae*, I-II, q. 3, a. 2, ad. 4.

Of course, this is not the wisdom that many of our contemporaries want to hear; for this reason, they will disapprove of virtues such as the counsels and of a notion of happiness that emphasizes the goods of the soul over the accumulation of external goods, over offspring when and however they are wanted, and over the affirmation of one's will or over the will to power. To assume vulnerability by "casting aside" riches, for example, cannot be understood simply from the goal of a natural perfection. As Aquinas tells us, when the forfeit of external things is adopted for the sake of Christ because of humility, then it is not to be disapproved, but rather to "be praised greatly." To become vulnerable to the eyes of the world, for the sake of Christ, requires a larger vision of things than that afforded by the wisdom of the world or the wisdom of the wise.

We need a new sort of humanism, a new sort of wisdom, to enter into that vision. Maritain, in *The Twilight of Civilization*, speaks of a "humanism of the Incarnation," of an "integral humanism," "which considers man in the integrality of his natural and supernatural being and which sets no *a priori* limits to the descent of the divine into man."[20] It is just this sort of humanism which, I believe, John Paul II has in mind when he says in different ways throughout his writings that man can only understand himself in Christ. As the former Pope puts it in *Fides et Ratio*: "The fundamental conviction of the 'philosophy' found in the Bible is that the world and human life do have a meaning and look towards their fulfillment, which comes in Jesus Christ. The mystery of the Incarnation will always remain the central point of reference for an understanding of the enigma of human existence, the created world and God himself."[21]

The Word of Wisdom, the wisdom of God revealed in Jesus Christ, provides us with a new sort of logic, based on both truth and love, in order to understand human vulnerability, suffering, and the meaning of life. In assuming human nature, the Divine Word also freely assumes

---

[20] Jacques Maritain, *The Twilight of Civilization* (New York: Sheed & Ward, 1943), p. 13.

[21] John Paul II, *Fides et Ratio* (Washington, D.C.: United States Catholic Conference, 1998), p. 118, no. 80, par. 3.

human vulnerability. For love of perfection, Christ frees Himself of riches and human affection so that, in perfect freedom and obedience, He unites His will to the will of God the Father. The *kenosis* or self-emptying of God is radical: "He emptied himself, taking the form of a slave, coming in human likeness, and found human in appearance, he humbled himself, becoming obedient to death, even death on a cross" (*Philippians* 2: 7-8). Aquinas argues that no one should doubt as to the pain truly experienced by Christ: "for true bodily pain are required bodily hurt and the sense of hurt. Now Christ's body was able to be hurt, since it was passible and mortal; neither was the sense of hurt wanting to it, since Christ's soul possessed perfectly all natural powers."[22] To this effect, Aquinas relies on Scriptural authority: "Surely He hath borne our infirmities and carried our sorrows."[23] Christ, Beauty itself–the splendor of the Father–is stripped of all glory in His passion and death on the cross; He willingly takes on disfigurement; as Isaiah graphically writes: "... there is no beauty in Him, nor comeliness: and we have seen Him, and there was no sightliness, that we should be desirous of Him: Despised, and the most abject of men, a man of sorrows, and acquainted with infirmity; and His look was as it were hidden and despised, whereupon we esteemed Him not" (*Isaiah* 53: 2-3). There is no external beauty in this description of "the suffering servant," of Christ; we are told that His appearance arouses no desire; He is rather despised and has been put to shame.

This is certainly not the beauty that the "wisdom of the world" exalts, and yet, despite the external aspect of a body deformed by affliction, Aquinas tells us that Christ had a certain divinity and thus beauty which shone from His face.[24] The internal beauty which radiates outward cannot be seen by everyone–not everyone sees the beauty of self-abasement and obedience, of that complete submission of the Son to the Father. A crucified God certainly inverts our ordinary

---

[22] Thomas Aquinas, *Summa Theologiae*, III, q. 15, a. 5.

[23] Ibid., sed contra.

[24] Mark Jordan, "The Evidence of the Transcendentals and the Place of Beauty in Thomas Aquinas," *International Philosophical Quarterly*, vol. XXIX, no. 4, issue 116 (December 1989): 407.

conceptions of the beautiful and challenges our way of seeing the world. In commenting on the obscurity or blindness which resulted from original sin, Aquinas says that man in his present state no longer sees God's radiance shining through the world; man is impeded as regards the vision of spiritual things "because he is distracted by and occupied with sensible things."[25] The wisdom of the cross and with it human vulnerability and suffering can take us out of that distraction and occupation, so as to make us realize that "the world is not the source of man's ultimate happiness"[26]–the world is precarious, vulnerable, subject to mortality and corruption, just as the human body is. That aspiration to wholeness or integrity, to the perfect good of happiness, cannot come from the world. It can only come to man from God. "This is why Christ speaks of God's love that expresses itself in the offering of His only Son, so that man 'might not perish but might have eternal life' (*John* 3:16). Eternal life can be given to man only by God; it can be only His gift. It cannot be given to man by the created world. Creation–and man together with it–is subject to 'futility'(cf. *Romans* 8:20)."[27]

## IV The Human Person's Perfection and Approval

So, if to understand human life and happiness in terms of mere self-preservation or in terms of the "pleasures of wealth and greatness" is totally inadequate, because of the futility to which man and the world are subject, then understanding and seeing oneself in the Word of Wisdom not only completes the "wisdom of the wise," which recognizes the superiority of goods of the soul, but offers us something radically new. In referring to the way in which God creates and re-creates, that is, restores what He has created after sin, Aquinas uses an important analogy: that of the Divine Artist, His art, which is His Wisdom or Word or eternal concept, and His artifacts or creatures; as Aquinas puts it:

---

[25] Thomas Aquinas, *Summa Theologiae*, I, q. 94, a. 1.

[26] John Paul II, *Crossing the Threshold of Hope* (New York: Alfred A. Knopf, 1994), pp. 55-56.

[27] Ibid., p. 56.

> [T]he Person of the Son, Who is the Word of God, has a common agreement with all creatures, because the word of the craftsman, i.e., his concept, is an exemplar likeness of whatever is made by him. Hence the Word of God, Who is His eternal concept, is the exemplar likeness of all creatures. And therefore as creatures are established in their proper species, though movably, by the participation of this likeness, so by the non-participated and personal union of the Word with a creature, it was fitting that the creature should be restored in order to its eternal and unchangeable perfection; for the craftsman by the intelligible form of his art, whereby he fashioned his handiwork, restores it when it has fallen into ruin. And hence man is perfected in wisdom (which is his proper perfection, as he is rational) by participating the Word of God, as the disciple is instructed by receiving the word of his master.... Hence it was fitting that by the Word of true knowledge man might be led back to God, having wandered from God through an inordinate thirst for knowledge.[28]

So, not only is the Word of God the exemplar of all creation, He is also the exemplar for man's re-creation, for his restoration. Man's perfection in wisdom thus requires an imitation of the exemplar. To be instructed in the Word of God means not only participation in the fullness of truth, but also in the fullness of love and beauty. Just as the Son is in total relation to the Father, surrendering His will to Him and loving the salvific will, so, too, man is called to do likewise. Since by sin man withdraws from the light of reason and of the Divine Law, then to return to the state prior to sin, it is necessary that man's will should have a movement contrary to the previous movement; man will need therefore to reunite himself to his ultimate principle through the path of humility and self-abasement which the Word of Wisdom delineates for us, contrary to the pride which is the beginning of every sin.[29]

In *Fides et Ratio*, John Paul II says: "Human perfection ... consists not simply in acquiring an abstract knowledge of the truth, but in a

---

[28] Thomas Aquinas, *Summa Theologiae*, III, q. 3, a. 8.

[29] See Thomas Aquinas, *Summa Theologiae* I-II, q. 86, a. 2, and I-II, q. 84, a. 2.

dynamic relationship of faithful self-giving ... [in which the] person finds a fullness of certainty and security."[30] It is in this interpersonal relationship that the person brings into play her capacity not only to know, but also to entrust herself to another, to others.[31] In the exemplar, in the Word of wisdom, we find just this self-giving, and, for this reason, He is commended as the Son in whom the Father is well pleased. So the vulnerability, pain, and suffering which are ours due to our bodily condition has a special significance. As C. S. Lewis puts it in *The Problem of Pain*:

> We are, not metaphorically but in very truth, a Divine work of art, something that God is making, and therefore something with which He will not be satisfied until it has a certain character.... We were not made primarily that we may love God (though we were made for that too) but that God may love us, that we may become objects in which the Divine Love may rest 'well pleased.' To ask that God's love should be content with us as we are is to ask that God should cease to be God: because He is what He is, His love must, in the nature of things, be impeded and repelled, by certain stains in our character, and because He already loves us He must labor to make us lovable.[32]

Our vulnerability, the pain and suffering experienced due to our precarious state, are meant, then, for our very perfection. We are to be perfected, restored, made lovable and pleasing to our creator through suffering. Lewis says: "... that is why tribulations cannot cease until God either sees us remade or sees that our remaking is hopeless."[33]

The person's vulnerability, affliction, and pain are meant to shatter the illusion that all is well and that we are self-sufficient and consequently need only to trust in ourselves (as may have happened in 9/11 in New York). It would seem then that, in order really to experience the beauty and grandeur that we so desire and for which in

---

[30] John Paul II, *Fides et Ratio*, p. 48, no. 32, par. 2.

[31] Ibid.

[32] C. S. Lewis, *The Problem of Pain* (New York; Macmillan, 1977), pp. 30 and 36.

[33] Ibid., p. 94.

this life we often delude ourselves, we ultimately have to face the dreadful.[34] A vision of the beautiful, an encounter with the absolute fullness of good, can only come to us as a result of purification, self-surrender, and trust.[35] Illness, affliction, sober the soul, and sobriety of this kind belongs to the essence of purity. We can only be purified and transformed by experiencing the dreadful, just as we paradoxically save our life when we lose it.

If vulnerability and suffering are for the sake of perfection, for experiencing eternal life and gazing upon the face of the beautiful, then how we are seen by others in our affliction is of little or no importance–how we are seen by God is what matters, for it is His approval that we really seek. And, in facing Him, we will be known by Him and know that we are approved or disapproved. As C. S. Lewis so graphically puts it: "In the end that Face which is the delight or the terror of the universe must be turned upon each of us either with one expression or with the other, either conferring glory inexpressible or inflicting shame that can never be cured or disguised."[36]

---

[34] Josef Pieper, *The Four Cardinal Virtues* (Notre Dame, Indiana: University of Notre Dame Press, 1966), p. 127.

[35] Thomas Aquinas, *Summa Theologiae*, II-II, q. 19, a. 12, sed contra et resp.

[36] C. S. Lewis, *The Weight of Glory* (Grand Rapids, Michigan: Wm. B. Eerdmans, 1965), p. 10.

# Beyond the Personal: Weil's Critique of Maritain*

Eric O. Springsted

Jacques Maritain and Simone Weil never met, although there was a brief exchange of letters between them. Maritain never cites Weil; she cites him explicitly in at least three places, but disparagingly. But therein hangs a tale, and one that in the telling reveals that although there never was a great exchange, and that Weil may well have been slightly vindictive, that nevertheless Maritain did play a significant role for Weil. However, it was one in which he chiefly inspired her to rise to a new level of thought by her conscious and deliberate attempt to contradict him.

## I

When Simone Weil arrived in New York in early July, 1942 with her parents as refugees, she had one plan of action fixed firmly in her mind. That was to return to the occupied portion of France, and indeed to be parachuted into it. Sometime earlier she had conceived a plan to parachute nurses into the front lines who would take care of the wounded in the heat of battle. There were, of course, very grave risks in such a venture, but taking them was at the heart of the plan. For, Weil believed, in such a war, one way that the Allies could show what they were fighting for was by risking themselves in an effort of brave self-sacrificial compassion.

It is virtually impossible to overestimate the importance of this mission to Weil. Its moral significance had captured her conscience, and she was desperate to do something for the war effort. Living in the comfort of New York, she felt like a deserter, and were she to be isolated from France much longer, she wrote, it would break her heart.[1]

---

* A slightly different version of this paper was published in *Harvard Theological Review* 98:2 (2005) 209-18. We thank *Harvard Theological Review* for permission to publish this version.

[1] Simone Pétrement, *La Vie de Simone Weil* (Paris: Fayard, 1973), p. 627, condensed and translated by Raymond Rosenthal as *Simone Weil: A Life* (NewYork: Pantheon, 1976), p. 475. Biographical facts are taken from this source.

She wrote numerous letters to anybody who might listen to her plan and help in its implementation or help her to get somebody in authority to listen. The recipients of these letters included an Admiral Leahy and probably President Roosevelt himself. When ultimately she did reach England, only to be stuck (she thought) writing reports for the Free French and having the plan declared as mad by De Gaulle, she resigned her post with the Free French, and fell into a despair that ended only with her death from tuberculosis in August, 1943.

It was in an effort to enlist his help in this plan that Weil wrote to Maritain shortly after her arrival in New York, figuring that he might not only be sympathetic but also that he might have some influence. Maritain was out of town but did reply on August 4. Although the correspondence has yet to be published, Pétrement, who had seen it, described his reply as friendly, saying that Weil's purpose was lofty and noble, and, although he did not know if her plan was practicable, that he would try to help her meet with appropriate authorities. He also advised her to meet with Alexander Koyré, and to discuss with Father Coutourier certain questions about her "spiritual position" that she had mentioned.[2] It was, of course, out of her meetings with Coutourier that the well-known and controversial "Letter to a Priest" emerged.

Aside from any promise, implied or explicit, to help, this might have been the end of the exchange. It clearly was for Maritain. But it wasn't for Weil. Instead, we find Maritain twice mentioned explicitly in *The Need for Roots*. The first is when, in discussing the soul's need for truth, Weil quotes his claim that all the greatest thinkers of antiquity accepted slavery, despite the very clear evidence of Aristotle, who says that there are people who did not. Since people reading Maritain might well not have the wherewithal to do the research themselves and would have to take his word on the matter, he has offended against the need for truth and ought to be hailed in front of a tribunal which could censure him.[3] (This is somewhat less silly than it sounds since it is

---

[2] Ibid., p. 627.

[3] Simone Weil, *The Need for Roots* (San Francisco: Harper and Row, 1971), p. 38. Cf. Jacques Maritain, *Les droits de l'homme et le loi naturale* (New York: Editions de la Maison Française, 1942), trans. Doris C. Anson, *The Rights of Man and the*

simply a "for instance" of a larger and very serious point about the responsibility of writers in a society.) The second instance is when, at the end of *The Need for Roots*, she directly quotes him as saying that "the notion of right is even deeper than that of moral obligation, for God has a sovereign right over his creatures and he has no moral obligation to them."[4] This thought absolutely appalled her, and she cites it as an example of what she deemed "the Roman conception of God," that is, a God who is like the emperor exercising sovereignty over subjects as slaves. This is actually a very important point, as I shall argue below. Nevertheless, it also indicates lack of pleasure. Finally, if Maritain is indeed the target in the essay "La personne et le sacré," as I and others have maintained,[5] then he is also one of the originators of personalism who is "warmly wrapped in social consideration," one of those "writers for whom it is part of their profession to have or hope to acquire a name and reputation."[6] One senses more than a little rancor here.

Why the antagonism? I suspect that to the degree her aggressiveness is personal it is because Maritain ultimately did not do anything to help after his original warm letter. It may well be the case that the warm tone of the letter and its kindness when he did not help was in the end taken by Weil as condescension, the sort of encouraging politeness one receives from great people, but that ultimately is designed to get rid of us. Feeling a sense of expectation, when disappointed we feel that we have been played for fools. Maritain may not have meant this, but Weil, who was very sensitive about these sorts of things, and had a lot of experience with them as she scouted for support for her project, might very well have thought he did.

---

*Natural Law* (London: Geofrey Bles, 1944), p. 57. Citations are from the English translation.

[4] Ibid., pp. 277-78; cf. Jacques Maritain, *Rights of Man*, p. 37.

[5] Cf. E. Springsted "Rootedness: Culture and Value," in D. Allen and E. Springsted, *Spirit, Nature and Community* (Albany, New York: State University of New York Press, 1994), pp. 178-179. Simone Fraisse, "Simone Weil, la personne et les droits de l'homme," *Cahiers Simone Weil* 7.2.

[6] Simone Weil, "Human Personality," in *Selected Essays 1934-43* (London: Oxford University Press, 1962), p. 17.

Now, if this were the sum of the exchange between Weil and Maritain, it is not entirely to Weil's credit. However, there is rather more, and it lies at a far deeper philosophical level. Indeed, it concerns the very idea of depth in human life.

## II

Weil finally reached London in November, 1942, and joined the Free French. She was given the task of examining the developing projects of the Resistance committees for the reorganization of France after the war. Her identity card states her title as "redactrice." She was bitterly disappointed on not being sent to France on a dangerous mission, and even more so as she could receive no serious hearing for her own project. Yet this was an incredibly productive time for her. Far from simply churning out the easily forgettable reports of a bureaucrat, she wrote in a period of little more than six months numerous essays on the spiritual and political renewal of France, what has come to us as the book *The Need for Roots*, as well as several other essays on politics, religion and ancient philosophy. Her thought in these works is at its most mature and most integrated. Indeed, she herself in a letter to her parents at the time suggests that her thought had taken such a turn that it had become more and more compact, more indivisible, as it grew.[7]

One of the most important of the works written at this time was the essay "La personne et le sacré," the first or among the first of the London works and a turning in Weil's thought. It both clears the decks of numerous ideas so easily assumed in thinking about the human being and human communities, clearly distinguishing Weil's own views, and introduces many of the great themes of the London writings, such as her notion of the "impersonal," and her argument that obligations absolutely have precedence over rights. It is above all an extremely original essay, and has a timeless quality to it, as many of her writings have.

Yet, despite this timeless quality it is also a highly contextual essay. One part of that context is, of course, the concern over just what France

---

[7] Simone Weil, *Seventy Letters* (London: Oxford University Press, 1965), p. 196.

should look like after the war, of how it would conceive and organize its laws, social concerns, and politics. In short, she was very concerned about how justice would be conceived, especially given all the competing voices. That much has always been recognizable and recognized. The other part of the context has not been so easily recognized, although if one looks carefully it is in fact easily recognizable. That context is Maritain's little book *The Rights of Man and Natural Law*, which for Weil was perhaps the chief competing voice.

There is no doubt that Weil had read *The Rights of Man*, which was published in French in New York in 1942, and that she could put a copy in front of her. The direct quote from *The Need for Roots* cited above attributing a "Roman conception of God" to Maritain is from this book,[8] which is also the source for Maritain's contestable claim about how the ancients viewed slavery.[9] While "La Personne et le sacré" never explicitly mentions Maritain, and has no direct quote from him, there are numerous indicators that it is a direct response to *The Rights of Man*. The most incontrovertible example is a point that can only be taken from Maritain's discussion of natural law in that book. There he calls the natural law an "unwritten law" and proceeds to cite Antigone as an example of it.[10] Weil notes, in a way that leaves no doubt as to what she is referring to, that "it is extraordinary that Antigone's unwritten law should have been confused with the idea of natural right (*droit*)."[11] Since this point is not an aside or a mere "for instance," but an essential one about the status of rights in the Greeks, and part of an extended argument about rights and their linkage to the concept of "person" and "personality," an essential theme of the essay and of Maritain's book, it is immediately clear that this essay is a response to *The Rights of Man*. The connection becomes even clearer when then one reads the essay in the light of its being a response, for Weil can then be seen to be explicitly attacking a number of points that Maritain has made about rights and the concepts of "person" and "personality" in *The Rights of*

---

[8] Jacques Maritain, *The Rights of Man*, p. 37.

[9] Ibid., p. 57.

[10] Ibid., pp. 34 and 35.

[11] Simone Weil, "Human Personality," p. 20.

*Man.* Simone Fraisse, who was the first one to notice the connection, points out: "On y trouve l'éloge de la personne, à laquelle sont associés les termes que Simone Weil refusait de lui reconnaître: le sacré, le respect, l'épanouissement, le droit."[12] One may also add to this list Weil's discussions of the relation of the person to the collectivity, and her equally subtle but insistent differences from Maritain on the issue of human labor.[13]

If this is a direct response, what sort of response it is needs to be considered, however. While rather thorough in covering a number of Maritain's points, it is not exactly a systematic critique, a point by point refutation. Nor is it, despite everything else, one that is entirely unsympathetic to Maritain's project. In fact, on any number of items of concern which they both canvas they might well agree: the deep problems of both individualism and totalitarianism, and the need to

---

[12] Simone Fraisse, op. cit., pp. 123-24.

[13] This issue is one that admirably illustrates Weil's approach to Maritain's book discussed in the next few paragraphs. Maritain spends considerable time defending the dignity of labor, and liberating it from the conditions of slavery and servitude (*The Rights of Man*, pp. 50-60). Weil would agree in the abstract. Where she disagrees is that, unlike Maritain, who thinks we ought to aim at progressive liberation from material necessity (pp. 22 and 27) and ought to subjugate nature (p. 26), she thinks that the value of labor is that it allows one to obey necessity and is an "opportunity to reach the impersonal stage of attention" ("Human Personality," p. 17). So, when Maritain outlines the rights of the working person (*The Rights of Man*, pp. 61-62), he chiefly considers issues of property, such as a just wage, ownership, insurance, and other benefits. Weil, for her part, comments: "Usually when addressing [the workers] on their conditions, the selected topic is wages; and for men burdened with a fatigue that makes any effort of attention painful it is a relief to contemplate the unproblematic clarity of figures. In this way, they forget that the subject of the bargain, which they complain they are being forced to sell cheap and for less than the just price, is nothing other than their soul. Suppose the devil were bargaining for the soul of some poor wretch and someone, moved by pity, should step in and say to the devil: 'It is a shame for you to bid so low; the commodity is worth at least twice as much'" ("Human Personality," p. 18). Here, she is contesting a general position about labor, and Maritain happens to be one who believes it.

establish the human being as ontologically related to God. For this reason, a point by point refutation would miss the mark, since it is a general approach to these problems that she is worried about. Indeed, to read it as a point by point refutation would suggest that Weil had let a rather unfair prejudice color her reading of Maritain and that she had in fact utterly misread him. Her attacks on the concepts of "person" and "personality" that she launches there are attacks on concepts of the empirical, social ego, and that is clearly *not* what Maritain thinks he is trying to get his readers to consider, and what he is trying to avoid by rooting the concept of person in a relation to God and calling it sacred. I think she understood this, and does not make him a strawman.

The response is more subtle and more pressing. Its nature is indicated in the sixth sentence of Weil's essay. In her opening lines, she makes a common sense appeal to a distinction between a sentence such as "You do not interest me," which is genuinely cruel and offensive, and one where we might say "Your person does not interest me," which, she notes, can be used in an affectionate conversation between friends. One might imagine, for example, in the latter case two friends pursuing a philosophical argument, and one musing about how amenable a position is to him. The other can, without offense, suggest that how well it fits his friend's personal preferences is irrelevant to discovering its truth, which is what they are both really interested in. Given this valid distinction, she then comments: "This proves that something is amiss with the vocabulary of the modern trend of thought known as Personalism. And in this domain, where there is a grave error of vocabulary it is almost certainly the sign of a grave error of thought."[14] The accusation therefore is initially not so much that Maritain has gotten hold of the wrong sort of problem or that he has failed to define his terms accurately, but that in using the term "personne" he has failed to get a hold on *le mot juste*.

That is not a trivial point, and certainly not for Weil, whose own concern for calling things by their right names was categorically imperative. The most charitable interpretation, then, of her objection is that no matter how carefully defined "personne" might be, and

---

[14] Simone Weil, "Human Personality," p. 9.

Maritain certainly went to some efforts to define it carefully, this would simply be *recherché*, and its subtle distinctions would be lost given the normal freight that the word carries. Weil is absolutely right on this. What is heard and celebrated when one says that the person is sacred is *not* that "one can find alone his complete fulfillment"[15] in the absolute of God, which is what Maritain thinks he means. What is heard is that the confused mass of desires that constitutes our social egos and aspirations, what we normally call the person or our personality, is sacred. When that happens, the sacred is created in our image. I think, given Maritain's intellectual influence among the Free French, Weil was particularly concerned to warn them on this point.

That is the most charitable interpretation, and leaves Maritain's own thought internally intact. However, while Maritain may have been less misled by his use of the term "personne" than his audience might have been, Weil believed that nevertheless he was still misled, and seriously so. He makes exactly the sort of mistake she fears will be made when one uses the term "personne" for what is sacred in a human being. The problem is Maritain's easy connection of "personne" to the notion of rights, which Weil thinks belongs to the realm of "words of the middle region,"[16] the realm of ordinary institutions. Rights are a matter of commerce and property, she claims, and are defined by *jus utendi et abutendi*. That, of course, makes them quite fit to deal with issues of personality and the social ego. But when then Maritain suggests ideas such as rights having priority over obligations because God has rights over creatures and not obligations she thinks something has gone very wrong, indeed. Not only has law belonging to property and commerce been applied rather unequivocally to the divine (she is being Plotinian here), the whole sense of the proposition runs counter to the more genuine Christian understanding of God. God acts out of his goodness and love to creatures, going out from himself to meet their needs. Obligations, as she understands them, are not laid on one–and they are not laid on God. They are a response of goodness to need, a matter of heart. To talk about rights preceding obligations in

---

[15] Jacques Maritain, *The Rights of Man*, p. 6.

[16] "Simone Weil, "Human Personality," p. 33.

the case of God is then utterly to mis-describe the nature of God's goodness and love as portrayed in the Gospel.

## III

The scope of this paper does not allow me to go much further into the substance of what may now be seen as a legitimate and important philosophical debate. I would briefly like, however, to say something more about Weil's deepest objections to personalism and about her original alternative in suggesting that what is truly sacred in the human being is the impersonal, and why she was so insistent on liberating the minds of her colleagues from Maritain's claims.

Weil has two important reasons for rejecting personalism. One is her considered view of what constitutes personality. Rather than seeing it, as Maritain did, as the highest and deepest dimension of our being, that wherein our freedom is most clearly expressed and needs most respect, in arguments similar to those of Foucault a generation later, she held that personality and its value are constituted by what she called "social matter." The person and the value we put on persons is historically contingent, and manufactured by the play of social forces. So, more often than not, when we focus on the person and personality, we tend to miss what is of genuine and lasting value in human aspiration. Moreover, since personality is born out of social struggle, there is always an element of contention involved in personality and in its expansion. As she points out quite observantly, rights, which are linked to the concept of the person, are always asserted in a tone of contention, and even inhibit movements of genuine charity.

The second related reason for rejecting personalism is that it doesn't actually protect and value humanity to the ultimate degree that it thinks it does, no matter how many rights are defined and how clearly. Even when one's rights are scrupulously guarded, Weil thought, one's deepest inner cries are not necessarily heard or responded to. Those lie behind easily defined words, and until one can hear the inarticulate word behind the words, one has not heard the human or what is sacred in her at all. Weil bases this claim in her own watching of court cases, where everything is done fairly, but somehow those who lack articulateness have a profound sense that good has not triumphed, that they have not been heard and even that they have been humiliated by the flow of fine words.

Now, given this critique of personality, Weil's counter-assertion that what really is sacred in a human being is the impersonal in him gains some plausibility and shows her own originality. For although the very word "impersonal" perhaps chills us as being unfriendly and abstract, a good part of Weil's point is that to isolate personality from the human being's striving for good, and to consider it all of her, is itself the very height of abstraction. When she recommends "impersonalism," she is therefore not trying to cut humans out of the world, but to make room for them. She is doing so by refusing to take aspects of the human striving for good that are essentially bound up with contingent historical circumstances to be the whole of humans. The human expectation for good is more than what counts as personality, and we are obliged to respect humans even when they show no signs of being persons (no matter what Peter Singer thinks). As she points out in another essay, the man laid upon by thieves and lying by the side of the road had become nothing more important than a stone; it is no wonder that the priest and the Levite walked by him. Yet the Samaritan somehow didn't let that limit him, nor did he let his Samaritanishness or the man's Jewishness limit him, either. So "impersonality" is meant to stand behind a stronger moral claim than can be generated from the notions of personality and rights.

The impersonal is for Weil absolutely prior to any individual aspects of the human. Now that wounds our vanity, for we like to think what we have made of ourselves is really important. But in the end the impersonal may alone be that which sustains our infinite love and concern–and what in us allows us to transcend our own personal aspirations in order to care for another. I refer here to a point made by Stanley Cavell. Cavell, in discussing Wittgenstein's dismissal of private languages, notes that often people object to that dismissal because they think that by taking away the privacy of, say, the way they want to talk about pain sensations, something important about our inner life is also taken away. He goes on to say:

> In a way this is true. I think one moral of the *Investigations* as a whole can be drawn as follows: The fact, and the state, of your

> (inner) life cannot take its importance from anything special in it. However far you have gone with it, you will find that what is common is there before you are. The state of your life may be, and may be all that is, worth your infinite interest. But then that can only exist along with a complete disinterest toward it. The soul is impersonal.[17]

What both Weil and Cavell seem to be saying is that if we are wholly and infinitely committed to making space for human souls in the world, it cannot be because of their interesting–or our interested–features. The commitment must be farther reaching than that. It must transcend the world of the personal, and be impersonal. For that is where the soul of the true lover and beloved dwells. It is not Maritain's point at all, I think. But I do think he in some way was responsible for Weil coming to it.

[17] Stanley Cavell, *The Claim of Reason* (Oxford: Oxford University Press, 1979), p. 361.

## THE PERSON IN AMERICA

John F. Morris

### I Persons and Personhood

Jacques Maritain begins *The Person and the Common Good*, with the following statement:

> Among the truths of which contemporary thought stands in particular need and from which it could draw substantial profit is the doctrine of the distinction between individuality and personality.[1]

However, Maritain goes on to note:

> The essential importance of this distinction is revealed in the principles of St. Thomas. Unfortunately a right understanding of it is difficult to achieve and requires an exercise of metaphysical insight to which the contemporary mind is hardly accustomed.[2]

Now, the concepts of "individuality" and "personhood" are certainly important in the contemporary American vocabulary. However, these notions–especially that of "personhood"–are rarely applied correctly, philosophically speaking. Indeed, the term *person* has become co-opted and corrupted in contemporary American public debate. Today, we find the terms *person* and "personhood" being given numerous social and political definitions that are influenced heavily by a naturalistic/reductionist view of reality. Contemporary political and ethical debates in America often revolve around questions of "personhood," which is only "asserted" of an individual based upon certain criteria established by some group in power. However, even though we find the term "personhood" being applied in many different ways, I will argue that there is a metaphysical basis for the concept *person* that is grounded in human nature. This metaphysical basis for *person* provides an objective foundation upon which we can judge the

---

[1] Jacques Maritain, *The Person and the Common Good* (Notre Dame, Indiana: University of Notre Dame Press, 1966), p.11.

[2] Ibid.

appropriateness of current debates regarding the "personhood" of certain individuals within society. Thus, when a prominent figure like Peter Singer claims that, "In regarding a newborn infant as not having the same right to life as a person, the cultures that practiced infanticide were on solid ground,"[3] we need not stand back and say, "*Well, that's an opinion we must respect in the name of tolerance and pluralism.*" Instead, it can be argued that such an assertion is, in fact, wrong. The error here is one of applying a malformed and impoverished understanding of "personhood," which in turn results from a malformed and impoverished view of the human *person.*

The sad fact today is that many contemporary philosophers have lost sight of the reality behind the concept of "personhood." And, this is not an error to take lightly. As John Kavanaugh, S.J., notes in his recent book, *Who Count As Persons*?:

> Underneath systems of racism, oppression, and sexual exploitation lie the fundamental dynamics of moral evil. Evil is a rejection of the truth of who and what we are as persons. It is a repression of the evidence that points to our truth. It is a denial of ethics itself, grounded in the reality of personhood.[4]

In this light, we see that the debate over the term *person* is not simply a matter of rhetoric. The dangers involved with allowing some members of society to determine who is a *person* and who is not are quite real, and jeopardize all of the vulnerable within a society. To respond to this particular evil that dwells within contemporary American culture, I will draw upon the insights of St. Thomas Aquinas and Jacques Maritain–two of the great defenders of the human *person*–in an effort to exemplify an authentic understanding of "personhood." I will also draw upon the work of Fr. Kavanaugh, and his more contemporary critique of American culture. In particular, I want to expand upon Kavanaugh's claim that:

---

[3] Peter Singer, *Rethinking Life and Death* (New York: St. Martin's Press, 1995), p. 255.

[4] John Kavanaugh, S.J., *Who Count As Persons?* (Washington, D.C.: Georgetown University Press, 2001), p. 107.

> The fact that we are persons is why we experience the world ethically, why we inevitably feel moral outrage and make judgments about value–even though we might not be able to justify or rationalize our outrage. I argue that if we are going to take morality seriously, we must know what being a human person means, who counts as a person, and what the implications of personhood are.[5]

In the end, my goal is to reaffirm (echoing the words of Maritain):

> ...the personalism rooted in the doctrine of St. Thomas and to separate... a social philosophy centered in the dignity of the human person from every social philosophy centered in the primacy of the individual and the private good.[6]

I realize this is no small task. But it is my conviction that as long as we hold on to our common human experience, we can continue to assert the truth of authentic "personhood" in the face of contemporary relativism, naturalism, and reductionism, thereby protecting and promoting the dignity of each and every human *person*.

### II What is a Person?

Let us begin by examining the term *person* itself. What does the term literally mean? Our English term "person" has its roots in the Latin word, "persona"–which itself is a combination of the phrase "per sonans," which means to "speak through," or even to "sound through." This Latin phrase is itself related to the older Greek phrase, "pros opon," which means "see through and out" in reference to a mask. And so, this phrase is an allusion to the masks worn by the actors, or "personas," represented in Greek plays. In discussing the etymology of the term *person* in his book, *Who Count As Persons?*, John Kavanaugh explains the connection here:

> To be a person is to be an expressive animal, a self-creating drama, a center of action, a narrative becoming conscious of itself, revealing and yet concealed through the embodiment of

---

[5] Ibid., p. 139.

[6] Jacques Maritain, op. cit., p. 13.

> mask. The mask is not a pretense–although it can be. It is a revelation, an expression, an externalization that is one with the actor.[7]

In sum, it is our ability to reveal ourselves to others–which, in turn, is only possible because we are self-aware that marks human beings as *persons*. This capacity for self-revelation is itself a part of our common, shared human nature.

For his own part, St. Thomas gives the following definition of *person* in the First Part of the *Summa Theologiae*, Question 29, Article 1, as he discusses the Trinity:

> ...in a more special and perfect way, the particular and individual are found in the rational substances which have dominion over their own actions; and which are not only made to act, like others; but which can act themselves; for actions belong to singulars. Therefore, also the individuals of the rational nature have a special name even among other substances; and this name is *person*.[8]

St. Thomas proceeds to clarify and nuance this definition, which is drawn in part from Aristotle and Boethius, throughout the remainder of his discussion on the Trinity. For example, St. Thomas explains that the human soul by itself is not properly referred to as a *person*; rather, in the case of human beings, the term *person* applies to human nature taken as a whole.[9] In Article 3 of this same question, St. Thomas refines his definition further: "*Person* signifies what is most perfect in all nature–that is, a subsistent individual of a rational nature."[10]

In this third article, St. Thomas also goes on to give an account of the origins of the term *person*. In his reply to the second objection,

---

[7] John Kavanaugh, op. cit., p. 62.

[8] Thomas Aquinas, *Summa Theologiae* (cited hereafter as *ST*), I, q. 29, a. 1, literally translated by the Fathers of the English Dominican Province, Volume I (New York: Benzinger Brothers, 1947), p. 156.

[9] Ibid., ad. 5; see, also, *ST* I, q. 29, a.2, ad. 3 (p. 157), and a. 4 (p. 159).

[10] Ibid., a. 3 (p. 158).

Aquinas explains why it is proper to apply the term person to God, even though the term did not itself originate from Sacred Scripture:

> Although this name *person* may not belong to God as regards the origin of the term, nevertheless it excellently belongs to God in its objective meaning. For as famous men were represented in comedies and tragedies, the name *person* was given to signify those who held high dignity. Hence, those who held high rank in the Church came to be called *persons*. Thence by some the definition of person is given as *hypostasis distinct by reason of dignity*. And because subsistence in a rational nature is of high dignity, therefore every individual of the rational nature is called a *person*. Now the dignity of the divine nature excels every other dignity; and thus the name *person* pre-eminently belongs to God.[11]

In this discussion, St. Thomas–recognizing the roots of the term *person* in the ancient tradition of Greek plays–reveals that all human beings are *persons* because of our common, shared, intellectual nature. This is a significant point, in that human society is still struggling to recognize this truth fully. Unfortunately today, not all human beings are considered *persons* in the metaphysical sense expressed in Thomas' definition. Nevertheless, the truth remains–even before the human intellect came to understand God as *person*, and before leaders of the Church were recognized as *persons*, and before other human beings were recognized as *persons* due to their subsistent, rational nature–all of these were indeed *persons* properly understood. This emphasizes that, in the Thomistic understanding, the term *person* is not simply the reflection of a social or political designation, but rather that *person* refers to a metaphysical reality that exists independently of whether or not that reality is recognized in the social or political order.

Now, what exactly is the metaphysical reality referred to here? The rational nature of a human being. As Maritain explains in *The Person and the Common Good*:

---

[11] Ibid., ad. 2.

> ...such are the two metaphysical aspects of the human being, individuality and personality, together with their proper ontological features. However evident it may seem, in order to avoid misunderstandings and nonsense, we must emphasize that they are not two separate things. There is not in me one reality, called my individual, and another reality, called my person. One and the same reality is, in a certain sense an individual, and, in another sense, a person. Our whole being is an individual by reason of that in us which derives from matter, and a person by reason of that in us which derives from spirit.[12]

Here Maritain emphasizes the Thomistic insight that human beings are *persons* in the totality of our being–physical and spiritual. In more contemporary terms, Kavanaugh argues that:

> To speak of a human as a personal nature is to refer to the fact of embodiment. The human cannot be reduced to some rigid or fixed model of nature. A human–paradoxically because of the "natural" endowment of self-consciousness–transcends any attempt to fully constrain human behavior. We humans, as personal animals, share an "open" nature because "what" we are is the kind of being endowed with distinguishing capacities of *self-conscious* embodiment whereby we are freed from any inflexible or determined "playing out" of our natural drives. We are not "owned by" our built-in capacities because one of our capacities is an endowment wherein we can own ourselves.[13]

What we need to pay special attention to is this notion of an "endowment," and what this means in terms of a being's nature. Everything that exists has an essence or nature. It is this essence or nature that makes a thing what it is. The essence of a thing is discovered by observing its activities and function (as Aristotle noted). However–and this is the crucial point–once we have discovered the essence of a particular "kind" of thing, the intellect recognizes that every individual of the same "kind" will possess that same essence,

---

[12] Jacques Maritain, op. cit., p. 43.

[13] John Kavanaugh, op. cit., p. 66.

even if it does not exhibit all of the activities of its essence. A baby eagle that has yet to fly is still every bit as much an eagle as its mother–the fact that the baby eagle has yet to exhibit flight itself does not make it any less an eagle. Nor would it be appropriate to say that the baby is only "potentially" an eagle, and that it will only become an eagle once it can actually fly. Rather, we say that the baby eagle possesses the endowment or capacity for flight. The absence of an expression of a being's endowments does not mean those endowments themselves are absent. They are present in the being's nature. This is what makes this argument metaphysical: an endowment refers to a reality that penetrates deeper than what is empirically observable.

Indeed, the whole "potentiality" argument today regarding the human *person* is based on fallacious reasoning. Consider, for example, arguments favoring embryonic stem cell research. One of the arguments used in support of such research is that a zygote, blastocyst, and embryo represent only "potential" human life. But contemporary embryology tells us that this is not the case. While a zygote, blastocyst, or embryo may potentially one day be an astronaut, a musician, or a future President of the United States, what it IS is quite clear–it is ACTUAL human life. Further, while it is true that an actual being also possesses many future possibilities, those possibilities must relate to *real* potencies within the being in question. What this means, practically speaking, is that if someone wants to say that a human zygote is only "potential" human life, then that zygote must also at the same time have the potency to become something else entirely–which contemporary genetics points out is untrue. In fact, from the very moment of fertilization, a human is distinguishable from a pig, a cow, and even from a chimpanzee–which we are told bears less than a 5% genetic difference from a human being. And so, it is inappropriate to refer to any zygote as "potential" human life, as if it could become something else.

Part of the error in thinking that a fertilized human ovum is only "potentially" human life rests upon the mistaken notion that human development goes through "ontological" stages – that is, stages in which the being is actually changed when it passes through. Embryologists point out that while terms like zygote, embryo, and fetus have become convenient for discussing the progress of human development, they do not refer to what could be called actual stages of development except in an artificial sense. Our growing knowledge of genetics, fostered by the Human Genome Project, affirms that human development is a continuum–not a series of stages.[14] Nor is this simply a case of favoring one set of characteristics for "personhood" over another, as some have suggested.[15] A fertilized ovum coming from human gametes is at its very moment of fertilization something actual–and what it IS, is actual human life. It is "human" because of its human genetic material, and it is "life" because it is a *self-developing* entity.[16] And, when we add the metaphysical insight that human nature includes the endowment for rationality, then we can see that a human being–even in its most immature stages–is also a *person.*

Thus, when we speak of human nature, we are not referring to a merely static reality that can be equated with what is empirically evident. Rather, human nature must be understood in a dynamic sense, in that human nature contains all of the endowments and capacities of

---

[14] For two key examples, see Lee M. Silver, *Remaking Eden: Cloning and Beyond in a Brave New World*, (New York: Avon Books, 1997), or Ronan O'Rahilly and Fabiola Muller, *Human Embryology & Teratology*, 3rd ed. (New York: Wiley-Liss, 2001).

[15] Jane English, "Abortion and the Concept of a Person," in *Biomedical Ethics*, 3rd edition, edited by Mappes and Zembaty (New York: McGraw-Hill, 1991), p. 447.

[16] The issue of *self-development* is crucial to understand, as it clarifies the confusion that some people raise regarding human gametes considered individually. Some try to argue that if one claims that the fertilized ovum is called "human life," then we must also call a human sperm or a human egg "human life" as well, since sperm and eggs are "alive" and they are "human." And so they try to reduce the argument that a fertilized ovum is "human life" to absurdity. But their approach fails, for the simple reason that sperm and eggs by themselves are not *self-developing.* Unless a complete genetic code is actuated within an ovum (either through natural reproduction, *in vitro* fertilization, or one of the various cloning techniques), there will be no new human entity or being. But once a complete genetic code is actuated, a new, *self-developing* entity begins to unfold. To put this in philosophical terms, at fertilization a substantial change takes place and a new being begins to exist.

human beings in general, even though all of those capacities may not be fully actuated within a particular, individual human being. Kavanaugh eloquently summarizes this point when he writes:

> One is either a human person or not a human person. A human person is an unfolding reality, a historical being in which personal endowments make possible the emergence of activities, among which are knowing, loving, and choosing freely. Many humans never "fulfill" their potentials, whether through a lack of maturation or opportunity. Many others can no longer fulfill their potential because of trauma to or aging of the human body. They are still persons, however, even though unfulfilled or injured.[17]

In sum, what makes a human being a *person* is the human essence itself, not how that human essence is exhibited to others.

### III The Contemporary Error–The Fallacy of "Personhood"

In light of the previous understanding of the human *person*, the contemporary errors that arise in discussions and debates over human "personhood" are more easily recognized. Consider, for example, the rhetoric of "personhood" that has arisen in the current debates over abortion. It is commonly asserted by pro-choice advocates that a zygote, an embryo, or a fetus is not a *person*, and therefore abortion remains the sole decision of a pregnant woman. Since no other *person* is involved, abortion becomes solely her choice. Now, the reason that it is argued that a zygote, an embryo, or a fetus is not a *person* is because zygotes, embryos, and fetuses do not exhibit the characteristics of "personhood." But what are the characteristics of "personhood"? One can find a number of different "lists" regarding what constitutes "personhood," but one helpful illustration is found in Mary Anne Warren's pivotal pro-abortion piece, "On the Moral and Legal Status of Abortion." In this often cited and anthologized article, Warren offers these criteria:

---

[17] John Kavanaugh, op. cit., p. 69.

> I suggest that the traits which are most central to the concept of personhood, or humanity in the moral sense, are, very roughly, the following:
>
> 1) Consciousness (of objects and events external and/or internal to the being), and in particular the capacity to feel pain;
>
> 2) Reasoning (the *developed* capacity to solve new and relatively complex problems;
>
> 3) Self-motivated activity (activity which is relatively independent of either genetic or direct external control);
>
> 4) The capacity to communicate, by whatever means, messages of an indefinite variety of types, that is, not just with an indefinite number of possible contents, but on indefinitely many possible topics;
>
> 5) The presence of self-concepts, and self-awareness, either individual or racial, or both.[18]

After offering some qualifying remarks about this list, Warren draws the following conclusion:

> Now if (1)-(5) are indeed the primary criteria of personhood, then it is clear that genetic humanity is neither necessary nor sufficient for establishing that an entity is a person. Some human beings are not people, and there may well be people who are not human beings. A man or woman whose consciousness has been permanently obliterated but who remains alive is a human being which is no longer a person; defective human beings, with no appreciable mental capacity, are not and presumably never will be people; and a fetus is a human being which is not yet a person, and which therefore cannot coherently be said to have full moral rights.[19]

The implications of Warren's position are clear–if one does not, cannot, or

---

[18] Mary Anne Warren, "On the Moral and Legal Status of Abortion," in *Biomedical Ethics*, p. 440; emphasis added.

[19] Ibid.

no longer can exhibit the characteristics of "personhood," then one is not a *person*.

To make this even clearer, we can turn to a later piece of Warren's, "The Moral Significance of Birth," in which she adds:

> Women are already persons in the usual, nonlegal sense–already thinking, self-aware, fully social beings–and fetuses are not. Regardless of whether we stress the intrinsic properties of persons, or the social and relational dimensions of personhood, this distinction remains. Even sentient fetuses do not yet have either the cognitive capacities or the richly interactive social involvements typical of persons.[20]

Forget the obvious fact that we are talking about human beings, who are of the same "kind" as we, and with whom we share a common rational nature–Warren asserts that if you do not act like a *person* then you are not a *person*. A review of pro-choice arguments that have been presented since Roe v. Wade in 1973 would show that Warren's argument is typical, and thus serves as an apt illustration of the emphasis on "personhood" as the determining factor for who does and does not count as a *person*.

In a slightly different, although still related, vein, Peter Singer uses a similar line of argument in his discussions of contemporary ethics. In his book, *Practical Ethics*, Singer addresses the permissibility of killing human beings based upon whether or not the being in question possesses these same characteristics of "personhood." Singer argues that:

> ...the fact that a being is a human being, in the sense of a member of the species Homo sapiens, is not relevant to the wrongness of killing it; it is, rather, characteristics like rationality, autonomy, and self-consciousness that make a difference. Infants lack these characteristics. Killing them, therefore, cannot be equated with killing normal human beings, or any other self-conscious beings. This conclusion is not limited

[20] Mary Anne Warren, "The Moral Significance of Birth," in *Bioethics, Justice, & Health Care*, eds.Wanda Teays and Laura M. Purdy (Belmont, California: Wadsworth, 2001), p. 480.

> to infants who, because of irreversible intellectual disabilities, will never be rational, self-conscious beings. We saw in our discussion of abortion that the potential of a fetus to become a rational, self-conscious being cannot count against killing it at a stage when it lacks these characteristics–not, that is, unless we are also prepared to count the value of rational self-conscious life as a reason against contraception and celibacy. No infant–disabled or not–has as strong a claim to life as beings capable of seeing themselves as distinct entities, existing over time.[21]

Even though Singer himself does not specifically argue in this passage that fetuses and newborns are not *persons*, he still employs what have become the basic characteristics of "personhood"–rationality, autonomy, and self-consciousness. His argument for the permissibility of killing the unborn or the newborn originates with the claim that infants and fetuses lack these characteristics of "personhood." But the key point of emphasis is that Singer, as Warren, asserts that both the unborn and the newborn lack the characteristics of "personhood" for the simple reason that fetuses and infants do not *exhibit* those characteristics.

As we compare the claims of Warren, Singer, and the many others who seek to deny "personhood" of the weak and vulnerable within human society, with the Thomistic understanding of the human *person*, we can begin to identify the lack of metaphysical insight within contemporary American social, political, and ethical debates. Various forces within society could be identified as causing this lack–naturalism, materialism, empiricalism, reductionism, and so on. But my purpose here is only to point out the error itself. Those who would deny "personhood" of the unborn, the comatose, and the near death, have replaced the reality of the human *person* with the concept of "personhood." In turn, they view the concept of "personhood" only from their naturalistic, empirical perspective of reality, and simply refuse to consider that there may be more to reality than "matter" and "sense data." To counter this, Kavanaugh argues that:

---

[21] Peter Singer, excerpted from *Practical Ethics*, 2nd Edition (Cambridge: Cambridge University Press), 1993. http://www.petersingerlinks.com/taking/ .htm.

> Human infants do not become persons when they start thinking they are persons. Thinking is just one stage of personal development, made possible by the capacity to do so. A woman in a sixteen-year coma does not cease being a human person and then suddenly have her personhood stuck back on when she revives. She was never in a vegetative "state." She was in the state of being a human person, endowed with human capacities and yet so massively damaged in the cortex that many of these capacities could not be exercised, few of them could be revealed, and for a while none could be externally acknowledged by others. What she regains upon revival are the organic conditions required for the embodied self-expression of these capacities.[22]

Every human being, by virtue of our shared, rational nature, is a *person.* The reality of our humanness is present, even when it is not externally revealed. But when this reality is not evident, the burden does not fall on the underdeveloped or damaged human being to prove its worth, but rather upon us to use reason to penetrate into the reality that lies before us in the unborn, the comatose, and the near death.

Indeed, I believe that the line of reasoning used by thinkers such as Warren and Singer is nothing more than a highly stylized version of the "straw-man" fallacy. After all, concepts do not just pop out of thin air. Human ideas are not innate. Rather, human knowledge is derived from our encounter with the real world. In this case, our concept of "personhood" is drawn from our experience of *persons* within the world. From the particular, individual beings we have encountered in our lived experience, we derive an idea of "personhood." However, as we explained earlier, our knowledge is not limited to particulars, but rather reflects an understanding of things in the world as "kinds" and "types." And so, one "kind" of thing that the idea *person* correlates with is a human being. This means that our understanding of "personhood" is drawn from our knowledge and experience of all human beings–including the unborn, comatose, and near death. To turn around and apply the concept of "personhood" in a manner that excludes some members of the human race strips the very idea of "personhood" of its

---

[22] John Kavanaugh, op. cit., pp. 67-68.

metaphysical basis–thus, our "straw man." Limiting the criteria of "personhood" ultimately to what can be exhibited, and therefore empirically validated, simply leaves no way to include human beings who are either still in their development or who have been damaged in some fashion. The concept is too narrow to include the fullness of the reality. In sum, if someone asserts criteria for "personhood" that will not include all human beings, then that notion is malformed and incomplete.

Now we must not gloss too quickly over these concerns raised by the notion of "personhood" and its restrictive applications. During the debates leading up to the Civil War in this country, it was consistently argued by proponents of slavery that the Africans were not fully *persons.* Male slaves could be counted as part of the census by Southern States, but not as representing a whole man. Yet, if a slave could escape to the North, or become free in some other manner, then he suddenly became a *person* and could become an American citizen. This fact illustrates the arbitrary manner in which "personhood" is assigned by various social groups. It is worth noting that at the same time male slaves could be partially counted in the population during a census as part of determining representation in the legislatures, women and children–both African and American–did not count at all. Throughout human history, women and children have not been fully treated as *persons.* It would also serve us well to reflect upon the atrocities committed by the Nazis upon the Jewish people during the Holocaust. The Nazi propaganda machine focused upon physical attributes of Jews that they argued were signs of genetic inferiority. The goal of Nazi propaganda was to argue that the Jews were dispensable because they were not full *persons.*

And so, given that to the naked eye Africans were much more similar to Americans, and Jews much more similar to Germans, and women much more similar to men, than the unborn, the comatose, the deformed and defective are to you and I, the risk of depersonalizing human beings who do not empirically look and act like us is great. Indeed, the greater the empirical differences, the easier it seems to be to exclude others as *persons.* If one carefully examines the rhetoric behind these and other similar arguments, one finds that the notion of "personhood" is most often applied in a manner that is designed to do just that–exclude certain individuals or groups from the larger group. Such exclusion marks those not deemed *persons* as vulnerable to the whims and desires of the larger group. Kavanaugh points out the serious dangers of this reductionist attitude towards the human *person* when he writes:

> To negate personhood, to deny its reality, to repress its moral truth, is the foundational negation of all ethics. To reduce men and women to the condition of replaceable and expendable objects is to deny their reality and to deny the foundation of the ethical impulse. It is the primary ethical negation. It is the primary ethical rejection. Thus, the positive formulation of the primary law of all ethical behavior is this: Affirm the reality of personal existence. Less abstractly, it requires the love of persons and the love of personal existence, for all love is the affirmation of the truth of the beloved as being good.
>
> The negative formulation is this: Do not treat persons as non-persons. Do not reduce persons to the status of an object.[23]

In the end, we may not be able to change the opinions of thinkers such as Warren and Singer, and others who share their empirical, naturalistic bent. Indeed, it is the contemporary disposition towards naturalism and empiricism that prevents many from seeing the metaphysical reality of the human *person*. However, that does not mean that we must simply accept their reductionist view of "personhood." Instead, we must continually assert the truth of what a human *person* is, and of who count as *persons*.

### IV Conclusion: The Person in America

The title of this paper is "The Person in America." That is why my comments have been restricted specifically to American social and ethical debates. But there is another reason why I specified "America" in this discussion, and it relates to Jacques Maritain's own feelings towards America as expressed in his *Reflections on America*. Maritain's "reflections" on America can be described quite simply as "hopeful" and "optimistic." Maritain saw in America the promise of greatness–

---

[23] Ibid., p. 108.

not as a superpower, or as an economic giant, but primarily as a genuinely human community. He tells us, "America is the only country in the world where the vital importance of the sense of human fellowship is recognized in such a basic manner by the nation as a whole."[24] As such, America should provide fertile ground for establishing the true *common good* of humanity, with its emphasis on democracy and human fellowship. Indeed, as Maritain notes at the end of *The Person and the Common Good*:

> In the final analysis, the relation of the individual to society must not be conceived after the atomistic and mechanistic pattern of bourgeois individualism which destroys the organic social totality, or after the biological and animal pattern of the statist or racist totalitarian conception which swallows up the person, here reduced to a mere histological element of Behemoth or Leviathan, in the body of the state, or after the biological and industrial pattern of the Communistic conception which ordains the entire person, like a worker in the great human hive, to the proper work of the social whole. The relation of the individual to society must be conceived after an irreducibly human and specifically ethiosocial pattern, that is, personalist and communalist at the same time; the organization to be accomplished is one of liberties.[25]

America, as the land of liberty, is the ideal place to establish an authentic human society that fully respects the human *person* as a being of inherent dignity and worth. And, to a certain extent, I would agree that America is the best refuge for the human *person*. I would ague that in America *persons* are given the widest range of rights and liberties in the world, and that the dignity of *persons* is supported at all levels of American society. The problem, however, is that Americans have failed to recognize exactly who count as *persons*.

Our own *Constitution* notes that life, liberty, and the pursuit of happiness are *inalienable* rights–that is, rights that cannot be taken

---

[24] Jacques Maritain, *Reflections on America* (New York: Image Books, 1964), p. 42.

[25] Jacques Maritain, *The Person and the Common Good*, pp.101-02.

from anyone. And yet we can find many examples of the failures within American society–both in our past as well as our present–in which these *inalienable* rights are indeed denied to certain human beings. However, I think that the crucial point to be emphasized here is that denying the *inalienable* rights of various marginalized members of our society, as well as failing to recognize that all human beings are *persons* and deserve to be treated as such, is a violation of the spirit and principles of America. I would echo the words of Maritian in his *Reflections on America* when he decries the evil of racism and the horrific acts that it leads to in American society. Of these evil actions that damage American life, Maritain notes, "They are a plague on it, and they are incompatible with its spirit, the sense of human fellowship inherent in its people, and the very tenets in which living together is founded here."[26] Later, Maritain adds:

> ...what we witness when we consider in a general way the race question in America, is the spectacle of a nation which struggles doggedly against itself, or, more accurately, against large segments of its own people, against a certain legacy of evil in its own mores, and against the demons of the human heart–in order to free itself of abuses which are repellent to its own spirit, and to raise its entire practical behavior to the level of the tenets and principles in which it believes and in the strength of which it was born.[27]

I believe that these words continue to ring true today regarding those in American society who would exclude the unborn, the newborn, the damaged, and the near death from consideration as *persons*. The exclusion of some members of our society surely flies in the face of what America, as the land of inclusion, stands for. These errors must continue to be repudiated, and America's promise renewed.

I close with these words of John Kavanaugh, S.J., who vividly reminds us of what is at stake here:

---

[26] Jacques Maritain, *Reflections on America*, p. 33.

[27] Ibid, p. 34.

In the recovery of personal existence, consequently, one final habit of life recommends itself: to expose our hearts and intellects to the “damaged,” the “handicapped,” the “defective,” and the “avoided.” They may reveal to us the deepest truths of our being and the inadequacy of all our philosophies. In avoiding the wounded we may well be avoiding the truth. For what is defective in them serves to remind us of the contingency that is one with our frail embodiment as persons. What we lose by ignoring them may be nothing less than the power of our humanity to call forth and bestow love.[28]

[28] John Kavanaugh, op. cit., p. 158.

# MARITAIN, CONNATURALITY, AND THE AMERICAN FAMILY[*]

James G. Hanink

## I Introduction

In *Reflections on America*, writing about marriage on "the American scene," Jacques Maritain laments "I am afraid a whole book would be necessary to attempt a satisfactory study of it."[1] Indeed, he continues, "the problem of the relations between the sexes seems to me to be still more important...in this country than that of the relations between management and labor, and even that of the relations between races."[2] Four decades later and just as provocatively, Robert George calls attention to our tendency to treat children as property. In *The Clash of Orthodoxies,* he links this abuse to a "fast eroding" understanding of sex and marriage.[3] Ironically, the traditional understanding is "under severe assault from people who have no conscious desire to reduce children to the status of mere means."[4]

For his part, however, George gives us a deliberately robust definition of marriage. It is "a two-in-one-flesh communion of persons that is consummated and actualized by acts that are reproductive in

---

[*]Anne Barbeau Gardiner helped me achieve much of the still insufficient unity of these reflections.

[1] Jacques Maritain, *Reflections on America* (Garden City, New York: Image Books, 1964), p. 82. What might American feminists make of this? Consider, for example, Catherine MacKinnon's inflammatory indictment: "[M]ale dominance is perhaps the most pervasive and tenacious system of power in history." For the defense, see Christina Sommers's "The Feminist Revelation" in Christiana Sommers and Fred Sommers, *Vice & Virtue in Everyday Life* (New York: Harcourt Publishers, 2001), p. 80.

[2] Ibid., pp. 82-83.

[3] Robert George, *The Clash of Orthodoxies: Law, Religion, and Morality in Crisis,* Foreword by John J. DiIulio, Jr. (Wilmington, Delaware: ISI Books, 2001), p. 80.

[4] Ibid., p. 80. If this is true, we need to renew the ancient prayer, "Forgive us our sins, both deliberate and indeliberate." It occurs in the Liturgy of St. John Chrysostom at the communion of the celebrants.

type."[5] Conjugal love needn't be motivated by a desire to reproduce, but an openness to life is critical. Children are gifts that supervene intercourse and fulfill the community that it actualizes. They are, he continues, "properly understood and treated–even in their conception–not as means to their parents' ends, but as ends-in-themselves."[6]

To be sure, its cultured despisers dismiss this understanding of sex and marriage as a relic of oppression. In doing so, they often rehearse for us how much in American life *has* changed of late, including the very texture of national debate. Manifestly, the Princeton of Jacques Maritain, Robert George–and Peter Singer–reflects such change.

Yet there are questions to raise about these, or any, changes. *What* is it that changes? And is the change for good or for ill? In any case, however changing the context, we remain the agents of our sexuality and the architects of family life. We can live in marriage wisely, or not. We can nurture our children wisely, or not. To do so would be impossible had we neither nature nor intelligible potentiality. Because we have both, there is a natural law that illuminates conjugal love and the nurturing of a family.[7]

---

[5] Ibid., p. 77. Elizabeth Anscombe, in a like vein, writes that the "good and the point of a sexual act is marriage," and that intercourse is to be a "reproductive type of act," adding "(I don't mean of course that every act is reproductive any more than every acorn leads to an oak-tree)": see her *Contraception and Chastity* (London: Catholic Truth Society, 1977), p. 21 and p. 5. Dorothy Day offers a still deeper dimension: "Our beds may be altars at which we kneel to pray, and on which we receive the sacrament of matrimony, giving and receiving in a communion which is a foretaste of the beatific vision." See her *On Pilgrimage*, Foreword by Michael O. Garvey, Introduction by Mark and Louise Zwick (Grand Rapids, Michigan: Eerdmans, 1999), p. 132.

[6] Ibid., p. 80. Like Karol Wojtyla in his *Love and Responsibility*, George draws on the language of Kant's Categorical imperative: see *Love and Responsibility*, trans. H.T. Willetts (New York: Farrar, Straus, Giroux, 1981), especially pp. 27-28.

[7] Perhaps here one needn't support this claim. Consider Maritain's precedent: "Since I have not time here to discuss nonsense (we can always find very intelligent philosophers, not to quote Mr. Bertrand Russell, to defend it most

Still, we often come to know this law with difficulty. To help explain this embarrassment, Maritain distinguishes between the ontological and the gnoseological natural law. Ontological natural law is within us; it shares our essential reality. Gnoseological natural law is that law insofar as we know and articulate it. Doing so, for Maritain, depends on *connaturality*, that is, a settled inclination to pursue the true or the good that prompts one to judge or act in particular cases.[8] Thus, Catherine Green characterizes connaturality in terms of an agent's having "formed himself in relation to the good."[9] Connaturality eludes the algorithmic and yet remains a *sine qua non* for human reasoning. Through connaturality our natural inclinations attune, as it were, our intellects to the dynamism of the human subject.[10]

Herein, though, the Christian thinker meets a pluriform dilemma. Our inclinations and intellects suffer from the wounds of original sin. Moreover, our inclinations are partly shaped by unjust social institutions. Dare we still hope that such discordant inclinations will attune our intellects? Can we articulate the role of natural law in marriage and family if our inclinations in their regard are dissonant? And how are we to frame a Christian understanding of marriage when, as Elizabeth Anscombe put it, society "has wrecked or deformed this human thing?"[11]

---

brilliantly), I am taking it for granted that we admit that there is a human nature" *Man and the State* (Washington, D.C.: The Catholic University of America Press, 1998), p. 85.

[8] Here I follow Ralph McInerny in *Art and Prudence: Studies in the Thought of Jacques Maritain* (Notre Dame, Indiana: University of Notre Dame Press, 1988), p. 163.

[9] Catherine Green, "It Takes One to Know One: Connaturality–Knowledge or Prejudice?," in *Jacques Maritain and the Many Ways of Knowing*, ed. Douglas A. Ollivant, Introduction by George Anastaplo (Washington, D.C.: American Maritain Association, 2002), p. 54.

[10] Jacques Maritain, *Man and the State*, pp. 89-92.

[11] Elizabeth Anscombe, *Contraception and Chastity*, p. 21.

## II The American Family: a Dilemma in Focus

In flagging the special dignity of children, Robert George sharpens the focus on the dilemma before us. "It goes without saying," he is nonetheless quick to say, "that not all cultures have fully grasped these truths about the moral status of children."[12] With equal paradox, it goes without saying, not all cultures fully grasp the truth that marriage is a two-in-one-flesh union of persons. Among these cultures is our own. It is this culture, and its America, which the Christian must confront.

But wait, says Dame Philosophy. A stern mistress she! How is a natural law thinker, if a Christian, in any position to confront an invasively secular culture? Well aware of the dilemma which George helps us specify, she is keen to pay it her regards. How better to do so than by restating its three vexing problems? First, as noted, there is the legacy of original sin. How can wounded inclinations harmonize damaged intellects? Second, our social institutions disorder our inclinations. How can they, sustaining this fresh damage, attune our intellects? And, lastly, how can one confront the culture in the language of natural law if one stutters in its articulation?

Yet even with her hard questions, our mistress serves us well. If she cannot now answer the questions she highlights, perhaps her challenge will help us do so. Let's address each in turn.

## III Elements of a Resolution

Consider, first, the wounds of original sin.[13] They have taken from us the original justice of our first parents. We retain, however, the core principles of our nature. Yet even these are intact only at their roots. Maritain comments: "What is... weakened by the first sin in the *human nature transmitted to all men* is... *the natural ordering* toward virtue, not so much as regards its root in the essence of the soul, but rather as

---

[12] Robert George, *The Clash of Orthodoxies*, p. 80.

[13] For Maritain's analysis of the effect of original sin on the speculative intellect, see my "The Wounds of the Intelligence," *Études Maritainiennes / Maritian Studies*, Vol. XVII (2001): 103-11.

regards the state of its development."[14] This weakening of natural inclination affects our pursuit of both the good and of the true, and painfully so in our marriages and families.

What, then, are we to make of this disordering? Rejoice that the roots of our nature are intact and recognize that only grace can bring us to flourish. Maritain writes: "If here and there, in what he does, a man arrives at the peak of his natural possibilities, it is because grace which raises him to the supernatural has also 'cured' him in the order of his nature."[15] Is not the theologian to pursue his vocation on his knees? Maritain asks philosophers to do the same.[16] Much more might be said on this score, but at another time.

Here we do better to turn to Dame Philosophy's second question. Our social institutions further disorder our inclinations. How, then, can these same inclinations attune our intellects?

Because this question is so pressing, we must first clarify what these inclinations are. Neither concepts nor judgments, they are rather the vital elements of connatural knowledge. Maritain sees them as a matrix of "congeniality."[17] He writes that "the intellect, in order to bear judgment, consults and listens to the inner melody that the vibrating strings of abiding tendencies make present in the subject."[18] With St. Thomas, he teaches that those things to which we have a natural

---

[14] Jacques Maritain, *Untrammeled Approaches*, trans. Bernard Doering (Notre Dame, Indiana: University of Notre Dame Press, 1997), p. 212.

[15] Ibid., p. 207.

[16] On this point, see Ralph McInerny's *Art and Prudence*, pp. 184-85.

[17] Jacques Maritain, *Man and the State*, p. 87. The expert gardener and the savvy horse-breeder, he says, exemplify this congeniality. Maritain also speaks of "connaturality or congeniality" in (among other places) his "On Knowledge Through Connaturality," a paper read to the Metaphysical Society of America in 1951 and reprinted in Jacques Maritain, *Natural Law: Reflections on Theory and Practice*, edited and introduced by William Sweet (South Bend, Indiana: St. Augustine's Press, 2001), pp. 15 and 20.

[18] Ibid., p. 92.

inclination reason naturally apprehends as good.[19] Reason, to be sure, must harmonize our inclinations; yet we also experience a natural inclination to act according to reason.[20]

Still, even the corrective interplay of reason and inclination can fail.[21] Focusing on inclinations as "tendential frameworks" and "dynamic schemes," Maritain laments "the warped... inclinations" that mingle with those that are healthy and more basic.[22] Defective inclinations are often "accidents of social evolution."[23] They disorder both individuals and "social structures," and thus block the recognition of core human rights.[24] Thus, he anticipates the "structures of sin" that John Paul II identifies as among the signs of the times.[25]

Here a comparison is helpful. Max Weber's identification of "the iron cage" of modernity also illustrates how social structures can disorder our individual inclinations.[26] Indeed, Charles Taylor speaks of a series of iron cages: atomistic individualism, technological tyranny, and the bureaucratic instrumentalizing of reason.[27] Each phenomenon takes structural forms; together they lead some to suppose that there is no antidote for our alienation. Could the pessimists be right? Can we even hope to escape these cages? Taylor is soberly hopeful. We ourselves

---

[19] Thomas Aquinas, *Summa Theologiae,* I-II, q. 94, a. 2.

[20] Ibid., a. 3. See, too, Maritain's reference to our "reason-permeated inclinations" in "On Knowledge Through Connaturality," loc. cit., p. 20.

[21] For perceptive comments on this critical balance, both for theoretical and practical reason, see again Ralph McInerny, *Art and Prudence*, especially pp. 148 and 163.

[22] Jacques Maritain, *Man and the State*, p. 93.

[23] Jacques Maritain, "On Knowledge Through Connaturality," loc. cit., p. 22.

[24] Ibid., p. 102.

[25] John Paul II, *Sollicitudo rei socialis* #36.

[26] Max Weber, *The Protestant Ethic and the Spirit of Capitalism*, trans. Talcott Parsons (New York: Charles Scribner's Sons, 1958).

[27] Charles Taylor, *The Ethics of Authenticity* (Cambridge, Massachusetts: Harvard University Press, 1992); see, especially, Chapter IX, "An Iron Cage?," pp. 93-108.

have built these cages. Still, we cannot dismantle them without political struggle.[28]

With clarification and comparisons in hand, let's return to the question at issue. How can our socially disordered inclinations attune our intellects? The Christian natural law thinker must surely engage the political dimension. But equally critical, and logically prior, is the dimension of epistemic insight. Here we might well turn to two great friends of Christian philosophy.

John Henry Newman famously contrasts the fickleness of notional assent with the force of real assent. In doing so, he highlights our capacity to challenge "received opinion." We can, if we choose, accept it; we can, alternatively, treat it as an hypothesis; or we can flatly reject it. Newman's examples of notional assent, it happens, begin with political institutions and their partisans. ("Such are the assents," he tells us, "made upon habit and without reflection; as when a man calls himself a Tory or a Liberal, as having been brought up as such.")[29] And while we can make little headway without our familiar notions, we are often enough "ashamed" when we come into contact with "real facts" that supplant them. That this experience is so familiar shows, if nothing else, that we *can* overturn the prejudices of our social and political ambience.

A second friend of Christian philosophy, Dietrich von Hildebrand, offers another affirmation of our capacity for critical insight. In the Prolegomena of his *Christian Ethics*, he makes an initial request. We are "to follow [his] analysis of the data step by step and to suspend all explanations which have been offered in former theories, reductions, or interpretations, many of which...leave no room at all for the data in question."[30] In urging this turn to the given, von Hildebrand is not advocating a superficial descriptive psychology. Nor does he confuse

---

[28] Ibid., esp. pp. 103-08.

[29] John Henry Newman, *An Essay in Aid of a Grammar of Assent*, Introduction by Nicholas Lash, (Notre Dame, Indiana: University of Notre Dame Press, 1979), p. 53.

[30] Dietrich von Hildebrand, *Christian Ethics* (New York: David McKay Company, 1953), p. 3.

the given with a concatenation of sense data. The given, rather, is an intelligible object which "imposes itself on our intellect" and which we can engage with "intellectual intuition."[31] Our theories and reductions and interpretations, we know, often have a flawed social and political genesis. The phenomenological realist asks that we ourselves judge their adequacy. Our capacity to do so shows that we can, at least in part, free our inclinations from damaging distortions.

Von Hildebrand's first example of the given is the grandeur shining through the martyrdom of St. Stephen (*Acts* 7.55-60). For Christians, it is a telling choice. Here, though, I offer a second example of a striking "datum" of experience. It might lead believer and non-believer alike to dispute the distortions of socially controlled inclinations. A recent General Electric commercial extolling the technology of 4D ultrasound shows, with vivid clarity, the face of an unborn child. In the background, we hear the familiar melody of the sixties' song "The First Time Ever I Saw Your Face."[32] No matter, now, the authority of the secular establishments. It is enough to *see* the living reality of the human face. Emmanuel Levinas offers us a philosopher's corroboration. But the truth is ready at hand for those who can see.[33]

Our capacity for epistemic insight, to which Newman and von Hildebrand attest, helps us overcome the cultural distortion of our inclinations. And, to be sure, only insofar as these inclinations are well

---

[31] Ibid., p. 10.

[32] On the internet, see www.gemedicalsystems.com/rad/us/4d/ commercial .html. I thank Fr. Frank Pavone, of Priests for Life, for calling attention to this line of reflection.

[33] See Emmanuel Levinas, *Entre nous: on thinking-of-the-other*, trans. Michael B. Smith and Barbara Harshav (New York: Columbia University Press, 1998), especially pp. 147-52. For praise of Levinas's contribution, see John Paul II, *Crossing the Threshold of Hope*, ed. Vittorio Messori, trans. Jenny McPhee and Martha McPhee (New York: Alfred A. Knopf, 1995), pp. 210-11. The Pope writes: "*The human face and the commandment 'Do not kill' are ingeniously joined in Levinas, and thus become a testimony for our age*, in which governments, even democratically elected governments, sanction executions with such ease." John Paul II might also see a work of Providence in the name of the newest Doctor of the Church: Therese of the Child Jesus of the Holy Face.

ordered can they attune the intellect in its articulation of natural law. It is, furthermore, just such insight and inclinations that at key moments help us identify and sustain human rights. These same human rights, in turn, challenge our disordered social institutions. They serve, as well, to animate the struggle for the institutions of a civilization of love. Noting this interplay of the epistemic and the political is critical.

We must, of course, be sober in our appeal to rights. Yet our insistence should be unwavering. Students of Maritain think at once of the United Nations and The Universal Declaration of Human Rights.[34] Article 3 states that "Everyone has the right to life, liberty and security of person." More particularly, the United Nations' Declaration on the Rights of the Child, in its Preamble, recognizes that "[T]he child by reason of his physical and mental immaturity, needs special safeguards and care, including appropriate legal protection, before as well as after birth." Article 6 of this Declaration insists that "[E]very child has the inherent right to life."[35] Are we sober in our appeal to these rights? Is our insistence unwavering? If so, then no government can tolerate, much less promote, abortion and infanticide without hypocrisy. Authentic rights, publicly affirmed, become levers by which we can displace the established *dis*order.

There is a special promise in the vocation of the family to serve as the *pivotal* institution of social healing. Consider, again, the language of The Universal Declaration of Human Rights: "The family is the natural and fundamental unit of society and is entitled to protection by society and the State" (Article 6). So it is that John Paul II in *Familiaris Consortio* #44 calls for a "family politics." Such a politics offers its own perspectives on hospitality and heritage, education and justice, and health and education. Such a politics, if it keeps its integrity, honors its unique genesis in conjugal love.

Thus, the poet-activist Wendell Berry, reflecting on his diurnal round, writes:

---

[34] Maritain explains his approach to this Declaration in *Man and the State*, pp. 76-80.

[35] See "Vatican Statement at Meeting of Religious Leaders on World's Children," New York, May 8, 2002 (*Zenit*).

*But on the days when I am lucky*
*or blessed, I am silent.*
*I go into the one body*
*that two make in making marriage*
*that for all our trying, all*
*our deaf-and-dumb of speech,*
*has no tongue.*

Marriage, for Berry as for the Catholic tradition, is a two-in-one-flesh communion. And Berry, with a spare eloquence, guides us from speech, in its many accents, to the communion of marriage. Doing so, he leads us to the deep and healing inclinations that it embodies. His meditation ends with these lines:

*The way of love leads all ways*
*to life beyond words, silent*
*and secret. To serve that triumph*
*I have done all the rest.*[36]

Maritain perhaps says as much. In foretelling "a new age... called upon to recognize and define the rights of the human being," he specifies that no question is more urgent than "the rights of that primordial society which is family society, and which is prior to the political state..."[37] Though a friend of poets and of silence, Jacques Maritain had a philosopher's calling to articulate the paths and power of love in the natural order.

So, too, does the Christian natural law thinker. We must, then, return to Dame Philosophy's third question. How can one confront one's culture in the language of natural law if one stutters badly in its articulation?

There are, I think, two promising lines to follow in answering her question. The first is that we look to the primacy of the person. This

---

[36] From Wendell Berry, *A Timbered Choir: The Sabbath Poems, 1979-1997* (Washington, D.C.: Counterpoint, 1998), p. 182.

[37] Jacques Maritain, *Man and the State*, p. 104.

"personalism" serves us at more than a one level. Thus, Maritain advocates a "personalist" society.[38] Karol Wojtyla recommends a Thomistic personalism.[39] W. Norris Clarke teaches us to do metaphysics on the basis of our experience as persons.[40]

A good novelist often evinces a personalist sensibility. In *Keep the Aspidistra Flying*, George Orwell gives us the ambiguous fictional character Gordon Comstock. No moral paragon, Comstock nonetheless sometimes stumbles onto the truth. When Rosemary, his only-too-recent girl friend, becomes pregnant, they consider abortion. Orwell describes his character's surprising insight:

> For the first time he grasped, with the only kind of knowledge that matters, what they were really talking about. The words 'a baby' took on a new significance. They did not mean... a mere abstract disaster, they meant a bud of flesh, a bit of himself, down there in her belly, alive and growing. His eyes met hers... For a moment he did feel that in some mysterious way they were one flesh. Though they were feet apart he felt as though they were joined together–as though some invisible living cord stretched from her entrails to his.[41]

---

[38] Ibid., p. 106.

[39] See his "Thomistic Personalism," in *Person and Community: Selected Essays*, trans. Theresa Sandok (New York: Peter Lang, 1993), pp. 165-75. As John Paul II, in *Fides et Ratio* #83, he urges Christian thinkers to go beyond anthropology to the metaphysics of the person.

[40] See W. Norris Clarke, *The One and the Many: A Contemporary Metaphysics* (Notre Dame, Indiana: University of Notre Dame Press, 2001), pp. 36 and 37. This is a theme to which he repeatedly returns.

[41] George Orwell, *Keep the Aspidistra Flying* (London: Secker & Warburg, 1959), p. 277. David P. Mills called my attention to this passage in Christopher Hitchen's *Why Orwell Matters* (New York: Basic Books, 2002), pp. 151-52. Hitchens, no apologist for Christianity, comments: "One could hardly wish, in a few sentences, for a clearer proof of the way in which Orwell relied upon the instinctual. The impalpable umbilicus unites the couple as well as the mother and child; to sever it prematurely, for any selfish motive, is to commit an un-nameable but none the less intelligible offence against

Such a passage helps illustrate both Newman's real assent and von Hildebrand's intuition of the given. Still more poignantly, the passage shows how the personal encounter of the other can give a new voice to what is already obscurely present.

A second point to explore, in discerning how we are to articulate the natural law, is axiological. Articulating natural law demands clarity about the good. We must continually distinguish between the *instrumental* good and what is good *in and of itself.* Maritain, with scientism in mind, writes that for "a philosophy which recognizes Fact alone, the notion of Value–I mean Value objectively true in itself–is not conceivable."[42] Just such thinking remains dominant, and natural law thinkers sharply dispute it.

To be sure, such a value distinction needs concrete illustration. Happily, it is ready to hand in Robert George's analysis of marriage, to which we can now return. The core of George's argument is as follows.[43]

(P1) Conjugal love, if reproductive in type, actualizes marriage.

(P2) Marriage is a basic and intrinsic good.

(P3) Actualizing a basic and intrinsic good is itself such a good.

(C1) Such conjugal love is a basic and intrinsic good.

(P4) Children supervene on, and are a fruit of, conjugal love.

(C2) Thus, children fulfill the union which conjugal love actualizes.

(P5) Instrumentalizing a basic and intrinsic good wrongly devalues it.

---

humanity." Orwell's Comstock has no access to ultrasound. But even a series of textbook pictures have their impact. "His baby had seemed real to him from the moment when Rosemary spoke of abortion; but it had been a reality without a visual shape–something that happened in the dark and was only important after it had happened. But here was the actual process taking place": *Keep the Aspidistra Flying*, p. 286.

[42] Jacques Maritain, *Man and the State*, p. 97.

[43] See Robert George, *The Clash of Orthodoxies*, pp. 77-80.

(P6) Non-marital sex acts are instrumentalizing, e.g., are carried out for mutual pleasure or some private good.

(C3) Thus, these instrumentalizing acts are morally disordered.

(C4) So marriage alone fully actualizes persons in their sexual agency.

Professor George, one supposes, sees the basic goods to which his argument refers as relational. Here, it is worth noting that John Crosby, following Dietrich von Hildebrand, encourages us to reflect more deeply on value as distinct from either instrumental or relational good.[44]

While his suggestion is helpful, a question arises. Might we not see a basic good as *both* relational *and* of value in itself? Marriage, to be sure, is a relational good. But might it not also be of immense value simply for what it is? Children, after all, are good in relation to conjugal union; they are also of priceless worth in themselves. Would not an understanding of some basic goods (*versus* merely instrumental goods) as both relational and of value in themselves enrich our axiology? (Note: an intrinsic relational good like friendship can *also* be an instrumental good as in, for example, "My friend got me the job.") This broader understanding, I think, clarifies the argument before us; it also increases its epistemic accessibility, since the good as "value in itself" seems especially self-revealing in von Hildebrand's intuition of the given.

Nor need there be any incompatibility between knowledge by inclination and knowledge by rational intuition. Each can enhance the other, and it seems that the former often sets the stage for the latter. The chief *caveat* is that Maritain's emphasis on inclination and von Hildebrand's call for a grasping of the given are to be seen as in harmony with reason rather than in opposition to it. Here, I think, Michael Harrington, then of the New York Catholic Worker, went wrong when he claimed to find in Maritain the thesis that natural law "is an inclination toward good, and a progressive understanding of the

---

[44] John F. Crosby, *The Selfhood of the Human Person* (Washington, D.C.: The Catholic University of America Press, 1996), especially pp. 174-85.

terms of that inclination, primarily through intuition, *not through reason.*"[45]

## IV A Skeptical Challenge

But now it is time for Dame Philosophy to renew her inquiry. Happily, space allows her but a single fresh objection. It is an objection to Maritain and to any one who shares his optimism. For Maritain is optimistic about the development of conscience, or the knowledge of natural law, by means of our knowledge through inclinations. In *Man and the State* he writes, "That progress of moral conscience is indeed the most unquestionable instance of progress in humanity."[46] A skeptic would dismiss his claim as bravado. Even Maritain, in the same text, refers to the "ever widening crises in the modern world."[47] Thus Dame Philosophy asks, by way of her closing objection, whether it would not be far better, and saner, to acknowledge that the signs of the times are disconcertingly mixed.

Yet here the Christian thinker can still stand with Maritain. There need be no conflict between the progress of conscience and the widening of crisis. If our crises widen, conscience can range more widely and more deeply. Evil, in the end, is emptiness. But the good we do endures. Distinguishing between the transitive and the intransitive dimensions of human action, Karol Wojtyla notes that the "transitive in our culturally creative activity [is] a result of the particular intensity of that which is intransitive and remains within our disinterested communion with truth, goodness, and beauty."[48] Here he anticipates Vatican Council II's teaching that Christ "hands over to the Father" the

---

[45] See Maurice Isserman, *The Other American: The Life of Michael Harrington* (New York: Public Affairs, 2000), p. 76; emphasis added. For Harrington's review, see "Man and the State," *Catholic Worker* 17 (May 1951): 4.

[46] Jacques Maritain, *Man and the State*, p. 94.

[47] Ibid., p. 76. His later work, *Peasant of the Garonne* (1966), and his earlier work, *The Twilight of Civilization* (1943) are decidedly somber.

[48] See Karol Wojtyla,"The Problem of the Constitution of Culture Through Human Praxis," in *Person and Community*, p. 271.

fruits of our struggle and that even now "the Kingdom is already present..." (*Gaudium et Spes* #39).

## Envoi

In the Christian struggle, Jacques Maritain's voice retains its force, and surely not the least so in America. His praise of this country was at times extravagant. Yet he was always aware of how high the human stakes were in the American experiment. Etienne Gilson recorded the *élan* with which Maritain met the challenge. "America offered Jacques Maritain a... difficult game to play. He hadn't sought it, but he accepted it, because I have always seen him accept a game provided it was difficult," and "this time again–and I am a witness–[Maritain] won."[49]

Today, the stakes are higher still. Nowhere is this clearer than in our own crisis of marriage and the family after thirty six years of a State-sanctioned silent holocaust.[50] To the extent that we are complicit in it, our inclinations are disordered. To this extent, our ability to love and to nurture is compromised. We are fortunate, then, that Maritain's engagement with the questions of truth and beauty and goodness offers so many lessons. Yet there is one imperative lesson about *how* we might advance Maritain's legacy. It is that we press on.

[49] Lawrence Dewan, O.P., brings this remark to our attention in his "Jacques Maritain and Toronto (A Visit to P.I.M.S. - S.M.C. Archives," in *Études Maritainiennes / Maritain Studies* XV, p. 16, footnote 8. Dewan's source is Etienne Gilson's "Jacques Maritain au Vatican," *La vie intellectuelle*, no. 2 (1945): 36-38. Gilson's verdict comes more than a decade before *Reflections on America* appeared.

[50] Sister Nirmala, M.C., Mother Teresa's successor, underscored one of the ways this crisis weakens the Church. Asked why, in the West, there are so few vocations, she replied: "In some of those countries there are few births; the family is no longer able to transmit certain values. Vocations begin at home, but too many families in the West are destroyed" (Calcutta, India, April 21, 2002 [ZENIT.org-Avvenire]).

# THE "NORMAL" PURSUIT OF *EUDAIMONIA*, AND THE POTENTIAL OBSTACLE POSED BY GENETIC MANIPULATION

William M. Joensen

Some of the prospective outcomes for genetic manipulations of human persons that are envisioned in clinical medicine are "happier" than others. Putative improvement in the human condition cannot be gauged solely by technical, practical successes. Other criteria obtain.

Human gene alteration is proposed for two reasons: to treat diseases and for "genetic enhancement."[1] Genetic enhancement refers to any alteration of "normal" genetic material related to our physical and cognitive capacities, and to the adjustment of human behaviors

[1] Laura Palazzani describes genetic enhancements as a class of "what might be termed 'alterative genetics' or eugenics; the constructive or innovative genetic intervention in the already existing 'normal' or 'healthy'–i.e. non-pathological-genetic heritage." Among the interventions of alterative genetics, she distinguishes: "a) interventions which remedy deficits which, without being specifically diseases, nevertheless leave the subject in a condition of inferiority in relation to the statistic average" and "b) interventions to strengthen one or more qualities above the average, in the subject and in his/her descendants (this is the case with ameliorative genetics)": see her "Genetic engineering and human nature," in *Man-made Man: Ethical and Legal Issues in Genetics*, eds. Peter Doherty and Agatha Sutton (Dublin: Open Air, 1997), p. 47 and n. 4.

Maxwell J. Mehlman recognizes the ambiguities surrounding the concepts of the "normal" and "normalcy" taken in both quantitative and qualitative senses. "Functionality" and "normal function" criteria reflect aspects of both statistical and qualitative approaches to human life, but "normalcy" is often translated from its physiological and ontological senses to a political connotation; "normalcy" here becomes an "opportunity range" that is as much external as it is intrinsic to the individual: see his "How will we regulate genetic enhancement?," in *Wake Forest Law Review* 34, no 3 (1999): 671-714; cf. Eric T, Juengst, "What does *enhancement* mean?" in *Enhancing Human Traits: Ethical and Social Implications*, ed. Erik Parens (Washington, D.C.: Georgetown University Press, 1998), pp. 29-47, a work in the Hastings Center Studies for Ethics, ed. Mark J. Hanson and Daniel Callahan.

connected with these capacities.[2] In this essay, I go further than merely anticipating unfortunate consequences for some genetic manipulations. My stronger claim is that genetic procedures that impinge upon persons whose lives are already genetically or functionally "normal," are inherently, morally objectionable.

In contrast to the sort of utopian "democratization" of human capacities and excellences that is insinuated with a unilateral pro-genetic manipulation agenda, I retrieve a more classical and more comprehensive view of human nature. I proceed by three steps, examining: (1) the necessity of moral virtue as a foundation for human friendship, (2) the proper meaning of the concept of the humanly "normal," and (3) their mutual application in political society relevant to proposed genetic interventions. Understandings of normality and moral virtue inform human friendship and political participation, and correlate with the human life well-lived.

Humans cannot truly know themselves without the help of other persons. However, the affirmation of common biological species identity–verified either by genetic or functional criteria, or in common experience–is not sufficient to guarantee that moral respect for human dignity will be tendered among persons. Human friendship and the broader contribution of political society are necessary in order for human achievement and the realization of *eudaimonia* to occur. *Eudaimonia* is the ultimate *telos* of human life. *Eudaimonia* is often

---

[2] Within the genus of gene enhancements, Roberta M. Berry identifies alterations of the genetic constitution of humans whose "purpose is to enhance appearance or functions that fall within the *normal* range for the human species" (emphasis mine): Roberta M. Berry, "From involuntary sterilization to genetic enhancement: the unsettled legacy of 'Buck vs. Bell,'" in *Notre Dame Journal of Law, Ethics, and Public Policy* 12, no. 2 (1998): 401-48, 439 n. 111. She delineates three categories of these "genetic enhancements": (1) "cosmetic enhancements–altering aspects of physical appearance such as height, eye color, facial features, and so on"; (2) "capabilities enhancement–altering faculties such as intelligence, strength, agility, and so on"; and (3) "behavioral enhancement–altering predispositions to display traits such as kindness, empathy, gentleness, or a particular sexual orientation" (pp. 439-40); cf. Maxwell Mehlman, op. cit., p. 675.

translated as "happiness," "blessedness," or "flourishing," but here Robert Spaemann's formulation of the "life that turns out well" is the basis of my treatment.[3]

My conclusion is that only those procedures that implicitly affirm the good of human existence in its normal state, and that promote virtuous striving and choice, will enable the achievement of *eudaimonia*, the life well-lived. Concepts of the normal and the virtuous represent criteria for evaluating prospective genetic alterations of human individuals in their pre- and post-natal states. Genetic manipulations that seek to enhance persons, absent present or future indications of disease, instead portend "unhappy" and "unfriendly"' results based on their deleterious impact upon human associations at the personal and political levels.

## I Genuine versus domesticated friendship

Jacques Maritain maintains that "Friendship is the animating form of society. Society depends on the perpetual gift and surplus derived from persons."[4] Human friendship reveals us to ourselves and

---

[3] See Jeremiah Alberg's Preface to Robert Spaemann's *Happiness and Benevolence* (with an afterword by Arthur Madigan), trans. Jeremiah Alberg (Notre Dame, Indiana: University of Notre Dame Press, 2000), p. xi, from the original: *Glück und Wohlwollen* (Stuttgart: J.G. Cotta'sche Buchhandlung Nachfolger GmbH, 1989); cf. Henry B. Veatch, "Modern ethics, teleology, and love of self, *The Monist* 75, no. 1 (January 1992): 52-70, p. 55.

[4] Maritain characterizes the reciprocal relation of human person to society as one of "whole to whole"; see Jacques Maritain, *The Person and the Common Good*, trans. John J. Fitzgerald (South Bend, Indiana: University of Notre Dame Press, 1966), pp. 47-89, originally published in New York by Charles Scribner's Sons, 1947. "The political task," says Maritain, "is essentially a task of civilization and culture": see Jacques Maritain, *The Rights of Man and Natural Law*, trans. Doris C. Anson (New York: Charles Scribner's Sons, 1949), p. 44. The necessity of friendship, the family and the polis for *eudaimonia* is articulated by the Millers in Aristotelian terms. They state, "The directly learned *hexeis* (such as ethical virtues, *technai* and *epistemêmai*) are themselves organized into the overall *entelecheia* of the whole psyche as its 'selfhood' by means of *phronesis* as well as by *philia* [cf. *Nicomachean Ethics* 8.5-8]. Both these levels of organization continue to be influenced by social

intensifies the kind of persons and society that we are. In the Aristotelian understanding of friendship, says Spaemann, "the subjective and objective perspectives of one's own life fuse with one another."[5] The one who is friend in the most authentic sense "possesses human virtues which make the person lovable for his own sake."[6] We

---

motivations and pressures exerted by social institutions (family, polis, culture, etc.), which have self-perpetuating mechanisms of their own at the societal level of integration. In addition, individual personal inter-actions (*philia*) influence the goals of behavior by means of mutual reinforcement": Alfred E. Miller and Maria G. Miller, "Aristotle's *entelecheia* as a paradigm for today's health problems: ontological explanation of the psyche as grounded in *Metaphysics H*," in *Philosophy and Medecine*, Vol. 1, ed. K.J. Boudouris (Alimos, Greece: Ionia Publications, 1998), 123-44, p. 130.

5 Robert Spaemann, op. cit., p. 55; cf. Aristotle *Nicomachean Ethics* (cited hereafter as *EN*) 3.4 1112b25, 8.9-9.11. Spaemann elaborates the self-discovery that occurs in the face of the humanly other: "We become really ourselves only in the face of the claim made by the irreducibly real." We move out of the centrality of our living, and thereby "discover the reality of the other, insofar as the other is not merely a correlate of our intentional situations. This discovery cannot be purely theoretical. Theoretically we press ahead to objects. Being oneself becomes possible only in free affirmation, in an act of acceptance. This act, however, in which life transcends itself and in this self-transcendence comes to a whole which examines its various states, is only possible through the highest powers of life. This self-transcendence of life is the rational: in its most elementary form we speak of justice; in its highest, of love" (pp. 90 and 91).

6 Ibid., p. 97; cf. p. 100. Martha C. Nussbaum explicates the dynamic of particularity affirmed in the Aristotelian doctrine of friendship in her *The Therapy of Desire: Theory and Practice in Hellenistic Ethics*, Vol. 2 (new series), Martin Classical Lectures (Princeton, New Jersey: Princeton University Press, 1994), pp. 67-68; cf. pp. 91-95 and 508-09, and also Aristotle, *Politics* 2.4 1262b22-24. "Love," comments Nussbaum, "is a profound attachment to another separate life, which must remain as a separate center of movement and choice, not being engulfed or fused, in order for the relationship of love to be possible at all. And in the loves Aristotle values most highly, the participants view one another as good characters, therefore as fully independent choosers of the good; if one controlled the other, even to the extent that a parent does a child, the love would apparently be less good as love" (p. 91).

are an occasion for another to act toward us as an end, and we are given the same opportunity to act on his or her behalf, thereby contributing to our individual good and the common good.[7]

Not all the affections evoked in the context of human friendship are pleasant. Judith Barad discusses the place of justified anger connatural to friendship in the context of Aquinas' doctrine.[8] "According to Aquinas," she states, "each person is this expanded self, comprised of other things and individuals we love and thereby with which we identify. By punishing a person who has injured those with whom we identify, we demonstrate that we are not simply isolated individuals, each pursuing his own egoistic concerns."[9] In other words, angry responses can be marks of virtuous character when they follow upon injustices visited upon those whom we love.[10]

---

[7] For insightful discussions of the Thomistic appropriation and development of Aristotle's doctrine on the love of friendship, see David M. Gallagher's "Person and ethics in Thomas Aquinas," *Acta Philosophica* 4, no. 1 (1995): 51-71; "Desire for beatitude and love of friendship in Thomas Aquinas," *Medieval Studies* 58 (1996): 1-47; and "Moral virtue and contemplation: a note on the unity of the moral life," *Sapientia* 51, no. 200 (1996): 385-92; see, also, Louis B. Geiger, *Le problème de l'amour chez saint Thomas d'Aquin*, Conférence Albert-le-Grand (Montreal: L'Institut d'Etudes Mediévales, 1952).

[8] Barad develops Aquinas's definition of anger as a "desire to punish another by way of just revenge": Judith Barad, "Aquinas and the role of anger in social reform," *Logos* 3, no. 1 (Winter 2000): 124-44, p. 124; see Aquinas, *Summa Theologiae* (cited herafter as *ST*), I-II, q. 47, a. 1. In Thomas's doctrine, anger corresponds with the virtue of justice. "It is essential to justice that judgment be accompanied by a strong feeling. It is inappropriate to judge merely dispassionately that some horrific act has occurred unless we are also angry. Anger should rely not only on correct rational judgments, but should also involve a desire to inflict just punishment for suffering. Justice is demanded by an angry, morally indignant person, who seeks to relieve anger by injuring the cause of his or her pain. The purpose of revenge is to relieve that anger and thereby promote justice": Judith Barad, op. cit., p. 127.

[9] Ibid., p. 135.

[10] Ibid., p. 136: "Zealous anger is a desire of vengeance insofar as it is really just. If we identify with someone we love, zeal may become aroused when that

In some quarters, there is call for genetic modification even of normal, aggressive instincts in humans. LeRoy Walters and Julie Palmer rehearse arguments for and against gene enhancements used to moderate and reduce aggressive tendencies in human beings. They consider cases both of identifiable sociopathology, and of the more general, "normal," aggressive tendencies found as part of the human condition.[11] While their recommendations for "normal" persons eschew coercive means of pacifying individuals, they incline toward a utopian, formalist program of diminished social aggression that in fact mitigates individual autonomy–and, I propose, threatens to destroy the irascible part of nature that fosters human inclinations to survival, to practice courage in the face of hostile objects, and to strive for justice in human relations.

While agenda such as those proposed by Walters and Palmer may indeed produce a "new world," such a world would be anything but brave or truly friendly. Healthy friendships between persons of virtue include situations where anger will be the appropriate response. When the genes that dispose individuals toward normal aggression are altered or deleted, the bodily substrate for experiencing anger is removed. The rationally-informed desire for justice will be correspondingly diminished. In effect, enhancement practices aimed at

---

thing is harmed.... Accordingly, zealous anger has its source in love, wanting good for someone else"; cf. Thomas Aquinas, *ST* I-II, q. 28, a. 4.

[11] See LeRoy Walters and Julie Gage Palmer *The Ethics of Gene Therapy*, Illustrations by Natalie C. Johnson (New York: Oxford University Press, 1997), pp. 101 and 123-28; cf. H. Tristram Engelhardt, Jr., "Human nature technologically revisited," *Social Philosophy and Policy* 8, no. 1 (Autumn 1990): 180-91, pp. 186-89. Walters' and Palmer's utopian premises are evident in their statements: "We assume that treated individuals would continue to be free to choose their own acts but would be more likely than the average 20th-century human to behave in a friendly manner"; "In our view, moral enhancement by genetic means would be a useful adjunct to other important programs like social and economic reform and education about ethnic, racial, and national groups that are different from one's own"; "We hasten to add that our goal would not be to achieve perfection in human nature but merely to moderate the influence of the violently aggressive tendencies that are clearly part of human nature as it has been transmitted to us" (p. 127).

pacifying normal persons excavate the foundations for noble friendship and for polities where justice, rather than raw power, predominates.[12]

**II Human nature and normality, and an alternative view**

Our organism with all its appetites coincides with our cognitive power in a distinctively human, analogous sense of "nature." Along with this more robust sense of human nature, there is a corresponding concept of human "normality" that admits the integration of biology and reason. To sustain the argument against the prospective genetically-induced diminution of friendship and political cooperation aimed at the common good, I draw from Georges Canguilhem's construal of the organically and ontologically "normal" as the dynamically self-sustaining, well-functioning, norm-issuing state of human engagement with the environment.[13] Normal, healthy human beings are unencumbered by biological self-consciousness introduced by some form of pathology.

This understanding of human normality is compatible with Aristotle's notion of hypothetical necessity; on the one hand, it admits material necessity and the determinate appetites that are part of our organic existence. On the other hand, however, human normality also indicates the presence of an analogous "second nature" achieved through the inculcation of cultural mores and customs, coupled with

---

[12] Cf. James G. Lennox, "Aristotle on the biological roots of virtue: the natural history of natural virtue," in *Biology and the Foundation of Ethics*, eds. Jane Maienschein and Michael Ruse (Cambridge: Cambridge University Press, 1999), p. 14; Aristotle, *EN* 2.6 1106b16-24; Thomas Aquinas, *ST* I-II, q. 47, a. 1.

[13] See Georges Canguilhem's *The Normal and the Pathological*, Introduction by Michael Foucault, trans. Carolyn R. Fawcett and Robert S. Cohen (Dordrecht, Netherlands: D. Reidel, 1978; reprint, New York: Urzone, 1991), pp. 174-75 and 261, from the original edition (Paris: Presses Universitaires de France, 1966); and *A Vital Rationalist: Selected Writings from Georges Canguilhem*, Introduction by Paul Rabinow with a critical bibliography by Camille Limoges, trans. Arthur Goldhammer (New York: Zone Books, 1994), pp. 35 and 137.

virtuous mastery over one's own inclinations. The second nature is posterior in experience and knowledge, though it is prior in being.[14]

The acquired, virtuous nature enables the directed expression–and not unilateral suppression–of bodily appetites within a greater scheme of human goods.[15] It is actualized in culture, but it is not arbitrarily determined by culture as a force that transcends and opposes human nature.[16] Vital meaning accompanies normality. *Nomos* expresses and enforces the humanly normal. We might say that the normal is truly an oblique notion of the humanly good.

---

[14] Spaemann distinguishes the "first" and "second" natures: "The happiness of one's own life remains unthematic as long as traditional, religious and social horizons retain their unquestionable validity so that the habits, through which these horizons are interiorized, have the character of being second nature. Only when their coercive force is loosened can our "first nature" assert itself against the second. And when this happens in a reflective manner, questions about the conditions for a happy life emerge, especially insofar as these conditions may or may not be fulfilled through our own action": Robert Spaemann, op. cit., p. 28.

[15] "We can come to have rational desires for some things and mere appetites for others," observes Douglas Rasmussen. "Our appetites and desires can be revamped or reshaped into rational dispositions by our intelligence so that what we ought to desire and what we in fact do desire can be in harmony. Moral virtue and practical wisdom are mutually interdependent, because the compossibility they seek is one of thought and feeling, not mere abstract goods": Douglas B. Rasmussen, "Human flourishing and the appeal to human nature," *Social Philosophy and Policy* 16, no. 1 (Winter 1999): 1-43, pp. 42-43.

[16] Yves R. Simon speaks of an obvious difference between human and other animal species, with whom we share some inclinations. He says, "Man's instincts let loose desires connected with the conservation and expansion of individual life and social life, but they do not suffice to direct those desires. If instinct is left to itself, the desires to which it has given birth will fail of their object, produce discord, and arrest life": Yves R. Simon, *Freedom and Community*, ed. Charles P. O'Connell (New York: Fordham University Press, 1968), p. 153. In regard to manipulation of embryos, genetic interventions, and the willingness to alter children for the sake of fulfilling parental desires, we submit, one might understand the "arrest" of life in the most deliberate and most ultimate sense.

Virtuous development allows the person to participate in a more sublime aspect of human dignity: moral dignity.[17] This moral dignity is compatible with human necessity and human vulnerability. Humans experience a sort of "earth-bound" gravitational dynamic of necessity and need coupled with our transcendent aspirations. There is a fundamental metaphysical tension immanent to human persons that affects the relation of the humanly "normal" to *eudaimonia.* We want to retain and reinforce our "selves," even as we desire to enrich, expand, and transcend ourselves.

Reason's appetitive impulse carries with it a self-annihilating tendency when it disregards the necessities of biological being. The powers of deliberation and choice presume the bodily matrix that is present in every human action. The radical, Platonic emancipation of human reason in the service of utopian, rationalist projects aspires to leave aside the human condition.[18] Reason unhinged from natural

---

[17] Josef Seifert cites Gabriel Marcel when he describes this level of moral dignity as a "conquest and not a possession": Josef Seifert, *What is Life? On the Originality, Irreducibility, and Value of Life,* Value Inquiry Book Series (Amsterdam: Rodopi, 1997), p. 105. Human moral dignity, says Seifert, "depends on the *good* use of freedom. This dignity is not inalienable nor does it automatically belong to us as persons.... This dignity differs from the purely ontological dignity of persons in that it knows opposites" (ibid.).

[18] Robert Spaemann, op. cit., p. 53. Cf. Robert Spaemann, "Genetic manipulation of human nature in the context of human personality," in *Human Genome, Human Person, and the Society of the Future*, eds. Juan de Dios Vial Correa and Elio Segreccia, Proceedings of the Fourth Assembly of the Pontifical Academy for Life , February 23-25, 1998 (Vatican City: Libreria Vaticana, 1999), 340-50, pp. 341 and 345-48. Leon Kass analyzes this "ecstatic yearning" of the human soul proceeding from the "promise" of life: "That so many cultures speak of a promise of immortality and eternity suggests, first of all, a certain truth about the human soul: the human soul yearns for, longs for, some condition or goal toward which our earthly activities are directed but which cannot be attained during our earthly life. Our soul's reach exceeds our grasp; it seeks more continuance; it reaches for something beyond us, something that for the most part eludes us. True happiness, a genuine fulfillment of the deepest longings of our soul, is not in our power, and cannot be fully attained, much less commanded. Our distress with mortality derives from the conflict between the transcendent longings of the

necessity results in corrosion of the "normal" capacity for humans to achieve a kind of "this-worldly" happiness.

Moreover, this "ecstatic" type of *eudaimonia* that aspires to set aside the human condition must be contrasted with the Aristotelian exposition of a more "middle-class," "normal" sense of "lives which turn out well."[19] The uniqueness of human existence consists in the association of the "normality" of human life with the *telos* of a qualified *eudaimonia*. This is the *eudaimonia* of the *Nicomachean Ethics*, where one aspires to the sort of happiness in life that is "the best that one can hope for" as human.[20] Spaemann states, "Normal, in its proper meaning, human happiness, is the leading of a life which turns out well."[21]

---

soul and the all-too-finite powers and fleshly concerns of the body": Leon Kass, "Mortality," in *Powers That Make Us Human: The Foundations of Medical Ethics*, ed. Kenneth Vaux (Urbana and Chicago: University of Illinois Press, 1985), pp. 7-28, p. 20.

[19] See Aristotle, *Politics* 4.9 1295a25-1295b3. There is a "paradoxical situation," says Spaemann, "that the thinking on a life which turns out well, which appears together with the very emergence of thought, has the character of 'Utopia'. It anticipates a kind of happiness which, at the same time, it acknowledges is unrealizable for human beings.... For Aristotle the polis is the place which, as compensation for the 'no place,' the *utopia*, of absolute turning out well, allows for 'happiness which is humanly possible'": Robert Spaemann, *Happiness and Benevolence*, p. 74.

[20] See Aristotle, *EN* 1.6 1096b33-35 and 1.10 1101a14-21. I take issue with many of Nussbaum's ethical conclusions regarding disputed topics in contemporary genetic and reproductive medicine: see Martha C. Nussbaum and Cass R. Sunstein, eds., *Clones and Clones: Facts and Fantasies About Human Cloning* (New York: W.W. Norton, 1998). However, I agree with her where she enjoins "abandoning the zeal for absolute perfection as inappropriate to the life of a finite being, abandoning the thirst for punishment and self-punishment that so frequently accompanies that zeal," so that we may compassionately regard "the ambivalent excellence and passion of a human life": Martha Nussbaum, *Therapy of Desire*, p. 510.

[21] Robert Spaemann, *Happiness and Benevolence*, p. 54. Rasmussen expresses the essence of a distinctively human perfection: "To 'perfect', to 'realize', or to 'actualize' oneself is not to become God-like, immune to degeneration, or

Hence, there is an intrinsic "antinomy of happiness" where theoretical and practical reason are in tension bordering on opposition if the "Aristotelian compromise" does not prevail in the lives of individual persons and in the life of the *polis*.[22] The contingency and vulnerability of the normal human condition can be overwhelmed by a rationalism that seeks to cancel human finitude. A new, artificial vulnerability is introduced, where life "metamorphoses" solely into reason, since organic life then becomes an instrumental infrastructure, subject to arbitrary manipulation and reorganization.[23] A spirit of rational revolution against the boundaries of normality discerned in human nature produces an abstracted, absolutized autonomy over oneself and others–pitted against all.[24]

---

incapable of harm, but it is to fulfill those potentialities and capacities that make one human. This is to achieve one's natural end or perform one's natural function": David Rasmussen, op. cit., p. 37.

[22] See James G. Lennox, op. cit., pp. 19-20; cf. Aristotle, *EN* 6.8 1141b23-24.

[23] We compare this metaphorical, pathological "metamorphosis" with the salutary impulse of *amor benevolentiae*, described by Spaemann: "If we understand love in the sense of *amor benevolentiae* as the becoming real of the real for us, then the same conclusion emerges. The measure of this becoming real is not a mean lying between two extremes, but is itself an extreme: the spanning of an infinite space between the negativity of reflection and the positivity of being. For the being awakened to reason, the metamorphosis of life through the Logos and the fulfillment of rationality with life is a process without end": Robert Spaemann, *Happiness and Benevolence*, p. 113 (cf. ibid. 63).

[24] Engelhardt explicitly endorses the prospect that the power of reason will not only discern the meaning of our human personhood, but will be technologically equipped to *determine* and *refashion* our nature; he asserts, "Thus human persons are cast into a moral predicament. No longer can they turn to an understanding of their nature qua biological species for a source of moral values. Instead, their destiny is to create and invent their own values. It will never be possible simply to discover the good for humans. Reason, in short, creates our destiny as humans. We must choose, for example, the extent to which we will pursue capacities that outstrip what has even been part of our nature or the nature of other animals": H. Tristram Engelhardt, Jr., "Reason," in *Powers That Make Us Human*, p. 88.

I compare one view of human nature that opposes the understanding of human identity I have advanced so far. The evolutionist anthropology proposed by philosopher Michael Ruse establishes a threshold for unlimited genetic intervention and individual eugenic choice to move forward.[25] Our evolved instinct to perpetuate our genes, and to ensure the best possible survival among our progeny, animates our attitudes toward prospective children. Our "salvation" lies in our biological succession. We desire that our children flourish and not only adapt to society, but excel in the social setting. And we are willing to go to great lengths, perhaps even to alter the genome of our potential progeny, in order to ensure these outcomes.

But our desires regarding our children, according to Ruse's model, are not so much for the sake of the child, but for our own sake. Our desire for personal preservation and satisfaction is the source and end for the coupling and the cooperation that generates our children. We might even risk our lives for our children and for others whom we embrace as essential to our genetic welfare, but we are both predetermined and self-interested in doing so.

It should be noted that Ruse's determinist, evolutionist ideology encompasses not just the practices of molecular science and of

---

[25] "All things considered," Ruse comments, "humans are in pretty good shape. The human plan does not call for drastic redesign.... Nor am I saying that humans are perfect. I started this essay by pressing the value of eliminating genetic disease; and, within limits, I would allow that healthy humans could stand some genetic fine-tuning. If I could live, reasonably active, for 150 years, I would jump at the chance": Michael Ruse, "Genesis Revisited: Can we do better than God?" *Zygon: Journal of Religion and Science* 19, no. 3 (September 1984): 297-316, p. 314; cf. Michael Ruse's *Taking Darwin Seriously* (Oxford: Blackwell, 1986); "Knowledge in human genetics: some epistemological questions," in *Genes and Human Self-Knowledge: Historical and Philosophical Reflections on Modern Genetics*, eds. Robert F. Weir, Susan C. Lawrence, and Evan Fales (Iowa City, Iowa: University of Iowa Press, 1994), pp. 34-45; *Monad to Man: The Concept of Progress in Evolutionary Biology* (Cambridge, Massachusetts: Harvard University Press, 1996); "Evolutionary Ethics in the Twentieth Century: Julian Sorell Huxley and George Gaylord Simpson," in *Foundation of Ethics*, pp. 184-224; and *Mystery of Mysteries: Is Evolution a Social Construction?* (Cambridge, Massachusetts: Harvard University Press, 1999).

parenting, but extends beyond these practices to the larger society. To Ruse, scientific education and research are practices of indoctrination. He observes,

> The successful scientist is precisely the person who is, at some level, morally and culturally insensitive, if not dead. If this does not come about through self-selection, then it is a function of the training, especially the long years spent in graduate and postdoctoral study. The sanctification of the great scientists of the past is part of the indoctrination–the ideology that science stands beyond ideology.[26]

Ruse regards this phenomenon with respect rather than with reproach. In contrast, I claim that this mode of doing science is not truly ascetic but "ecstatic" in a corrupt sense. The moral aspect of persons is disregarded–both in the human object under study and in the one who does research. Scientists shed their regard for ethical good and evil. The neutrality of knowledge is joined to the "canonization" of predecessors and colleagues. Science is seen to be superior to all other disciplines. Ethics and politics are subordinated to the aspirations of "hard" scientists, whose projects extend far beyond their theoretical object.[27]

Hence, rationalism and evolutionist materialism combined conduce to an overt constructionism that is both biologic *and* cultural in character. There arises an artificial vulnerability of human life whose *telos* is extrinsically imposed as idea and precept rather than as freely-sought achievement.

---

[26] Michael Ruse, *Mystery of Mysteries*, p. 461.

[27] Proctor concludes, "The principle of neutral science, together with the doctrine of subjective value, constitutes the fundamental political ideology of modern science." Further, "Science is no longer a marginal phenomenon fighting for the right to exist. It has, in some sense, become the ethos of an age.... In this context, science has become a political force in its own right, neutrality serves to camouflage interests, to remove the moral and political from the realm of discourse itself": Robert N. Proctor, *Value-free Science? Purity and Power in Modern Knowledge* (Cambridge, Massachusetts: Harvard University Press, 1991), pp. 269 and 270.

Against this trend, I argue that if the immanent *telos* of nature is not embraced as measure and goal for the trajectory of human reason and human striving, then the relation of *entelechy* and *eudaimonia* is severed. The task confronting all humans is to reverse the estrangement characteristic of modernity that "pries off" human purposes from the ultimate human *telos*, and instead attempts literally to "incorporate" rational choices within the comprehensive practical contingencies that characterize human life.

One either accepts that one's existence is conditioned by nature, or one ends by canceling the very conditions of human existence itself, let alone the possibility of fulfilling that existence.[28] In the latter case, genetic manipulation abets a speculative project that reduces human life to a ruse, a counterfeit–a Hitchcockian "McGuffin" intended to distract, amuse, and mislead, rather than a remedy that helps display the human and guide us to our ultimate human end.

The net result in genetic enhancement scenarios is that the bond between individuals revolves around self-preservation instincts, power transactions, and the cultivation of pleasure. The exercise of political power contingent upon the consent of the many makes for a very fragile alliance indeed.

## III Actual enhancement in the realm of the personal and the political

There is a manner of helping other individuals that respects their humanity, and there are other ways of intervening that distort or deny both the nature of patients and the medical end.[29] There are intrusive

---

[28] Cf. Robert Spaemann, *Happiness and Benevolence*, p. 160.

[29] Cf. Grant Gillctt, "Virtue and truth in clinical science," *Journal of Medecine and Philosophy* 20, no. 3 (June 1995): 285-98, pp. 297-98; and William A. Galston, "Liberal democracy and the problem of technology," in *Technology in the Western Political Tradition*, eds. Arthur M. Melzer, Jerry Weinberger, and M. Richard Zinman (Ithaca, New York: Cornell University Press, 1993), pp. 229-52, p. 238. Spaemann proposes, "Help is neither a spontaneous expression of life, nor is it *poiesis*, making, creative activity.... It always presupposes a tendency, which is supported by it and which needs its support. All specifically ethical action is of this kind. It distinguishes itself from the immediateness of spontaneous expressions of life and also from technical or

or coercive acts that are actually antithetical to nature. The body ceases to be seen as an integral good of the human person whose sense of wholeness and health–periodically and perhaps, chronically–becomes an issue.[30] Medicine is successful when persons are helped to recover physical and mental health.[31] It cannot be judged successful when it seeks to change normal human persons into a different nature than they were first presented or anticipated to be.[32]

---

artificial actions, even when it is only a certain modification of these actions": Robert Spaemann, *Happiness and Benevolence*, pp. 104-05; cf. ibid., p. 174.

[30] Gerald P. McKenny, "Enhancements and the ethical significance of vulnerability," in *Enhancing Human Traits*, p. 230; Robert Sokolowski, "The art and science of medicine," in *Catholic Perspectives on Medecine and Morals*, Vol. 34, Philosophy and Medecine, eds. Edmund D. Pellegrino, John Langan, and John Collins Harvey (Dordrecht, Netherlands: Kluwer Academic Press, 1989), pp. 263- 75, p. 265; cf. Kass, who comments, "The technological triumphs are held to validate their scientific foundations. Here, perhaps, is the most pernicious result of technological progress–more dehumanizing than any actual manipulation or technique, present or future. We are witnessing the erosion, perhaps the final erosion, of the idea of man as something splendid or divine, and its replacement with a view that sees man, no less than nature, simply as more raw material for manipulation and homogenization": Leon Kass, *Toward a More Natural Science* (New York: The Free Press, 1988), p. 37 (originally published in 1985).

[31] Against the positivist concept of "normal," Spaemann asserts that in the Corpus hippocraticum [sic] the concept of *phusis* "serves to distinguish the healthy as the normal from the sick as the abnormal. Here normality is not, however, a statistical concept. If 90 percent of all people were to have headaches, they would not therefore be the healthy by which the other 10 percent had to measure themselves, but the reverse. For headaches are opposed to that natural tendency to self-preservation and well-being, which is characteristic of all natural beings": Robert Spaemann, *Happiness and Benevolence*, p. 163; cf. Georges Canguilhem, *Ideology and Rationality*, p. 129; and H. Tristram Engelhardt, Jr., "Germ-line genetic engineering and moral diversity: moral controversies in a post-Christian world, *Social Philosophy and Policy* 13, no. 2 (Summer 1996): 47-62, pp. 61-62.

[32] Engelhardt comments, "Human nature, which is still a relatively unalterable given, would become a cardinal point in the human refashioning of the

Human life achieves *eudaimonia* to the degree that it sustains itself in the face of life's contingencies–even as persons seek to transcend themselves. Human reason allows us to see the necessary aspect of human life, and to recognize that the moment we affirm "livingness," we also affirm that we are in the presence of the normal, the natural, *phusis*, soul–the ultimate principle by which our lives and our happiness are measured, perfected.

Human beings enter by reason into a "reality-space" that is limitless; hence, they are never fully satisfied in this world. We are challenged to accept that our lives bear contingency and insufficiency that can only be obviated by extinguishing the possibility that our lives will turn out well–or that they will be identifiable to us as real human lives when all is said and done.

There are, nonetheless, two alternatives in which human contingency is validly reduced without negating the alternatives to which we have already averted to. In an analogous, non-pejorative sense, both alternatives actually "enhance" human life. The first form is the already discussed acquisition of virtue. The indeterminacy of human nature, wherein human potencies may be determined to either act well or badly, is conditioned through the habitual use of personal freedom for the sake of human goods. Actual deeds are prior to the realization of virtuous potential.[33] Human ends and human purposes are brought into consistent alignment in the person of virtuous character. The challenge for humans is to achieve personal self-mastery and not to seek to exercise moral domination over other persons, as occurs in non-therapeutic genetic manipulation.[34]

---

human condition. Whether understood as the gift of God or merely as the deliverance of spontaneous mutations, random selection, genetic drift, cosmic happenstance, and biochemical constraints, human nature has until now been regarded as placing constraints on human freedom": H. Tristram Engelhardt, Jr., "Germ-line," p. 51.

[33] Robert, Spaemann, *Happiness and Benevolence*, p. 57; cf. ibid., 44.

[34] Seifert recalls Aristotle's axiom that the human person "is lord over the existence or non-existence of his actions": Josef Seifert, *What is Life?* pp. 45-46; cf. Aristotle, *Eudemian Ethics* 1223a.

Virtuous persons demonstrate a greater degree of determination over their individual actions and over their whole lives. Virtuous persons diminish chance's dominion over happiness. Virtuous persons acquire a habitual, natural autonomy in lives that still include human contingency.

For us, obviously, as in the Aristotelian worldview, virtue alone is insufficient for achieving *eudaimonia*; the apparent obstacles and accidental forces we confront in fact play a necessary part in the rounding out of a complete life.[35] Persons who are virtuously inclined to their own flourishing ultimately actually welcome numerous elements of life beyond their control, even if they do not concede the responsibility for life's turning out well to extrinsic forces.

Persons of good character are more acute in their perception of the facts of life and illness. They are able to distinguish between misfortune and disease, and restrict their solicitations of medical assistance to instances where disease is suspected or known to be present.[36]

---

[35] Nussbaum describes the dynamic of virtuous constancy and chance affirmed by Aristotle: "A life containing only (the state of) virtue, but no action from it out in the world (where the agent's efforts encounter the buffetings of chance), will not be judged by a reasonable person to be complete and lacking in nothing. In fact, says Aristotle, nobody would hold the view that the state of virtue is sufficient for *eudaimonia*, 'unless he were defending a theoretical position at all costs' [*EN* 7.12 1153b16-21; cf. 1.5 1096a1-2]": Martha Nussbaum, *Therapy of Desire*, p. 63; see *EN* 1.7 1097a15-b21.

[36] P.S. Greenspan illustrates the reductive attitude implied in recourse to genetic alteration by drawing an analogy with a presently available medical procedure: "Self-control via genetic engineering might be said to involve treating *oneself* as an object on the model of current strategies regarding more mundane self-control issues that depend on medical intervention. Consider weight loss via liposuction: the sort of control one exercises by signing up for the operation is not an exercise of 'willpower' such as that involved in dieting. Nor is it admirable in quite the same terms. It may be a sign of *courage*, but it does not involve the sort of self-training in temperance as a new trait of character that we have on the Aristotelian account of virtue. It involves giving up on virtue in at least one area": "Free will and the genome project": P.S. Greenspan, *Philosophy and Public Affairs* 22, no. 1 (Winter 1993): 31-43, p. 42.

Misfortune may be grounds for social and political remedies, but it is not a legitimate reason to solicit clinical intervention–to medicalize social injustice. Actual or projected social disadvantages are not acceptable moral grounds for the genetic manipulation of otherwise normal, healthy humans.

The second salutary reduction of contingency in human life is provided through the aforementioned role of the *polis*. Like Aristotle, Spaemann associates "normal" *eudaimonia* with the normal citizen. A humanly qualified form of fulfillment is available to the many, and not just the few:

> The happiness of the citizen is normal, human happiness. The polis founds and makes possible normality.... The reduction of contingency of virtue, i.e., the habitualization of reasonableness, is made possible and strengthened by the reduction of contingency by normality which is guaranteed by the polis. The ethics of Aristotle is a hermeneutic of this normality.[37]

We have earlier linked the natural and the normal. Normality is also significant for politics. There is a good sense in which someone may "politicize" human necessity, incorporating it into reasoned deliberation and decision.[38]

Culture enfolds natural ends in different layers of human meaning. Our awareness that there is variation among different cultures does not

---

[37] Robert Spaemann, *Happiness and Benevolence*, pp. 57-58.

[38] David O'Connor discusses Aristotle's thesis of the contingent character of the common good, depending on the virtues and vices of individual citizens. Some persons manifest a kind of "teleological misdirectedness" that affects both the individual's participation in the community and the realization of the common good. O'Connor states, "The obstacles to and limitations of community life are to be found in the same sorts of misorientation that account for simple vice. Virtue serves the community primarily by orienting individuals toward the end of virtuous activity, an end that can really be common and shared": David O'Connor, "The aetiology of justice," in *Essays on the Foundations of Aristotelian Political Science*, eds. Carnes Lord and David K. O'Connor (Berkeley, California: University of California Press, 1991), pp. 153, 163, and 164.

compulsorily relativize the humanly natural.[39] To the contrary, says Spaemann, awareness of variation elicits the generic concept of "that which is right by nature" and allows cultures to be compared.[40]

The concept of human personhood offers a means to evaluate disparate doctrines of society, culture, and human self-understanding. The priority of the concept of person is a criterion of good moral order within a particular culture. Alternatively, the modern imposition of the social whole upon the atomized individual makes him a subordinate part, valued only for his contribution to the larger structure.[41]

---

[39] Engelhardt, Jr., makes the opposing claim, and so concludes, "There is an obligation to tolerate numerous different approaches to caring for the human genome and respecting generations": H. Tristram Engelhardt, Jr., "Human nature genetically re-engineered: moral responsibilities to future generations," in *Germline Intervention and Our Responsibilities to Future Generations*, ed. Emmanuel Agius, et. al, Vol. 55, Philosophy and Medecine, eds. H. Tristram Engelhardt, Jr., and Stuart F. Spicker (Dordrecht, Netherlands: Kluwer Academic Publishers, 1998), pp. 51-63, pp. 61-63; cf. H. Tristram Engelhardt, Jr., "Human reproductive technology: why all the fuss?," in *The Beginning of Human Life*, eds. F.K. Beller and R. F. Weir (Dordrecht, Netherlands: Kluwer Academic Publishers, 1994), pp. 89-100, pp. 89-91; and H. Tristram Engelhardt, Jr, "Germ-line," p. 47. But, in this account, the toleration of different approaches makes the construal of "respect" tendentious and conventional.

[40] Robert Spaemann, *Happiness and Benevolence*, p, 163.

[41] Anita Silvers criticizes Norman Daniels for mixing certain political presuppositions with assessment of clinical needs: Anita Silvers, "A fatal attraction to normalizing: treating disabilities as deviations from 'species-typical' functioning," in *Enhancing Human Traits*, pp. 95-123, p. 103. Against Silvers, we find that Daniels explicitly rejects the medicalization of individual differences in normal capabilities. However, we also think that Daniels has a very "thin" ontology; he says, "It is important to note that I am not trying to save the appeal to a natural baseline here because there is something magical or metaphysically basic about it.... Rather, the natural baseline both facilitates and reflects moral agreement about the urgency of medical care": Norman Daniels, "The genome project, individual differences, and health care," in *Justice and the Human Genome Project*, eds. Timothy F.

Constructionism locates the concept of person among cultural conventions rather than as a given kind of individual rational life meriting respectful attention. The person whose nature is construed as mere convention is more susceptible to technical manipulation.[42] These manipulations ignore individual boundaries present in a distinct subject with unique powers linked by relationships extending into the present, past and future. The person is one who is normally capable of attentive presence, of friendship, of endurance in love.

Genuine human dignity demands and directs development toward virtuous excellence for the sake of others and oneself. With genetic enhancements, instead of moving toward intrinsic completion, perfection, *entelechy*, we settle for constricted notions of what it means to be human, whole, capable. We strive to alter our appearance or our capacities, and yet, in effect, we arrest our development. We settle for mere seeming rather than affirming the human form we already are,

---

Murphy and Marc A. Lappé (Berkeley, California: University of California Press, 1994), pp. 110-32, pp. 126-27.

[42] Engelhardt articulates a moral distinction made in constructionist anthropology between respect for life *qua* life versus respect for persons *qua* persons. The distinction raises the issue of whether there is such an entity as a "human non-person," which is beyond the scope of our investigation, though it should be apparent that we think there is no such entity. Engelhardt says, "Some initial sense of the respect due to life can be advanced as reflecting a regard for important values. The first involves respect for life as an affirmation of life's value, the second involves valuing the diversity of life, the third recognizes a dignity in life that should not be violated, and the fourth a concern to respect life out of sympathy with living organisms, disposing us not to cause unnecessary suffering": H. Tristram Engelhardt, Jr., "Respect for life and the foundations of bioethics," in *The Ethics of Life*, eds. Denis Noble and Jean-Didier Vincent, trans. Noel Castelino, UNESCO Ethics Series (Paris: United Nations Educational, Scientific, and Cultural Organization, 1997), pp. 21-36, p. 26; cf. H. Tristram Engelhardt, Jr., "Persons and Humans," and Tom L. Beauchamp, "The failure of theories of personhood," *Kennedy Institute of Ethics Journal* 9, no. 4 (1999): 309-24; for an opposing position defending the personhood of all individual human lives, see Robert Spaemann, "Is every human being a person?" trans. Richard Schenk, *The Thomist* 60, no. 3 (July 1996): 463-74.

let alone the other humanly excellent qualities that have nothing to do with attractiveness or "personality" in the popular sense.[43]

Human species identity and human personhood do not possess degrees. Human dignity is not contingent on the level of functioning or on an individual's state of health.[44] The dignity of human freedom, conscience, achievements, and love follow from the foundational dignity of human life and the *telos* immanent to human personhood. The virtuous coordination of all the varied human inclinations in voluntary actions composes the pursuit of the ultimate end for human persons, the "life that turns out well."

Some elective forms of cosmetic surgery, steroid use, and other extrinsically induced enhancement practices by contemporary athletes are well-documented, and testify to the medically enabled exercise of personal autonomy turned against oneself or another.[45] We can confuse

---

[43] Alasdair MacIntyre speaks of the systematic errors that occur in our own practical reasoning when we rely uncritically on the dominant norms of our social environment. These errors are exposed in our attitude toward the disabled. He says, "If we are unable to free ourselves from these sources of error, we will continue to obscure what it is in both ourselves and others to which we ought to be responding in different contexts and we ourselves will continue to lead distorted lives. Note that this does not mean that we ought not to distinguish what is pleasing in appearance from what is unpleasing and both from what is horrifying, or that we should not continue to recognize that a handsome appearance and an engaging manner are good things to possess. But we will be mistaken as to the nature and limits of their goodness, if we allow ourselves to be seduced by their attractiveness into undervaluing those qualities and arguments that have to make themselves known through disfigurement and disablement": Alasdair MacIntyre, *Dependent Rational Animals: Why Human Beings Need The Virtues*, The Paul Carus Lecture Series, no. 20 (Chicago: Open Court Publishing, 1999), pp. 137-38.

[44] See Josef Seifert, *What is Life*, p. 387: "The life of a person is of a value that infinitely transcends just that of health."

[45] Whitehouse, Juengst, Mehlman and Murray analyze the issues surrounding cognitive enhancement delivered by non-genetic means (namely, by drugs) from a moral and metaphysical perspective. They state, "Increased memory, new insights and better reasoning could all lead to new values, new perspectives on one's relationships, and new sources of pleasure and

our transcendent inclinations for a life well-lived with the happiness that is achievable in this world. Once we are aware of the distinction between the theoretical satisfaction of all desires and the state of wholeness and fulfillment that is commensurate with our normal human condition, the ability to evaluate proposed genetic alteration procedures as being in accord with nature or opposed to it follows.

Every intervention or manipulation involving any part of an individual's genetic material (whether chromosomal or mitochondrial) is an action performed upon the whole person.[46] Procedures that interfere with the integrity of an individual genome absent therapeutic need encroach upon the dignity of persons. Non-therapeutic interventions invariably reflect human purposes directed to moral objects other than human health, and regard persons as means rather than as moral ends. Enhancement interventions insult human dignity; they are morally deficient and therefore objectionable.[47]

---

irritation. That does not mean the enhanced will literally lose their identities and become different people, any more than someone with disease does. But in the figurative sense intended by caregivers of people with this disease, it may be that after some point the cognitively enhanced will no longer be recognizable by those who knew them before their enhancement": Peter Whitehouse Jr., Eric Juengst, Maxwell Mehlmann, and Thomas H. Murray, "Enhancing cognition in the intellectually intact," *Hastings Center Report* 27, no 3. (May- June 1997): 14-22, p. 26; cf. Leon Kass, "The moral meaning of genetic technology," *Commentary* (September 1999): 32-38, p. 36.

[46] Seifert enlists the concept of "participation" to describe the dignity of the human genome: "The human genome possesses a unique value which we may call a dignity by participation (in the dignity of persons). This dignity of the human genome derives from its intimate linkage to the dignity of the human person himself. In man the content of 'this admirable linguistic document of the genome' possesses an entirely new and sublime dignity through its connection to human nature and to a human person": Josef Seifert, "Respect for the nature and responsibility of the person in acquiring knowledge about the human genome and in the application of human biotechnology," in *Human Genome, Human Person*, pp. 351-94, p. 374.

[47] Cf. Glenn McGee, who foresees that as genetic tests and therapies will move into the realm of improvement, "parents will make choices about the best means and *appropriate ends* of enhancement": Glenn McGee, "Genetic

Enhancement procedures digress from the traditional end of medical practice–the good of healing.[48] More significantly, gene enhancements neglect or deny the ultimate human *telos*, *eudaimonia*.[49] Enhancement imposes a degree of fixity and formality that nature itself does not contribute. Non-therapeutic gene interventions are a precocious, constructed determination rather than a naturally, morally achieved one. Paradoxically, enhancements are ontologically restrictive and not liberating. Therapeutic manipulations respect the ontological priority of human ends. Enhancements instead favor *poiesis* over medical *praxis*, giving priority to imposed purposes.

Genetic enhancement schemes in themselves add traits or supplement traits only by subtracting or suppressing others whose expression may be considered within the realm of the humanly

---

enhancement of families," in *Pragmatic Bioethics*, ed. Glenn McGee (Nashville, Tennessee: Vanderbilt University Press, 1999), pp. 168-80, p. 169.

[48] Comparing genetic enhancement to cosmetic surgery, Agneta Sutton says, "Cosmetic surgery sometimes serves a medical end by promoting the physical or mental health of the patient. But enhancement interventions intended to improve a child's intellectual or physical abilities would not serve the traditional ends of medicine. Enhancement genetic engineering intended to produce designer children would tend to cater to the demands of parents or society rather than be tailored to the best interests of manipulated individuals.... Interventions involving children would inevitably be serving ends external to the healing profession": Agneta Sutton, "The new genetics and traditional Hippocratic medicine," in *Man-made Man*, pp. 46-57, p. 68.

[49] For example, Whitehouse et al. speculate whether one of the major concerns with "cognitive enhancers is that they may promote a hypertrophy or overvaluation of our cognitive abilities, to the detriment of other human capacities such as empathy, emotional depth, visual creativity, or perceptiveness. Whether cognitive enhancement would necessarily come at the price of a reduction or eclipse of other capacities is uncertain. As with the concern about treating the body as a machine to be manipulated, turning an empirical claim into a moral one requires an argument showing that such treatment, on the whole, harms rather than furthers human flourishing": Peter J. Whitehouse et al., "Enhancing cognition," p. 20.

"normal."[50] Acts of enhancement intentionally disregard and deform the dignity of human persons, regarding the value of the whole person on the basis of particular traits or genetic "parts." Enhancement interventions introduce a moral deficit in the actions of the genetic manipulators where an organic or mental deficit may or may not already exist. Genetic enhancements, therefore, are intrinsically bad actions.

Nature and personal vulnerability are not opposed; the form of appearances and human limits in relationships are part of nature. In our human interactions, our own nature as well as that of other persons comes forth. Our moral obligation as citizens within the polis is to minimize the effects of chance in individual human lives only insofar as we provide "normal" conditions that will promote the general pursuit of happiness.[51] We cannot take upon ourselves the primary responsibility for *producing* happiness or fulfillment for others. *Eudaimonia* is not an extrinsic product wrought by thoroughly

---

[50] Michael Shapiro identifies the radical novelty of "enhancement" *in se* consistent with a "disorder model" for medical intervention; he states, "Enhancement does more than 'nullify' or 'cancel out' the disorder. It replaces it with a state that is not 'natural' for the subject being altered.... Think, for example, of someone who has been afflicted with some physical or mental disorder from birth and has thus never known another state. For her, amelioration or cure may well be viewed as enhancement–yet the intervention seems fairly unproblematic because of its 'location' within a disorder model for justifying intervention": Michael H. Shapiro, 1999, "The impact of genetic enhancement on equality," *Wake Forest Law Review* 34, no. 3: 561-638, p. 574.

[51] Robert Spaemann, *Happiness and Benevolence*, pp. 110-11, 169-70. Daniels contests society's putative obligation to provide enhancement technologies–genetic and otherwise–to further human happiness. He states, "We have obligations to provide services whenever someone desires that a medical *need* be met.... Enhancement does not meet a medical need even where the service may correct for a competitive disadvantage that does not result from prior choices. Accordingly, medicine has the role of making people *normal* competitors, not *equal* competitors": Norman Daniels, "The genome project," pp. 121-22; cf. Michael H. Shapiro, "Impact," pp. 604-05.

egalitarian social conditions; it is a personal achievement.[52] The "life that turns out well" is a *telos* that we must individually, voluntarily, consistently pursue.

The accommodation of the "human condition" in the well-ordered soul and in the good *polis* is essential for human flourishing. In contrast to a Hobbesian view of human existence, the anthropology I have proposed here maintains that human life is not inherently inimical to those who live it, whether we consider the lives of individual persons or the community of human relationships at large. The formation of human lives so that they will acquire the virtuous dispositions that make flourishing possible in the first place is a task that is usually contingent upon having virtuous parents. It also depends upon a larger social order where human vulnerability is met by prudent choices of means to assist, but not eradicate, vulnerable persons.

Gene therapy, delivered within the appropriate ethical guidelines, is consistent with this possible prudent assistance. In contrast, gene enhancement, a form of manipulation that ignores normal human capacities and the inclinations natural to life in favor of some speculative purpose proposed by parents, clinicians, politicians, or other entrepreneurs, is morally objectionable.

Human contingency may be felicitously moderated by the development and exercise of virtue within a political community. Persons who are active in, and supported by, a political culture that

---

[52] Berry opines, "The connection between a person's ability to lead a good life–as measured by happiness, success, or any other conception–and a set of capabilities–such as intelligence, memory, strength, or agility–is anything but obvious. Only if we limit our conception of the good life to a life lived with enhanced capabilities or a life lived with an abundance of that which enhanced capabilities enables us to attain, whatever that might be, must we conclude that the connection is secure. It is true that, intuitively, we believe there must be a connection. But this is likely because we now associate high-status jobs and social position with certain capabilities or with that which these capabilities enable their bearers to attain. But, for example, athletes have not always been so well paid and widely admired. Just as with personal appearance, the value we attach to capabilities is, at least in part, a matter of passing fancy": Roberta M. Berry, "From involuntary sterilization," p. 444.

elicits the virtuous excellences of its individual citizens not only are more likely to have their basic life necessities met. They are better equipped to lead human lives that will turn out well–lives considered both "worthy" and "happy," because they know themselves and have a better grasp of the genuine conditions for *eudaimonia.*

# INDEX

## A



## B



## C



## D

## E



## F



## G



## H



## I



## J



## K



## L

# Contributors

**Martin Andic** was professor emeritus of philosophy at the University of Massachusetts, Boston. Dr. Andic edited, with Henry Le Roy Finch, *Simone Weil and the Intellect of Grace* (Continuum, 1999). Dr. Andic also wrote many articles, such as, "Freedom," in *The Christian Platonism of Simone Weil*, eds. E. Jane Doering and Eric O. Springsted, (University of Notre Dame Press, 2004); "Is Love of Neighbour the Love of an Individual?" in *Kierkegaard: The Self in Society* eds. G. Pattison and S. Shakespeare (St. Martin's Press, 1998); "Simone Weil and Kierkegaard," *Modern Theology* 2 (1985): 20-41. He was a member of the American Maritain Association and the Kierkegaard Circle at the University of Toronto. Dr. Andic died in 2005.

**Joseph Allan Clair** is in the Ph.D. program in the religion department at Princeton University. His research is on the political thought of Augustine of Hippo. He earned an M.A. in philosophy from Fordham University and an M.T.S. from Duke University's School of Divinity.

**John A. Cuddeback** received a Ph.D. in philosophy from the Catholic University of America and is associate professor of philosophy at Christendom College in Front Royal, Virginia. His teaching and lecturing focus on themes in ethics, especially natural law, common good, friendship, and contemplation. He is the author of *Friendship: The Art of Happiness* (Epic, 2003), as well as several articles that have appeared in previous volumes published by the American Maritain Association, and in the English-language edition of *Nova et vetera*.

**Christopher Cullen**, S.J., is associate professor of philosophy at Fordham University. He is the author of *Bonaventure* (Oxford, 2006), and other publications on medieval philosophy. From 2001-2004, he was vice president of the American Maritain Association. He is associate director of Fordham's Center for Medieval Studies.

**James G. Hanink** is professor of philosophy at Loyola Marymount University, Los Angeles. Thomism, personalism, and political philosophy are his chief interests. His work has appeared in a variety of academic journals, as well as in the Catholic press. Prof. Hanink is an active member of University Faculty for Life.

## CONTRIBUTORS

**William M. Joensen**, Ph.D., a priest of the Archdiocese of Dubuque, teaches philosophy at Loras College in Dubuque, Iowa, where he is also director of spiritual formation for the St. Pius X Seminary program. His primary interests are in philosophical anthropology, the history of philosophy, and philosophy of medicine. Fr. Joensen is a member of various bioethics committees in his diocese, and also serves as chaplain at Clarke College in Dubuque.

**Robert P. Kraynak** is professor of political science and director of the Center for Freedom and Western Civilization at Colgate University. He is author of *Christian Faith and Modern Democracy* (2001) and editor with Arthur M. Melzer of *Reason, Faith, and Politics* (2008).

**John F. Morris,** Ph.D., is professor of philosophy in the Department of Philosophy at Rockhurst University in Kansas City, Missouri. His specialties include medieval philosophy, as well as contemporary ethics and medical ethics. Dr. Morris has also served since 2005 as the Special Advisor to Bishop Robert Finn for the Diocese of Kansas City/St. Joseph on the issues of stem cell research, cloning, and human embryos. Dr. Morris has presented and published numerous papers on these topics. Most recently, Dr. Morris published an anthology on medical ethics from the Catholic perspective titled *Medicine, Health Care & Ethics: Catholic Voices* (The Catholic University Press of America, 2007), which he edited and in which he authored a chapter on stem cell research. He resides in Overland Park, Kansas, with his wife, Carol, and two sons, Michael and Kevin.

**Ralph C. Nelson** was professor emeritus in the political science department at the University of Windsor (Ontario, Canada). After receiving his Ph.D. from the University of Notre Dame, he worked at the University of Windsor from 1963-1993. He co-edited, with Anthony O. Simon, the book authored by Yves R. Simon, *Foresight and Knowledge* (Fordham University Press, 1996). He wrote various articles, such as, "Two Masters, Two Perspectives: Maritain and Gilson on the Philosophy of Nature," in *Wisdom's Apprentice: Thomistic Essays in Honor of Lawrence Dewan, O.P.*, ed. Peter A. Kwasniewski (The Catholic University of America Press, 2007); "Moderating the Philosophy of Rights," in *Philosophical Theory and* *the Universal Declaration on Human Rights*, ed. William Sweet (University of Ottawa Press, 2003); "Beyond the Sovereignty of Good," *Études Maritainiennes* 10 (1994): 124-41. He was a long-time member of the American Maritain Association. Dr. Nelson died in 2008.

**Matthew S. Pugh** is associate professor of philosophy at Providence College. He previously taught at Ohio Dominican College, Ohio State University, and the University of St. Thomas in Houston, Texas. He is the author of numerous articles, and the co-editor of *Analytic Thomism: Traditions in Dialogue* (Ashgate, 2005). His interests include Thomistic metaphysics and epistemology, Asian philosophy, and virtue ethics. Dr. Pugh is currently working on a book tentatively entitled, *On Being and Existence in Aquinas: a New Interpretation of Esse.*

**Alice Ramos** is professor of philosophy at St. John's University in Queens, New York, where she has taught since 1987. She holds a Ph.D. in philosophy from the University of Navarra in Spain and a Ph.D. in French literature from New York University. Her publications include a book written in Spanish titled: *Signum: De la semiótica universal a la metafísica del signo* (EUNSA) and two edited books for the AMA: *Beauty, Art, and the Polis* (2000) and *Faith, Scholarship, and Culture in the 21st Century* (2002), and numerous articles in areas such as Thomistic metaphysics and ethics, Christian anthropology, and Kantian ethical theology. She is the recipient of grants for scholarly work both in the United States and in Europe, a past president of the American Maritain Association (2002-2004) and a former member of the executive council of the American Catholic Philosophical Association (2006-2008). She is currently working on a manuscript which is a collection of her own essays on truth, goodness, and beauty.

**Teresa I. Reed** is professor of philosophy and dean of the School of Arts and Sciences at Marymount University in Arlington, Virginia. She received her Ph.D. from the University of Notre Dame. Her memberships include the American Catholic Philosophical Association (executive council 1997-2000), American Philosophical Association, American Maritain Association, and Gabriel Marcel

Society. She is a realist philosopher whose scholarly work now focuses on the philosophy of time and the work of Gabriel Marcel.

**Francis Slade** is emeritus professor of philosophy at St. Francis College, Brooklyn, New York, where he was chairman of the Department of Philosophy for many years. He holds degrees from the Catholic University of America and the University of Notre Dame.

**Eric O. Springsted** is co-founder of the American Weil Society and has been its president since 1981. He has been chaplain and has taught at Illinois College, Princeton Theological Seminary, and General Theological Seminary (New York). He is the author and editor of eleven books, including six on Simone Weil, and of numerous articles on Weil and on philosophy and theology.

**John G. Trapani**, Jr., Ph.D. is a professor of philosophy at Walsh University in North Canton, Ohio. During his 35 years at the university, he has served as chair of the philosophy department and the humanities division and is also the founder (1976) and director of the university's annual Philosophy-Theology Symposium. Current President of the American Maritain Association, his book in the AMA series, *Truth Matters*, was released in 2004. In addition, John is also a professional musician, and bandleader of the 17-piece John Trapani Big Band, founded in 1977.

**Timothy Valentine**, S.J., earned his Ph.D. in philosophy from Columbia University. He served as an assistant professor at Fordham University's School of Education and as an instructor in philosophy at the United States Military Academy at West Point, New York. He also holds an M.A. in music and music education from Columbia University's Teachers College and an S.T.L. from Weston Jesuit School of Theology. He is currently serving as a chaplain in the U.S. Army.

**Henk E.S. Woldring** is professor of political philosophy at the Free University in Amsterdam and a member of the First Chamber (Senate) of the Parliament of the Netherlands for the Christian Democratic Party since 1999.

Breinigsville, PA USA
16 November 2009
227635BV00002B/2/P